Modernization of China

Modern China Series

Modernization of China

Tian Guang
Luo Kanglong
Chen Qian

North American Business Press

Modernization of China

ISBN: 978-1-948915-24-3

NORTH
AMERICAN BUSINESS
PRESS

North American Business Press
Atlanta, Georgia
Miami, Florida
New York, New York,
Toronto, Canada

FIRST PRINTING, 2022

About Modern China Series

As one of the oldest civilized regions globally, China has emerged as a "new world" because it embraces its essence and heritage and links them to viable economic strategies. In the last 25 years, China has made tremendous strides by doing so. The country and its people have every right to take pride in these accomplishments. Many Chinese leaders and intellectuals anticipate continuing growth with these successes under their belt. Furthermore, China's plans and strategies are often based upon this premise.

There is tremendous interest in the U.S. on the Chinese economy and business environment. China has emerged as a global superpower, and scholars and business people in the U.S. are keenly interested in learning how this will affect them and do business with China. In response to growing interest from international and Asian scholars, North American Business Press is pleased to announce our Modern China Series (MCS) books. It is the first book series about modern China in the U.S., garnering tremendous interest in the U.S. and worldwide. With our first book reaching stores in September 2011, this initiative develops relationships between NABP and Chinese scholars. They desire to promote their academic and applied business writings to the rest of the world.

We have had an overwhelming demand for the Modern China Series from both authors who would like to publish in the series and people who would like to read the books. There are currently ten books published in the series, and we have a couple of dozen books that we are considering for the series. The books have been viewed by tens of thousands of people from the U.S. and the rest of the world.

We have published books on several areas revolving around the Chinese business environment. We have a few that focus on the best practices in marketing in China; some are compared to "best practices" in doing business in China, and a few on the outlook of the Chinese economy.

The market for the Modern China Series is enormous. There are tens of thousands of scholars that are keenly interested in the continued growth of the Chinese economy and the implications that it will have on the business world. Even more significant are the millions of business people interested in the impact that China will continue to have on the global economy. It is difficult to pin down the exact demand for the series, but it Is enormous.

We have big plans for growing the Modern China Series. It can be one of the most significant economic/business series ever produced. We are very selective with the books we will add to the collection, but we encourage scholars who think they have unique and exciting perspectives on China to submit their book manuscripts. From the readers' perspective, we are committed to producing high-quality books regularly so that readers should expect a steady stream of insightful books to be coming out for many years to come.

This initiative is headed by Dr. Robert Tian, a renowned researcher and academic, who spearheads our efforts in partnering with foreign authors and administering the day-to-day operations of this series. Dr. Tian, a Vice-President with North American Business Press and Editor of this series, spends much of his time in Beijing, Shanghai, and other Chinese cities, focusing on developing and managing our interests with authors and universities. Below is the list of the books we have published:

Enterprise Strategy: New Horizon authored by Zhang Xiuyu

Governance of Private Enterprises in Modern China authored by Zhong Qin

The Art of War and Enterprise Strategy Management authored by Fu Shouzhi

Marketing Issues in Modern China edited by Robert Guang Tian et al.

The Footprints of the Academician authored by Fu Zhouzhi

Marketing and Economics in Modern China (I) edited by Xiaoguang Qi et al.

Marketing and Economics in Modern China (II) edited by Wang Tianjin et al.

An Islamic Heritage in China authored by Ma Zhanming

China Environmental Anthropology authored by Wang Tianjin, Tian Guang, and Ma Jianfu

Can China Rule the New World? Authored by Tian Guang and Chen Gang

Critiques on Pan-marketization authored by Li Cunlin, Liu Hongfei, and Tian Guang

Economic and Business Anthropology in China edited by Xiaoguang Qi and Tian Guang

China-Mongolia Economic Corridor authored by Eerdun Taoketao, Zhang Zhe, Wang Gang, and Wei Lisi

Anthropology of Chinese Foodways authored by Tian Guang and Chen Gang

Urbanization of Rural China authored by Li Taohong

Child Rearing in Rural China by Jiang Youchun and Yang Yunyi

Belt and Road vs. China and World by Tian Guang and Chen Gang

Modernization of China by Tian Guang, Luo Kanglong and Chen Qian

Table of Contents

Preface

China is a socialist developing country, and the Chinese people have chosen the CPC as the core of their leadership. After a long and bloody struggle, the Chinese people preferred China's current social system and proved to be the most suited to China's national conditions. For a long time, the Chinese people have followed the concept of state governance with the CPC at the core and the central leadership over local governments, top-down. The spirit of the CPC's important conferences and the main views of its core leaders will surely be implemented in China's modernization drive. Due to the particularity of China's national conditions, China's modernization also shows important characteristics of The Times. Therefore, to study China's modernization, we must first understand the CPC's important conference spirit. To predict the development trend of China's modernization, we must first understand the core ideas of China's leaders.

In November 2021, the Sixth Plenary Session of the 19th CPC Central Committee was held in Beijing. The meeting grasped the overall strategic vision of the Great Rejuvenation of the Chinese nation and major changes unseen in the world in a century. The meeting stressed that the new era of socialism with Chinese characteristics is a new era of building on past achievements and forging ahead into the future. Under the new historical conditions, China will continue to reap the achievements of developing socialism with Chinese characteristics, complete the building of a moderately prosperous society in all respects, and build itself into a great modern socialist country. The Chinese people of all ethnic groups will work together to create a better life and gradually achieve common prosperity. Ultimately, China will realize the Chinese dream of national rejuvenation, and China will continue to make greater contributions to humanity. The resolution's content shows that China has made major achievements in building socialist modernization. We have laid a good material foundation and gathered strong spiritual strength to realize the second Centenary Goal and the rejuvenation of the Chinese nation. It also marks that China has entered a new era of comprehensively building itself into a great modern socialist country.

In the modernization process, the Communist Party of China (CPC) and the Chinese government's conventional approach to governance are to regularly sum up experience, draw lessons in time, and adjust the direction of development and national policies in the process of constant reflection. China's coastal regions and big cities have seen rapid economic growth in recent years. In contrast, western regions, which lag, have also seen accelerated development thanks to targeted poverty alleviation and rural revitalization. Not only have many classic cases of modernization been practiced and promoted, but many scholars have also reflected on some lessons of failure and put forward policy suggestions. This kind of development model, which encourages bold pilot projects, applies them on a large scale when feasible, and controls development costs within an appropriate range, has stimulated strong internal impetus for China's modernization process. A review of the historical process of China's socialist modernization and a comprehensive and systematic summary of its positive and negative experiences are of great significance for China to better realize its goal of becoming a modern power and for other countries to learn from.

The essence of modernization is human modernization. Generally speaking, the human being is the unity of three-fold subjectivity: human class partiality, group partiality, and individual partiality. In reality, the human essence is the sum of all social relations. China has 1.4 billion people, and its development goal is to modernize a huge population. After more than four decades of reform and opening-up, China has solved the problem of absolute poverty, and people's living standards have improved significantly. China will continue to build a modern socialist country with Chinese characteristics to promote its sustainable development and its people better. A "two-step" approach is planned over the coming decades to achieve this goal. The first step is to build on a moderately prosperous society in all respects and realize socialist modernization in the next 15 years from 2020 to 2035. The second step is to build China into a great modern socialist country that is prosperous, strong, democratic, culturally advanced, harmonious and beautiful from 2035 to the middle of the 21st century.

The above contents review CPC leaders' modernization concept and reflect the development direction of China's modernization practice in the future. China needs to improve its governance system and capacity and hopes to explore a modern and sustainable development path that balances ecological, economic, cultural and social benefits as soon as possible. This book is a historical summary of the socialist modernization process with Chinese characteristics from different fields and perspectives.

Chapter 1 is authored by Dr. Wang Shaojie, an associate professor at the Business School of Hunan University of Humanities and Technology, Mr. Wang Yazhou， a doctoral student at Huaxia International Business School, Sinawa University, Thailand， and Wu Yiqun, Master Degree candidate at Business School of Hunan University of Humanities and Technology. It discusses the centennial exploration of anti-poverty in China. The authors address poverty as a "stubborn disease" perplexing human society. Since its birth, the Communist Party of China has eliminated poverty in China as its goal and continued to adhere to it. Especially since the 18th CPC National Congress, with the birth of the idea of targeted poverty alleviation, the Communist Party of China has led the people of the whole country to conquer China's last poverty fortress in one fell swoop. This great achievement has important reference value for the anti-poverty cause of the international community.

Dr. Tian Guang and Dr. Luo Kanglong, a professor of Culture & History administration at Jishou University, Hunan, authored Chapter 2. It explores the theoretical basis and development process of Chinese economic anthropology. The authors indicate that Chinese economic anthropology started relatively later compared with that in the West;

however, under the guidance of Marxist theory and based on the needs of China's economic development, it gradually formed unique advantages in its development process. This chapter probes and analyzes the scholarly contributions of the pioneers of Chinese economic anthropology; especially, it takes Marxist economics as the starting point to examine Professor Shi Zhengyi's theoretical contributions to the development of Chinese economic anthropology and its practical significance.

Chapter 3 is authored by Dr. Chen Qian, a Culture & History administration lecturer at Jishou University, and Dr. Tian Guang. It examines the modernization and social governance in Minority Areas in Western China. The authors emphasize that the modernization of the Minority Regions in Western China (the MRIWC) plays a vital role in the country's overall modernization progress. As the modernization process continues, the MRIWC can adequately deal with social governance issues by drawing lessons from typical cases like the Western Hunan Zila Tribute Rice trademark registration case. The MRIWC must construct cooperation governance patterns through the multiple subjects and adjust measures to local conditions by flexible governance means that are "lawful, rational, and affectional." It will accelerate the modernization of the MRIWC and help China build itself into a more advanced country.

Dr. Li Taohong, an associate professor of anthropology at Dali University, Yunnan, is the author of Chapter 4. This chapter discusses urbanization's unique path and process in old Shiyang Town. The author addresses that urbanization is a significant process in present China's history. Due to the long history and large territory associated with various cultures, the urbanization path and process differ from place to place. Taking old Shiyang (stone sheep) town in Dayao County of Yunnan Province as an example, this study probes a unique urbanization process and pattern in rural Southern China by examining the role salt resources played from a historical perspective.

Chapter 5 is authored by Dr. Jiang Youchun, a professor of Jishou University, and Yang Yunyi, a Doctoral candidate at Xiangtan University,

Hunan. It studies the relationship between cultural capital and the development of the rural economy in China during economic transformation. The authors indicate that cultural capital is an essential endogenous power for developing a rural economy. As many enterprises with intensive cultural capital and relatively high marginal product arising in China, cultural capital advances the development of the rural economy to promote the advanced organizational methods to allocate resources. It also upgrades human capital and increases the number of rural labor forces employed in the industries with a relatively high marginal product and abundant cultural capital. Moreover, the industries with intensive cultural capital expand the coordinated development of the markets and initiatives for the rural economy.

The authors of Chapter 6 are Dr. Tian Guang, Dr. Shu Xiaohui， a professor of economics at Huaihua University, Hunan, and Mr. Li Yangkuo, an economics lecturer at Huaihua University, Hunan. It explores the significant impact of China's national economy caused by the COVID-19 pandemic. The authors emphasize that in Post-Coronavirus China, the macro-economic development situation must be undergone new and substantial changes with a trend from a production-driven economy to a consumption-driven economy. With the transformation and upgrading of the consumption structure and the continuous promotion of structural reforms on the supply side, the essential role of consumption in economic development will be more sustainable. The new model for China's economic and social development is to cultivate new consumer markets, continuously increase people's income level and consumption capacity, and accelerate the construction and growth of crucial consumptions. It should become a new and long-term policy for China's macro-economic development.

Chapter 7 is authored by Dr. Tian Guang and Dr. Liu Yu, a professor of business administration at Shantou University, Guangdong. It studies the independent planning system and metropolitan development. The authors indicate that the optimal allocation of public management and administrative resources has played a key role in the fundamental economic development in China in recent years. The new administrative system of large cities (metropolises) with independent planning has become an innovative format to utilize the soft renewable resources of administration, a new attempt to reform the economic system by the Chinese government. The greater Chaoshan area needs to be agglomerated and unified to develop the regional economy by implementing an independent planning system. Agglomerating and integrating Shantou, Jieyang and Chaozhou into the greater Chaoshan Special Economic Zone with an independent planning system is practically feasible and has a decisive strategic significance in promoting the overall economic and social development of the whole eastern Guangdong area.

Chapter 8 is authored by Lu Yujie, a Doctoral candidate of communication at the University of Chinese Academy of Social Science, Beijing, and Lu Liqing，an Associate Professor of Zhejiang Gongshang University, Zhejiang. It examines the impacts of western films on contemporary China. The authors collect discourse data of Chinese audiences and scholars on ten outstanding Western masculinist films that flowed into China over several years. It found that five main categories, which consist of situational content of films, the relationship between the film and the West, the interaction between the film and Chinese audience, negative identification factors, and cognitive, motivational approaches. Dynamics adjust Western films' cross-cultural communication effect in China. It constructs a model of factors affecting the communication effects of western masculinist films in China.

Chapter 9 is authored by Dr. Li Jiangjun，an associate professor of Business Management, Han Shengyue and Liang Rui, both are MA graduate students at Beijing University of Civil Engineering and Architecture (China). It explores enterprise reform and China's modernization. The authors declare that enterprises have experienced a complex process of change in China's modernization, which has promoted or restricted the process of China's modernization. From the perspective of government function adjustment, this chapter studies the enterprise transformation process in China's modernization from a historical perspective. Although micro problems such as corporate governance and principal-agent are very important, they are only the second problem. The first problem should be the adjustment of government functions. The Chinese government carried out the social transformation of market economy orientation after 1979. From then, the enterprises have become modern enterprises in the market economy. The findings of this chapter are of great significance to enhance the institutional innovation of enterprises and promote the process of China's modernization.

From different angles and aspects, the authors of the above chapters analyze and describe the relevant issues in China's modernization. Due to the authors' limitations, the contents contained in this volume cannot reflect the entire picture of China's modernization. What we can provide to the readers is to show several specific aspects during the modernization in China. We sincerely appreciate our readers' understanding (Tian Guang, Luo Kanglong, Chen Qian).

Acknowledgment

We sincerely thank all the Chinese scholars who did much to inspire our ambitions to make this book. In addition to the works by all the participants, we have also referred to hundreds of articles and books published both in Chinese and in English. We thank Dr. Gao Jian, Dr. Jiang Youchun， Dr. Jiang Lifang, Dr. Li Rong, Dr. Liu Yu, Dr. Ma Jianfu, Dr. Ma Zhanming, Dr. Shu Xiaohui, Dr. Wu Hexian, Dr. Xu Zonglin, Dr. Zhao Peihua, Dr. Zheng Muqiang, and Professors Le Guobing, Li Dekuan, Wang Tianjin, Zhang Shaoping, and Mr. Li Yangkuo for their insightful comments on and constructive suggestions to the initial manuscript, without their encouragements and supports this book may not be able to get published in time.

We would like to thank the editorial team of North America Business Press for their encouragement and dedicated work. The Academic and Scholastic Publishing Foundations of Huaihua University, the College of Culture and History Administration of Jishou University financially supported publication this book.

Foreword

Modernization and the Chinese Dream

Yang Tingshuo

To realize the great rejuvenation of the Chinese nation has been the greatest dream for the Chinese people since the beginning of the 20th century. The "Chinese dream" is a great historic economic and social project that requires all the Chinese people to work hard together. Since the reform and opening-up started 40 years ago, significant achievements have been made in China's economic and social modernization. However, there are still problems that need to be addressed and resolved. It is undoubtedly necessary to explore the causes of the issues and strategies to remedy the defects. To realize the Chinese dream, Chinese people need to innovate their economic and social modernization concept. They need to create a new type of country with stronger comprehensive national strength and finally realize the dream of the great rejuvenation of the Chinese nation.

Introduction

In 2012, Chinese President Xi Jinping put forward the strategic concept of the "Chinese Dream" to realize the great rejuvenation of the country, the prosperity of the nation, and the happiness of people. The realization of this concept will be a great leap forward in the chronicle of China (Li, 2012). According to Xi Jinping, the "Chinese Dream" embodies the long-cherished aspirations of generations of Chinese people, along with the overall interests of the Chinese nation and the Chinese people.

The "Chinese Dream" is the common aspiration of every Chinese descendant and is a great project for the benefit of the Chinese nation for thousands of generations to come (Guo, 2014). The Chinese dream is not isolated and not connected with the outside world, but it shares people's aspirations worldwide. Undoubtedly, the reform and opening-up have greatly enhanced China's comprehensive national strength and provided broader space for China's rise and the creation of the Chinese miracle. The organic unity of the "Chinese Dream" and the "Community with a Shared Future for Mankind" focus on political and economic construction in the new era.

Chinese people must also realize that the competition of the comprehensive national strength of all countries in the world is becoming more intense. As such, China is facing many challenges. There are also many problems in constructing socialism with Chinese characteristics, among which roads, theoretical issues, system issues, and culture are the core ones. Seizing the opportunities and meeting the challenges has become the most pressing issue facing the Chinese government and people.

The realization of the "Chinese Dream" is a very complicated project of economic and social modernization. In this process, China needs to deal with many complex and changeable issues, continually absorb ancient and modern ideas at home and abroad, and innovate a higher and more creative art of guidance. Under the guidance of correct theories, the effect of "right direction," "high efficiency," and "good outcome" can be achieved (Tian & Dai, 2012). Only by striving to overcome difficulties can China accomplish the great project of the Chinese dream and realize the great rejuvenation of the Chinese nation.

Achieving the Chinese Dream Requires Correct Theoretical Guidance

Marx pointed out in the preface of *Das Kapital* that the modernization of social and economic forms is a natural and historical process (Marx, 1975). Human society is an organic unity of economic, political, cultural forms, and natural environment. Marx has described various social structures in detail in his classical works. He predicted that society would allow people to display their creative abilities in all-around ways instead of limiting human development to a narrow range. Humanity has also summed up the fundamental laws of material civilization, political civilization, spiritual refinement, and ecological civilization through various and multi-level experiences and lessons in social practice.

Excellent and brilliant achievements have been made through implementing various practical activities that conform to the objective laws. Understanding the "four civilizations" is particularly profound in China's modernization drive. In the process of human social development, the universal law of its development shows that the "four civilizations" are mutually conditional, mutually purposeful and mutually reinforcing (Huang and Shen, 2012). Once political and spiritual civilizations are formed, they have relative independence and historical inheritance with their particularities of development. Therefore, the realization of the Chinese dream must be guided by the theories of developing socialism with Chinese characteristics and must be based on the unique national conditions of China, be realistic, and conduct a detailed analysis of specific issues.

General Secretary Xi Jinping once pointed out that innovation has always been a vital force to promote the modernization of a country and a nation. He believes that China is a big developing country and is vigorously promoting the transformation of the economic development model and the adjustment of economic structure. Thus, the nation must implement the strategy of innovation-driven modernization to develop comprehensive innovation centered on scientific and technological innovation. China needs to stick with the direction of demand orientation and industrialization. At the same time, China needs to subscribe to the dominant position of enterprises in innovation to make full use of the decisive role of the market in the allocation of resources and the institutional advantages of socialism. They also need to enhance scientific and technological progress to economic growth, form new sources of growth power, and promote sustainable and healthy economic development (Li, 2010). 2006 to 2020 is a crucial stage of China's socialist commercial construction. The Chinese people face the ever-changing international situation and rare opportunities for peaceful world modernization.

The realization of the "Chinese Dream" requires significantly enhancing the ability of independent national innovation. It must go along with several scientific and technological achievements that significantly impact the world to promote steady economic and social modernization, safeguard national security, and provide strong support for the comprehensive construction of a beautiful and happy home. China needs to have an elevated level of material and spiritual civilization to achieve a substantial increase in social productivity to rank at the forefront of the world's core competitiveness (Liu & Li, 2018). Therefore, developing socialism with Chinese characteristics and building an innovative society are mainly embodied in the following aspects:

Autonomous innovation is the foundation

The 21st century is an era of the rapid modernization of science and technology and the continuous emergence of inventions and creations. The competition between countries is essentially the competition between overall national powers represented by economics, military, and culture. In recent years, the comprehensive national strength of China has developed to a certain extent. However, there is still a particular gap between the United States and other developed countries (See Table 1 for details). Without autonomous innovation, it is difficult for the country to break through the restrictions of various intellectual property barriers and fundamentally solve the significant strategic problems its modernization and national security face. The word "autonomous" in front of innovation emphasizes that Chinese intellects are the main body of innovation.

China needs to complete the process of scientific and technological innovation to acquire independent intellectual property rights, upgrade the technical level of the national industry, and master the core technology in some fields. President Xi Jinping emphasized autonomous innovation when he visited the Guangdong-Australia Cooperative TCM Science and Technology Industrial Park in Hengqin New Area. He pointed out the significance of accelerating the enhancement of the ability and strength of autonomous innovation and emphasized the development of the real economy. Independent innovation is the foundation of national economic and social modernization, the strong driving force of national modernization, and the indispensable lifeline for the survival and growth of the Chinese nation. Only by enhancing the ability of comprehensive innovation from the global perspective of a broader world can China win first place in basic science and frontier technology research. It will enhance key technologies and strengthen the core competitiveness, promote comprehensive national strength to form strong governance and seize opportunities, calmly respond to various challenges, and strive to advance the cause of socialism with Chinese characteristics.

Table 1. GDP ranking and growth of relevant countries in 2018

GDP Ranking	Country	Billion (US dollars)	Billion (Chinese Yuan)	The growth rate in 2018
1	The U.S.	19362.13	130810.6	1.27%
2	China	12945.41	82712.19	12.25%
3	Japan	4884.49	32999.61	2.01%
4	Germany	3651.87	24672.03	1.38%
5	France	2574.81	17395.42	1.12%
6	Britain	2565.05	17329.48	2.08%
7	India	2439.01	16477.95	12.78%
8	Brazil	2080.92	14058.7	3.30%
9	Italy	1921.14	12979.22	2.02%
10	Canada	1640.39	11082.47	4.07%

Source: National Bureau of Statistics of P. R. China

Common prosperity is the goal

The goal of realizing the Chinese dream is the country's prosperity, the revitalization of the nation, and the people's happiness. The realization of the "Chinese Dream" of the great rejuvenation of the Chinese nation and the construction of a win-win "Community with a Shared Future for Mankind" are essential components of President Xi Jinping's socialist thought with Chinese characteristics in the new era. These are organically integrated into the political construction of socialism with Chinese features (Dong & Su, 2018).

Forty years of reform and opening-up have yielded fruitful results, which have confirmed this correct political understanding. In developing socialism with Chinese characteristics and building an innovative country, the Chinese people are the main body of the practice of autonomous innovation and the beneficiaries and participants of the achievements of independent innovation. The cumbersome task of historical transformation lies on their shoulders, which should be equipped with Mao Zedong's pioneering spirit of "Yu Gong Yi Shan (The Old Man Who Moved Mountains)." The people should be fully involved in formulating reform plans and designs. The innovative ideas and fresh impetus from ordinary people should be fully absorbed. All "left" and "right" speech interference that hinders constructing a socialist market economic system with Chinese characteristics should be removed. People's minds and dreams should be emancipated, and innovation should be encouraged to scale the developmental peak bravely.

There are joys and sorrows as far as the current economic and social situation is concerned. The people have personally realized the happiness of the reform and opening-up, so they sincerely support the reform with pleasure. At the same time, there are problems between the modernization level of the South and the north, and the widening gap between the West and the East is most noteworthy. Besides, the difference between the actual disposable income of urban and rural residents also continues to widen (see Table 2 for details).

Table 2. Changes in per capita disposable income of urban and rural residents from 2013 to 2018

Year	2013	2014	2015	2016	2017	2018
Per capita disposable income of urban residents (RMB)	26,467	28,844	31,195	33,616	36,396	39,251
Per capita disposable income of rural residents (RMB)	9,430	10,489	11,422	12,363	13,432	14,617
Per capita Disposable Income Difference betChina en Urban and Rural Residents (RMB)	17,037	18,355	19,773	21,253	22,964	24,634

Source: National Bureau of Statistics of P. R. China

In addition to the widening income gap, there are also some problems in other areas, such as the inconvenience caused by the absence of public services, uneven distribution of educational resources, endless disputes between doctors and patients, etc. These situations are unprecedented problems in the previous economic construction. Therefore, China should use innovative thinking and explore ways to solve these problems. In the final analysis, improving people's sense of happiness and making them truly feel satisfied is the real cohesive link of China's strength and the safety valve of the Chinese society. Through active reform practices that can replace the old by bringing forth new, China continues to expand its opening-up to the outside world and deepens the reform of the economic system. Some deep-seated problems exposed will be solved to ensure the legitimate rights and interests of the people and allow the reform results to be shared collectively (Tian & Dai, 2012).

New rural construction is the critical point

Since the Third Plenary Session of the Eleventh Central Committee of the Communist Party of China was held in 1978, the reform began in the countryside and soon swept across the whole country. In March 2016, the 13th Five-Year Plan pointed out: "Agriculture is the basis for building a well-off society in an all-round way and realizing modernization. China must speed up the transformation of agricultural modernization mode by focusing on building a modern system of the agricultural industry, production and management. China needs to improve the efficiency and competitiveness of agricultural quality, and take the road of agricultural modernization with high output efficiency, excellent product safety, reasonable resource conservation and an environment-friendly system (Niu, 2016)." The plan emphasizes that economic work should focus on rural areas, vigorously building and developing new countryside construction, and implementing a precise poverty alleviation policy. At present, China's agriculture bears the supply of commodity grain and oil to survive the world's largest population. It takes the enormous competitive pressure brought about by the integration of the world economy.

Therefore, China should use the scientific modernization concept to explore and analyze problems, use innovative technologies, methods, and policies suitable for China's rural areas to guide and promote agricultural modernization, create green GDP, and implement new rural construction. In this course, deepening the reform of the economic system is of great importance. China should reform all unreasonable regulations and policies that block autonomous innovation, form a social atmosphere that encourages innovating independently and establish and improve the institutional mechanism that encourages independent innovation. Only in this way can China seize the opportunity, enhance the ability of autonomous innovation, and realize industrial restructuring (Li and Gao, 2013). Therefore, China should focus on solving the problems left over by the history of rural education and newly emerging challenges and cultivate talents for constructing the new countryside. As the rural area is vast with various situations and robust, the government should reform the working methods, promote the administration according to laws, speed up the construction of the rule of law and the service-oriented and effective government, and promote the continuous development of rural work.

Be brave to participate in world market competition

The competition in the world market is a war without smoke. China needs to complete autonomous innovation with a high-spirited posture and struggling spirit to occupy the commanding heights of international economic competition. Compared with the emerging high-tech level of patented technology in developed countries, China's science and technology level is still relatively low (see Fig. 1 for details). Faced with such a reality, China must face the competition of commercial science and technology, keep climbing, and persist in doing. In Japan, the high-tech industry is technology-intensive, fast-renewable, and effectively resource-saving. It has formed a specific scale of a market that can penetrate and drive the modernization of other related industries (Yu, 2010). Therefore, insisting on autonomous innovation and reflecting its achievements through enterprises' product manufacturing can help occupy an essential part of the industrial chain of world economic integration. Otherwise, the market will ruthlessly eliminate it because of the loss of vitality. Certain efforts should be devoted to tracking the fields of technological inventions dedicated to developed countries and keeping up with them. The field of science is of considerable significance to national modernization and security. The Chinese should seek new technological breakthroughs, concentrate their efforts on tackling fundamental problems, and continuously expand the international market share by the principle of suitability for national conditions and strength characteristics.

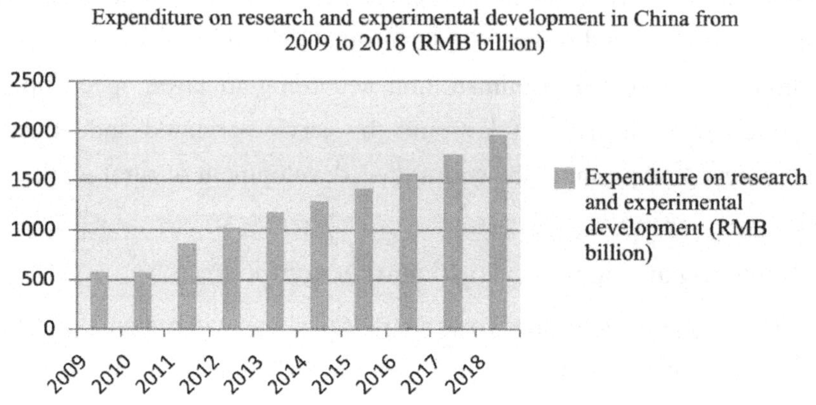

Figure 1. Expenditure on research and experimental development in China from 2009 to 2018 (RMB billion, based on data from the National Bureau of Statistics of P. R. China)

Since China joined the WTO in 2001, it has entered the competition of the international commercial market on a large scale. The total import and export volume has increased significantly. It produces some products with independent intellectual property rights to meet the demand of the world market. There are launches of commercial satellites, shipbuilding industries, etc. In the field of consumer goods, clothing, toys, hardware, tourist shoes, and products of other businesses made in China have been sold all over the world, and China has become the "world factory" in this field (see Table 3 for details) (Sun, 2011). China should continue to formulate new, targeted, operational policies for scientific and technological reform. The state should guide scientific and technical competence in general projects by managing significant project systems and market systems to ensure China's competitive advantage of science and technology at various levels.

Table 3. China's total import and export volume from 2009 to 2017

Year	Total import and export volume (RMB billion)	Total export volume (RMB billion)	Total imports (RMB billion)	Import and Export Balance (RMB billion)
2009	15,064.806	8,202.969	6,861.837	1,341.132
2010	20,172.234	10,702.284	9,469.95	1,232.334
2011	23,640.195	12,324.056	11,316.139	1,007.916
2012	24,416.021	12,935.925	11,480.096	1,455.829
2013	25,816.889	13,713.143	12,103.746	1,609.398
2014	26,424.177	14,388.375	12,035.803	2,352.572
2015	24,550.293	14,116.683	10,433.61	3,683.073
2016	24,338.646	13,841.929	10,496.717	3,345.212
2017	27,810.1	15,331.119	12,478.981	2,852.138

Source: National Bureau of Statistics of P. R. China

At present, China's economy has reached a relatively large scale, and the reform has entered into a critical stage, beginning to touch the "bone" that is difficult to tackle. Continuing to maintain the growth rate of the national macroeconomic economy and operating in the rising range of low prices is the focus of the national strategy at present and in the future. China should creatively implement macro-control policies to improve structural problems in economic operation further, alleviate the contradiction between energy and its transportation, and promote socialism with Chinese characteristics.

Eliminate the Influence of the "Pan-Marketization" Thought Trend

Developing socialism with Chinese characteristics aims to realize the Chinese dream, build an innovative country, and enhance comprehensive national strength. Therefore, all aspects of domestic affairs will be involved, all positive factors need to be mobilized, and appropriate construction and management methods should be adopted differently. However, according to the basic principles of Marxism, the economic development of a country has objective regularity. People need to adopt appropriate methods to act according to this regularity and give full play to their subjective initiative within the allowable scope of the balance. Other social fields also have their social values and development laws, so the way people act should be regulated by corresponding theories.

Developing a socialist market economy is undoubtedly an effective way to realize the Chinese dream. However, the market economy is not equal to "pan-marketization." The so-called "pan-marketization" tendency mainly refers to the gradual trend towards the market operation of some basic and public welfare departments such as science, education, culture, and health. However, when general welfare sectors such as health and education are "pan-marketized," the problems in the reform of the economic system are severe. The aim of adhering to the principle of the reform about the socialist market economy is to hope that China's educational concept can be innovatively developed, quality education can be implemented for all, and educational equity can be ensured. Therefore, to remove the obstacles to realizing the Chinese Dream, China must be conscious of the bad influence of the thoughts about the "pan-marketization" trend.

Trading principles should not be applied in the field of public service

One of the critical goals of the reform is to establish a socialist system of the market economy with Chinese characteristics that are compatible with the current situation of China. Article 15 of the People's Republic of China (namely, the revised version adopted by the Second Session of the Tenth National People's Congress on March 14, 2004) stipulates that "the state should implement socialist market economy." It is, after the reform exploration of "giving priority to a planned economy, supplemented by market economy" and "carrying out planned commodity economy," the reform guideline approved by the National People's Congress conforms to both the Marxist value system and China's national conditions (Sun, 2004). Based on the severe reflection on the theory and practice of social and economic modernization in China before the reform, the reform path was finally determined in the Constitution. In the past, under the unitary planned economic system, people's interpretation of market information was easily influenced by one-sidedness such as subjective understanding. Market activities are easily dominated by their narrow individual will.

In contrast, the violation of market law will inevitably lead to the distortion of the economic market and causes difficulties for market law to play an objective role. To change this abnormal and distorted economic system, it is necessary to scientifically understand and respect the market law and act according to the actual code to play a fundamental role in allocating resources. Numerous factors of production can flow through the market, the distribution of resources can be optimized, and transaction costs can be reduced. In this way, China can improve the operational efficiency of the whole economic system. Therefore, it is necessary to adhere to the reform (Sun, 2010).

With the rise of the Pan-market reform, people regard profit-seeking and maximization of capital gains as the only principle to regulate social relations, disturbing people's rational analysis and scientific thinking of social conditions. The actual market-oriented reforms carried out in some places have shown prominent characteristics of reducing the proportion of the state-owned economy and strengthening the share of privatization. Eventually, many state-owned enterprises were sold cheaply, resulting in a significant loss of state-owned assets. If such practices are not stopped and rectified, the ruling foundation of the state power will be severely eroded by the hidden crisis. The long-term practice of socialist construction has also clearly shown that in-depth reform cannot be "market-oriented." These include leadership systems, government agencies, ideological theory, judicial, military, ethnic and religious affairs. The government departments cannot have any tendency towards privatization. Reforms in the fields of science and technology, education, culture, sports, medical treatment, health, and environmental protection cannot be privatized entirely on the principle of "market orientation." Similarly, to reform many non-profit and non-governmental organizations in society, China should also eliminate the market's overall privatization. It would be tantamount to indulgence, which would only weaken the ruling power of the Communist Party, make the so-called rights and interests of vested interest groups over-inflate, and endanger the people's fundamental interests (Liu, 2007).

Even in the economic field, for the sake of national security and public social interests, there will inevitably be some public resources and public goods that are impossible or not allowed to be traded on the market, let alone be privatized. The popular economics textbooks of American universities point out that "the materials or funds to produce public goods such as defense and armaments should be controlled by the government" (Mcconnell, 2005). Can China marketize and privatize its defense industry? The answer is negative, and all countries worldwide have the same answer.

Moreover, a real market economy needs a market environment with equal status of market players, open and transparent market rules, standardized and orderly trading processes, fair and reasonable market management, and an appropriate market environment under the rule of law. The consequences of privatizing key industries related to the national economy and people's livelihood, such as the national defense industry, are unimaginable. Implementing the so-called completely free "marketization" of a private economic system is impossible in contemporary human society. Therefore, China must strengthen its national management to deepen economic policy reform. To conduct economic and social activities following the objective laws of the economy, obtain the best social and economic results using as few resources as possible and the optimal combination, and make an effort to coordinate the modernization of the economic and social environment. China must never allow the reform of the "self-improvement of the socialist system" to be distorted into "market-oriented reform" as such misleading is more ill-intentioned than childish (Liu, 2013).

Extreme Negative Benefits of the "Pan-marketization" Theory

In real life, the degree of marketization is not enough. A typical example is an argument of "high salary nourishes integrity." Compared with countries with a long history of the market economic system, the salaries of civil servants in Chinese governmental institutions are relatively low. Civil servants should have wages commensurate with their status and contributions in common sense. Their hard work should be reasonably rewarded, and the remuneration should increase along with the modernization of the economy.

Nevertheless, this does not mean that a high salary nourishes integrity. The "high salary nourishes integrity" theory refers to a market trading principle: to buy integrity for the public at a high price. It is not advisable to apply the law of market transactions to the political field. As a noble act, honesty cannot enter the market transactions, nor can it be bought with money. In political life, market principles should not be adopted. China should emphasize politics, responsibility, and morality rather than cash. It is undeniable that the trend of "pan-marketization" has brought troubles to China. In the reform process, the starting point of the so-called "pan-marketization" argument completely deviates from the interests of the state and the government in the very beginning, by the fallacies of which the economic and social chaos that once appeared in some regions (Tian, Dai & Qi, 2012).

What needs to be reflected and corrected is that some local administrators interpret marketization as the privatization of society and the government's getting rid of the burden. Under the guise of "market-oriented operation," some functional departments of local government have abandoned many responsibilities they should assume, not to mention that the market is full of "counterfeit and inferior" products and "pitfalls and abductions." Even some public schools, hospitals, and institutions engaged in public welfare undertakings have rightly begun to carry out "market-oriented reform" for the sake of "money" and "interests."

More chilling is that some government agencies are trying to use their power as "capital" in exchange for the interests that are biased towards or in line with the nature of small groups. In many places and units, the allocation of public resources has been transformed into their interests through "market-oriented operation." The market principles of "capitalization of power" and "equivalent exchange of values" are also widely used in officialdom. Corrupt cases of buying government positions, as well as embezzlement of public funds, occur quite frequently.

What is more worrying is that in pan-marketization, the pace of economic transformation in some places is too abrupt. Without other alternative measures, many workers in urban enterprises and rural farmers have lost many of their social benefits, including labor insurance and retirement benefits for urban workers and labor subsidies for rural peasants in the period of communes. Besides, the "buyout of the length of service" measures in some local enterprises are inappropriate as numerous laid-off workers, and their families have been affected. The number of laid-off workers affected by these measures is enormous, making the problem of employment, which has been very acute and prominent, even worse, thus forming potential and the destructive army of laid-off workers.

Moreover, due to the bankruptcy of small and medium-sized enterprises in cities, the number of employment opportunities decreases, which reduces employment opportunities for a large surplus rural labor force going to cities. It has become another grim fact. The misguided reform process is very radical, which interferes with the standard order of socialist countries and is very destructive. It also confirms an old Chinese saying that the heart of Sima Zhao is well known to passers-by.

Now, China must expose this evil to the world and let passers-by know it (Yang, 2016). The messy waves caused by the argument of the "pan-market" have led to some radical policies or practices, which have jeopardized the stable navigation of China's modernization. Therefore, to realize the great rejuvenation of the Chinese nation, China must firmly criticize the trend of "pan-marketization" in the theoretical and ideological field, eliminate the severe harm it has caused, and revise the radical reform policies and practices with the tint of generalization. Only this way can China turn the grand blueprint of the Chinese Dream into reality.

New Concept of Economic and social modernization Must Be Condensed

The successful practice of China's reform and opening-up tells us that it is impossible to grasp the complexity of modern society by relying solely on economic analysis in a country with a large population and significant differences in regional conditions. In other words, pure marketization may not solve all the problems in modern society. Applying China's stern economic theories mechanically and the arguments that attempt to influence or even manipulate the reform process can only push out some practical radical methods under the label of deepening reform. It often disturbs the harmonious atmosphere of the harmonious atmosphere Chinese society.

Enhance the county's innovative ability to participate in international competition

Developing socialism with Chinese characteristics and building an innovative country is inevitable in Chinese history. On the one hand, China is thriving at this stage; on the other hand, it has reached a critical historical period. The country must redesign its strategic layout according to the changes in the international situation and the reality of the domestic social economy. Otherwise, it will lose a once-in-a-lifetime historical opportunity. China's global strategic issues are significant and should not be underestimated. A Community with a Shared Future for Mankind confirms the implication of national rejuvenation. The construction of a

"Community with a Shared Future for Mankind" aligns with the world development mode, which has changed from focusing only on realizing self-interest to the win-win pattern.

China has completed its preliminary industrialization and has developed at an alarming rate in some areas. The country is gradually equipped with the potential strength to become a world power. World history has repeatedly shown that the growth of an emerging power often means the decline of the hegemonic dominant country of the previous generation. However, based on the actual status of a socialist country, China has repeatedly declared and proved that China is on a path of peaceful modernization and will never seek dominance and hegemony. Building a Community with a Shared Future for Mankind is China's plan for world modernization in the new era (Ren, 2018).

Since the resource space of the world market is limited, countries that desire to be the world's hegemon will never allow China to become stronger gradually. A small part of people in these countries must desperately contain China and advocate the threat of China's rise as a great power. Therefore, China should have its global strategic layout, and the critical point or value orientation of this strategic layout is to maximize China's national interests. On this issue, a national strategy for the new period is needed. Once has a correct national plan and implemented step by step, China will grow into a developed country with international competitiveness in 50 years to realize the dream of the great rejuvenation of the Chinese nation.

It is gratifying to note that the introduction of the Chinese dream is the crystallization of the wisdom of the whole nation centered on the leadership of the CPC Central Committee, with Xi Jinping as the core. It is full of the philosophies of coordinated modernization and maintains the healthy thinking of developing socialism with Chinese characteristics. Through the supplement in the construction practice, such thinking will inevitably lead to developing the national economy into a new world (Xie & Xie, 2014).

Grasp the correct direction of developing a socialist market economy

Xi Jinping pointed out at the 40th anniversary of the reform and opening-up, China must unswervingly consolidate and develop the public sector of the economy. The government needs to unswervingly encourage, support and guide the modernization of the non-public economy, give full play to the decisive role of the market in the allocation of resources, give better play to the role of the government, and stimulate the vitality of all types of market players." The core issue of the economic system reform is to deal with the relationship between the government and the market. In contrast, the focus and difficulty of establishing the socialist market economic system will be the reform of the state-owned enterprises, which represents separating the ownership of means and materials of products from products. The state-owned enterprises have established a modern system and gradually become the main market body in China. Insisting on autonomous innovation has laid a solid foundation for China to become innovative.

Therefore, China should firmly prioritize economic development, stress that science and technology are the first productive force, and produce high-tech and high value-added products to participate more actively in international commercial competition. According to statistics, China's gross domestic product increased from 367.9 billion yuan in 1978 to 82.7 trillion yuan in 2017, with an average annual real growth rate of 9.5%, which is much higher than that of the world economy of 2.9% in the same period. China's share of the world's gross domestic product has risen to 15.2% from 1.8% at the beginning of the reform and opening, and it has contributed more than 30% to world economic growth.

China's total import and export of goods increased from 20.6 billion US dollars to more than 4 trillion US dollars. The cumulative use of foreign direct investment exceeds 2 trillion US dollars, and the total amount of outbound investment reaches 1.9 trillion US dollars (Liu & Zhang, 2018) (See Figure 2 for details). The strategic goal of building an innovative country can be achieved by establishing a socialist market economic system, insisting on autonomous innovation and establishing famous commercial brands that can enjoy a global reputation.

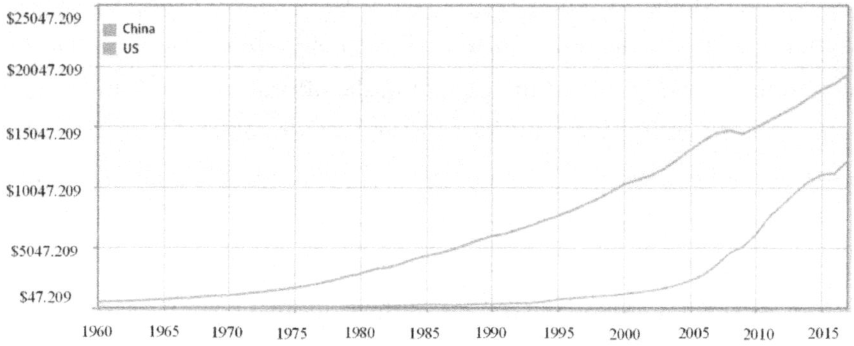

Figure 2. Gross Domestic Product between China and the United States from 1960 to 2018 (billion)

However, establishing a socialist market economic system is by no means the mechanical "marketization" of the whole country. The social responsibility of an advanced political party must not be swept away by the trend of "pan-marketization." The substantive expression of market economic theory, in some respects, is purely technological, which has its limitations and does not apply to all social phenomena. Therefore, China should criticize the trend of "pan-marketization." Only after dispelling erroneous statements can the correct theories be established and developed.

The goal of the socialist market economy is to ensure that the country is prosperous, that the people are well-off and healthy with better rights and interests, and that all Chinese people live in a safe and beautiful country. The words and deeds of Pan-marketization are misunderstandings of the market economy and distortions of market-oriented reform. One more step forward in truth is a fallacy, and turning marketization into "pan-marketization" is the first step towards delusion. Socialism with Chinese characteristics has entered a new era, and China's economic development has also introduced a new era.

To solve the problems about the relationship between the government and the market and to better play the role of the government, it is necessary to continually improve the property rights system and market-oriented allocation of factors to achieve effective incentives for property rights and free flow of production elements. It is essential to improve the management system of state-owned assets and consolidate the basic socialist economic system. It is necessary to deepen the reform of fiscal, taxation and financial systems and enhance the ability of financial services to the real economy (Wang, 2019).

Maintaining the common interests of society

How to develop a socialist market economy with Chinese characteristics? There are a great many suggestions from domestic scholars. The recognized core issue is how to carry out social change or social reconstruction. There are also many problems reflected in the reform of the market economic system, among which two need to be pointed out.

Firstly, the market economy is not equal to the market society. Former French Prime Minister Jospin has a famous argument: "market economy, not the market society" (Han, 2013). The market economy is indeed an effective economic system for allocating resources. However, its principles cannot wholly penetrate or dominate social life. In recent years, the reforms in some fields have made frequent mistakes and even caused severe harm, such as the reform of the medical market and the reform of education industrialization, which to some extent, has a direct relationship with the "pan-marketization."

Secondly, the socialist market economy needs to be based on public ownership and distribution according to work. Modern sociology believes that any economic system is embedded in the social foundation. It is difficult to operate normally without a proper social foundation, even with a perfect market economy.

To build a perfect socialist market economy in China, on the one hand, China needs to continually practice socialism with Chinese characteristics and combine it with the market economy to achieve higher efficiency. On the other hand, China should avoid blindness, prevent and avoid systemic economic risks and crises when practicing socialism in the way of resource allocation of the market economy, and treat and use it from a rational perspective (Liu, 2012). China must end capitalist exploitation and safeguard the common interests of the people, which are necessarily national interests.

Building a Community with a Shared Future for Mankind requires balancing the common interests of all countries in the world. Only by grasping the common interests can China understand socialism. Once the common interests are grasped, the ownership relationship and its structure, as well as the distribution relationship and its structure, will also be grasped so that China will not deviate from reality, lose direction, lag the times, or go beyond the stage. From building a Community with a Shared Future for Mankind and common interests, this foreword analyzes the relationship between public ownership, planned economy, and distribution according to work, which further deepens the understanding of Marx's socialist conception and construction of the great Chinese dream of rejuvenation.

Excellent national culture is the soul of economic construction

The Chinese culture, which has continuously been refined and honed by the Chinese nation in its thousands of years of development, is an inexhaustible driving force for the Chinese country to resist aggression and oppression and seek independence and prosperity since modern times. Although the history of the Chinese nation is full of changes, it has always been moving forward in a high-spirited manner because of its profound historical origin and deep cultural foundation, and the tremendous indomitable spirit of the Chinese people. During the period of reform and opening-up, China has once imitated the market economy theory implemented by the western industrialized countries, whose technological analysis method is worth studying and drawing lessons from it. The advanced concepts in the market economy theory should continue to develop and flourish.

However, suppose China wants to combine socialism with the stable market economy with Chinese characteristics and form a theoretical system of economics. In that case, they must have enough support such as logic, self-consistency, science, specialty, concreteness, and accuracy. To realize this grand systematic project, the Chinese people must have full cultural confidence. Cultural self-confidence is fundamental national self-confidence and an indispensable spiritual force for social progress. Since it was put forward, cultural self-confidence has experienced the development of "three self-confidence" to "four self-confidence." It is the more accurate take of "Chinese self-confidence" by the Party and the state government, the requirement of exerting the unique charm of Chinese culture, and the perfect response to the export of active western cultures (Hu, 2017).

Since the reform and opening-up, the theory of the socialist market economy in China has been the development of Marxism. However, this theory still has many imperfections that need to be adjusted more carefully. To proceed from China's actual situation, China should not mechanically quote some market economic theories that seem to have no flaws from theoretical or technical perspectives. Such practices neglect the critical element of "different national conditions" and put the construction of China's material civilization on a non-existent basis without seeking truth from facts. Therefore, given the problems in the economic system reform starting from China's national conditions, drawing lessons from its political, economic, cultural and historical traditions, the following points should be paid attention to:

Firstly, Measuring the degree of social modernization only by GDP and people's living standards by per capita GDP will deviate from China's national conditions, which are relatively scarce in resources, and the cultural traditions and national habits formed since ancient times. It will encourage the so-called advanced consumption and credit consumption, which will lead to a vicious circle of consumption if it lasts for a long time, and ultimately lead to the decline of people's actual consumption level.

Secondly, the excessive emphasis on economic benefits will fundamentally neglect social equity, resulting in unfair distribution of social wealth, polarization, and gradual accumulation of dissatisfaction among the masses to varying degrees. The goal of shared prosperity cannot be achieved.

Thirdly, although people can realize that the modernization of material civilization is the foundation of social progress, they always emphasize spiritual enlightenment. Still, in real life, they do not carry forward the fine culture of the Chinese nation but pay too much attention to the material foundation, which causes many young people to look down on the rich cultural heritage handed down to them. They lost the initiative, national confidence, and pride in constructing spiritual civilization (Guo, 2014).

Conclusion

To realize the great economic and social project of the Chinese Dream requires the removal of all obstacles on the way forward, a new outlook of economic and social modernization, adjustment of the strategic objectives and approaches of current economic and social modernization appropriately. In the final analysis, economic modernization is to achieve the well-being and shared prosperity of the whole people. Therefore, China must put material and spiritual civilization in the right place: material culture is the foundation of socialist economic construction, and spiritual enlightenment is the direction of socialist progress. Only by promoting each other can China achieve the goal of building a moderately prosperous society in an all-around way and realize the Chinese dream.

All kinds of negative phenomena caused by the trend of Pan-market economy theory have made some people feel confused or even dissatisfied with the development of the market economy. Scholars have made different interpretations in analyzing the causes of such negative phenomena. They believe that in the face of the "pan-market" problem in the modernization of the market economy, China needs to have a deeper understanding of the theory of the socialist market economy and the specific content of the great strategic concept of realizing the Chinese dream.

For many particular problems in the reform, starting from the appropriate content, including whether some reform measures are biased towards individual interest groups or whether some slogans or incorrect values are propagandized, China needs to seriously layout facts and rationalize instead of blindly following the crowd. Only such a severe approach can ensure that the process of marketization is "impartial" and that China will become a socialist country with characteristics of democracy, the rule of law, fairness and justice, vitality, stability and order, and harmony between man and nature.

While realizing the great social project of the Chinese Dream, China should consolidate the economic foundation and highlight the importance of national defense construction supported by high-tech means. Socialist modernization will not be realized with strong enemies outside the country and disunity inside. On the other hand, China needs to establish a systematic theory of promoting innovative countries from domestic social and economic modernization. It needs to firmly hold on to the center of economic construction and combine the "one belt and one road" initiative with the structural reform of the supply side to effectively build a modern economic system in the new era (Bao & Bi, 2016).

China should adjust the balanced modernization of the national economy and society. It also needs to create the fullest employment environment as the direction and take the achievement of the universal compulsory education and social security as the stage goal to ensure that the people can live a prosperous life and the country can be strong and prosperous. When necessary adjustments are made to the mechanism or economic and social modernization strategy, China must completely abandon the fallacy of "pan-marketization." Otherwise, the Chinese leadership cannot explain it to the whole nation. After these strategic adjustments are made, necessary reforms will be made to the existing administrative system, and adequate supervision mechanisms will be established to curb corruption at the management level from the source (Zhang, 2005).

In a word, from the perspective of modernization, China must innovate the concept of economic and social modernization, regard social equity and shared prosperity as the criteria for rebuilding the social family and strive to build an innovative society aiming to realize a "Community with a Shared Future for Mankind." The market economy theory still needs to be enriched; however, it must be re-interpreted and sublimated. In the fierce competition of comprehensive national strength, China has no other choice but to remove all obstacles that hinder the realization of the Chinese dream, overcome difficulties, and make the country better and more prosperous. Only this way can China realize the grand goal of the collective planning of the national leadership and finally make the great dream of national prosperity, national rejuvenation, and people's happiness come true.

Chapter 1
Centennial Exploration of Anti-poverty in China

Poverty is a "stubborn disease" perplexing human society. Since its birth, the Communist Party of China has eliminated poverty in China as its goal and continued to adhere to it. Especially after it came to power in 1949, eliminating poverty has become the mainline of the Communist Party of China's governance for more than 70 years. Especially since the 18th CPC National Congress, with the birth of the idea of targeted poverty alleviation, the Communist Party of China has led the people of the whole country to conquer China's last poverty fortress in one fell swoop. It will realize the all-around well-off society that the Chinese nation has dreamed of. This great achievement has important reference value for the anti-poverty cause of the international community.

Introduction

In 2020, the Communist Party of China led the Chinese people to complete the great feat of completely eradicating extreme poverty in a large country with a population of 1.4 billion for the first time in human history. China has been ending the "myth" of human struggle against poverty for thousands of years and creating a new era of human struggle against poverty. Today, looking back and Rethinking the 100-year great anti-poverty process led by the Communist Party of China is of great value to human anti-poverty cause in the 21st century and China's overall rural revitalization of industry.

"As long as theory persuades people, we can master the masses; as long as the theory is thorough, we can persuade people." A great cause needs the guidance of great ideas. Otherwise, it can only result from "blind people touching elephants." Since the Opium War, the Chinese nation has been trampled on the ground by the Western powers. These Western Powers had completed the Industrial Revolution for a century. Countless people with lofty ideals charged without me to explore the path of national rejuvenation and people's liberation from poverty. This process has experienced several failures, and the Chinese nation has paid a heavy price. In 1921, in the red boat on the South Lake of Jiaxing, the Chinese nation found the scientific thought - Marxism, which guided itself out of the impasse.

The original intention of the red boat was to realize the Chinese nation's liberation from poverty and great rejuvenation under the guidance of Marxist scientific thought. This original heart is deeply rooted in China's national conditions and China's profound historical and cultural traditions. It is naturally linked with the Chinese people and has become the firm revolutionary and ruling belief of the Communist Party of China. The Communists who hold high the banner of scientific thought have historically undertaken the historical task of the great rejuvenation of the Chinese nation. In this process, countless Communists threw their heads, shed blood, sat through the bottom of prison, died, defended the scientific thought of saving the nation in danger with fresh lives, and practiced the dream of letting the people get rid of poverty. Thus, the consciousness of leading the working people out of poverty began to awaken and lit a great ideological lamp against poverty. This lamp lights up the road of hope of the broad masses of people at the bottom in hardship, thus igniting the magnificent anti-poverty passion of a great nation. Since the 18th National Congress of the Communist Party of China, Marxist anti-poverty thought has been Sinicized into the thought of "targeted poverty alleviation." It is precisely under the guidance of poverty alleviation in this new era that the Chinese people, under the leadership of the Communist Party of China, have overcome difficulties, overcome obstacles, and finally completely overcome poverty and won a great victory.

Marx's whole world outlook is not a doctrine but a method. It does not provide ready-made dogma but provides the starting point and method for further research. While adhering to Marxism, the Communist Party of China has developed Marxism, forming Mao Zedong thought, Deng Xiaoping Theory, the important thought of Three Represents, the scientific outlook on development Xi Jinping's socialist ideology with China's characteristics in the new era. Today, the anti-poverty thought formed in the 100-year anti-poverty process under the leadership of the Communist Party of China is becoming one of the important guiding ideologies of anti-poverty for all humankind and the public spiritual wealth of human society. Therefore, the anti-poverty thought of the Communist Party of China will become the guiding light for most developing countries to fight against poverty in the 21st century and shine on the people of developing countries to get rid of poverty and move towards prosperity.

The core political force and System construction supports anti-poverty

Poverty is the "stubborn disease" of all humankind. History shows that it is impossible to cure poverty without the leadership of the core political forces. Since World War II, the anti-poverty practice of developing countries shows that the anti-poverty without the leadership of core political forces is unsustainable, especially the anti-poverty with simple material investment. For example, the international community has invested trillions of dollars in poverty alleviation support on the African continent in the past few decades, but the poverty here has not decreased. At this level, poverty eradication is the greatest political goal of all humankind.

Since the birth of the Communist Party of China on the red boat, the original intention of the Communists is to lead the great rejuvenation of the Chinese nation, get out of poverty and move towards a well-off society. This great original intention is the political guarantee for the Chinese nation to overcome poverty and the core political leadership to lead the Chinese nation out of poverty. Therefore, under the strong leadership of the core political force of the Communist Party of China, the Chinese nation will completely overcome poverty in 2020 and realize the people's well-off dream for thousands of years. In this long epic history of fighting poverty, the Chinese Communists have always been forefront. Especially since the 18th National Congress, under the background that China has entered a new era of society, the political forces with the Communist Party of China as the core have gathered the forces of China's democratic parties and social organizations to launch a final charge against China's poverty. From the central government to local governments, from Zhongnanhai to remote villages, the cadre team of the new era under the leadership of the Communist Party is fighting on the front line in the fight against poverty, and some cadres fall on the front line in this fight against poverty. It is the existence of this core political leadership that can condense the scattered social forces into a majestic anti-poverty force. It also organizes the scattered villages unprecedentedly, integrates them into China's fast-moving train, and realizes the miracle that one person, one village, and one nation must not fall behind in the journey of China's modernization.

Let us look back on China's great poverty Resistance War. It gives important enlightenment to the future development of China and the future development of all humankind: cultivating sustained and strong core political forces is the key to a nation and country's development and getting rid of poverty. The "super macro" factor of China's economic operation and development under the leadership of the Communist Party of China is the leadership of the Communist Party of China. It is the existence of this powerful political force that has firmly maintained the internal logical consistency of China's economic and social development for more than 70 years[3]. Looking back on the anti-poverty cases in developing countries since World War II, the anti-poverty behavior is intermittent due to the lack of political power to continuously play a leading role. Many behaviors fall short, and the effect of completing their work in one battle cannot be achieved. In many areas of Asia, Africa, and Latin America, there is even the problem of supporting poverty more and more, making an area in the trap of poverty for a long time. From the perspective of China's anti-poverty practice, these regions lack a core political force similar to the Communist Party of China, which adheres to the original intention and dares to make up its mind at the critical moment. In the process of development after World War II, although these regions obtained the independence of national sovereignty, without the leadership of sustainable core political forces, political forces of different factions took turns to control the state power, resulting in poor sustainability of national development policies. In the end, the order of development was disrupted due to the continuous transformation of political forces. The pattern of orderly anti-poverty has never been formed.

Poverty is not only an economic problem, a cultural problem, but also an institutional problem. In the lack of an efficient scientific system, it is difficult for a country to make substantive progress in its anti-poverty cause. Because different systems choices directly affect the generation, growth, and distribution of a country's national wealth, this impact is an economic problem and a political system problem for social development[4]. The original intention of the Communist Party of China is to establish socialist public ownership. Therefore, the Communist Party of China has locked its goal on the mainline of economic development. The next 28 years of revolutionary struggle revolved around the mainline of this system to realize the original intention.

After the founding of the new China, the Communist Party of China led the Chinese people to choose the socialist system firmly. Through this system, we firmly grasped the bullnose of national wealth distribution. We also implemented the original intention of the red boat in every field of socialist public ownership construction, scientifically solved the problem of social equity evolution that has plagued China for thousands of years, and promoted the great liberation of China's productive forces. It has laid a solid foundation for China's socialist building. After the reform and opening up, the initial intention of the Chinese Communists evolved to the stage of establishing the socialist market economic system, which scientifically solved the efficiency problem of the operation of socialist public ownership. Since the 18th National Congress, with China's socialist construction entering a new era, the Communist Party of China has further improved China's socialist system in the practice of national construction - "socialism with the deep integration of promising government and effective market under the leadership of the party." Under the guidance of the new era thought, China has invented the anti-poverty system of "targeted poverty alleviation" through the Communists, which has completely brought the Chinese people out of the "trap" of poverty and towards an all-around well-off society. Therefore, the Communist Party of China led the Chinese people to scientifically correct the distortion of national wealth distribution in the past development process through the construction of a socialist system [4]. We have explored a socialist development path that coordinates fairness and efficiency, and under the leadership of the Communist Party of China, we have overcome poverty in China.

It can be seen that the key to the success of China's anti-poverty cause lies in support of continuous system construction. Through the construction of the socialist system, China has comprehensively established the people's democratic system, effectively ensured that the people are the masters of the country, and realized the Chinese experience of development for the people and around the people. Adhering to the people's dominant position has fundamentally guaranteed that all state power belongs to the people and avoided China falling into the "trap of medium-sized countries." From this, we have built a well-off society in an all-around way, guaranteeing the people's right to survival, development, life, and health, and personal rights of citizens.

China's practice of "institutional anti-poverty" tells all humankind that a basic scientific anti-poverty principle is to build a national system suitable for China's national conditions. It is based on scientific analysis of China's national conditions, improves China's system through continuous practice, forms its development advantages and promotes its development. Instead of following the existing systems of some countries and comprehensively copying the systems of other countries to build their own country. The fundamental reason for the slow progress of anti-poverty in developing countries after World War II is that many developing countries over believe in the institutional teachings of "European and American teachers." They followed suit in the national system construction and development process and lost the initiative and development initiative. The Communist Party of China has led the Chinese people through the arduous exploration to build a national system that meets the interests of the greatest majority - the socialist public ownership system, through which we can ensure fairness and justice in development. Only in this way can a country's anti-poverty cause be effectively promoted. Because for a country's development, the system is the decisive factor, and the system problem is fundamental and overall. China has established the socialist system as a public norm that the whole country must abide by it. It is important to build an institutional bridge between the individual interests and the group public interests; form a strong social resultant force, Integrate highly dispersed individual interests into public interests and realize the integration of individual interests and public interests. It is the core of the practice of institutional poverty in China.

Education construction anti-poverty human resources

"Education is the foundation of a hundred-year plan; ten years of trees and a hundred years of people." After 1949, new China always grasped this main line of education and began to explore how to dig out the "poor roots" of the Chinese people from the level of education and culture. When new China was founded, illiteracy accounted for 80% of the country's 550 million people. The illiteracy rate in rural areas was more than 95%. The second census in 1964 showed that the illiteracy rate decreased from 80% to 52% among those residents over 15. More than 100 million people have taken off the hat of illiteracy. On January 1, 2001, the Chinese government announced that China had achieved the strategic goal of basically popularizing nine-year compulsory education and eliminating illiteracy among young and middle-aged people on schedule. By 2019, China's gross enrollment rate of higher education will exceed 50%, and China has entered the stage of popularization of higher education. Under the leadership of the Communist Party of China, through seven years of hard work, new China has achieved the popularization of higher education in a large developing country with a population of 1.4 billion, which is a miracle in the history of human education. In 2020, the consolidation rate of nine-year compulsory education will be 95.2%, and the popularization of compulsory education will reach the average level of high-income countries in the world. In 2020, the gross enrollment rate in senior high school education will reach 91.2%, exceeding the average level of upper-middle-income countries [6]. The educational achievements of more than 70 years in New China have laid a solid intellectual foundation for China's complete elimination of poverty, which has also injected new momentum into China's sustained anti-poverty action.

From this, we can find that the great poverty alleviation practice through education in China shows a basic truth to all humankind: "if you want to enrich your mouth, you must enrich your brain first." The Chinese Communists who led the Chinese people to "two bags" were rich. The new oath system on that red boat was established in China that year until the general secretary Xi Jinping solemnly swore "precise poverty alleviation" in the eighteen-hole village representative Party Central Committee in Xiangxi. In this hundred-year course, poverty alleviation through education has been running through the party's poverty alleviation work, and "supporting wisdom" and "supporting ambition" are implemented in "poverty alleviation." China's experience in poverty alleviation through education for most developing countries is the basic project for the country to get rid of poverty. Only by continuously promoting its education can a country or region lay a solid human resources support for the local poverty alleviation. It helps cultivate a leading talent echelon for the local prosperity, and poverty alleviation through education is the basic poverty alleviation that uproots the root of poverty.

Having a healthy physique is one of the important conditions for people to get rid of poverty. Before the founding of new China, the endemic diseases that plagued Chinese people for a long time became important reasons for their extreme poverty. After the founding of new China in 1949, the Communist Party of China led the people of the whole country to fight a resistance war against local diseases. By the end of the last century, China eliminated plague, cholera, schistosomiasis, which were eliminated in 1958, and disappeared in the early 60s. On June 30, 72021, WHO passed the malaria elimination certification by the WHO. This great national health project has provided healthy human resources support for China to eliminate poverty. Over the past 70 years since the founding of the people's Republic of China, China has established and improved its local health system, the national public health expenditure has continued to grow, a wide coverage medical and health security system in line with national conditions has been fully established, the construction of public health facilities has been continuously strengthened, the control system of infectious diseases and endemic diseases has been sound and remarkable results have been achieved, and the nutrition and physical fitness of residents have been greatly improved, The level of maternal and child health has been greatly improved, the health emergency system has been basically completed, the emergency response capacity for public health emergencies has been comprehensively strengthened, the development pattern of national fitness has initially taken shape, the national health level has been significantly improved, and China's per capita life expectancy has doubled (Yang Weizhong. 2019). When new China was founded, the average expectation of Chinese residents was only about 35 years old. Still, it increased to 77.3 years old in 2019, ranking at the forefront of developing countries and close to the level of some developed countries. China has built the world's largest social security system, including medical care, subsistence allowances, and pension. In

2020, basic medical insurance will cover 1.36 billion people. By April 2021, 1009.61 million people had participated in basic old-age insurance in China.

It can be seen that the construction of the national public health security system is another supporting project for China to get rid of poverty in an all-around way. The reason why the Chinese government has been able to continue to build this public health project for more than 70 years stems from the original intention of the Communists. When the red boat rippled the South Lake, the Communists saw the poor and weak China and the miserable situation that the people at the bottom were plagued by diseases and could not get rid of poverty. Therefore, the Communists vowed to eliminate the people's diseases, Give the people a healthy body. Today's achievements in the construction of China's public health project stem from the original intention of the Communists and their determination to serve the people wholeheartedly. In particular, on behalf of all the Communists, general secretary Xi Jinping issued a declaration on precision poverty alleviation and poverty eradication in a remote mountain village. China's national public health and health project completed the territorial coverage and solved the problem of ensuring the health of all the people.

China's national health engineering construction experience in the past 70 years is of great significance and reference value to most developing countries in difficulties. The practice of China's medical care and anti-poverty under the leadership of the Communist Party of China shows that national health is one of the preconditions for it to get out of poverty. Implementing a good national public health care project can effectively improve the national physical quality, which is an important basis for people to get rid of poverty. In the process of continuous anti-poverty for more than 70 years, China has explored and issued various forms of public health support policies in different periods and gradually solved the problems of "poverty caused by illness" and "loss of development ability due to illness" in stages and levels. Especially since

2020, under the background of the global epidemic, the problem of "poverty caused by disease" has become unprecedented in developing countries lacking public medical projects. China's experience in the construction and management of public medical and health projects is of great value to most developing countries.

Sustained infrastructure and Ecological environment governance

"To be rich, build roads first" is a phrase familiar to most people in China's development process in the past few decades. Under the support of this concept, new China has worked hard to plan the national transportation industry in the development process of more than 70 years. By 2020, the national railway mileage will reach 146300 kilometers, including 38000 kilometers of high-speed railway. The double-track rate is 58.5%, and the electrification rate is 72.8%. The national railway network density is 152.3 km / 10000 square kilometers (China Railway Statistical Bulletin, 2020). The total highway mileage is 5.1981 million kilometers, including 161000 kilometers of expressways. The navigation mileage of inland waterways is 127700 kilometers. There are 2592 berths of 10000 tons or above in ports across the country; 241 civil aviation airports, 48000 kilometers of UHV transmission lines and 115000 kilometers of natural gas and crude oil transmission pipelines have been certified (China Statistical Bulletin on the Development of Transportation Industry, 2020). This great achievement in constructing transportation infrastructure has been achieved in more than 70 years. However, the rise of modern transportation in China is marked by the purchase of the first steam engine ship by China Merchants in 1872, 65 years behind the West. In 1876, China built its first railway, imported its first car in 1902, built its first highway in 1906, and started China's aviation industry in 1929. By 1949, China had 21800 kilometers of railways, 80700 kilometers of highways, 73600 kilometers of inland waterways, and 161 berths at major coastal ports. Compared with the comprehensive transportation system formed in western countries in the same period, China's transportation is very backward. The overall appearance of transportation infrastructure and equipment is small, poor quality, low capacity, and partial layout. Compared with the vast land and large population, there are little modern transportation infrastructure and transportation equipment.

After founding the new China, the Chinese government has made a continuous investment in infrastructure construction, laying a solid foundation for China to get rid of poverty in an all-around way. After more than 70 years of continuous construction, China has achieved full coverage of high-speed transportation networks in remote areas from the great northwest to the great southwest. Especially in the great southwest, infrastructure construction under extremely complex geological conditions is an unprecedented challenge in the history of human infrastructure. China has completed this challenge. Those almost isolated regions are quickly guided into the modern system, realizing a great leap forward in development and finally eliminating poverty.

While carrying out unprecedented road construction projects, China began large-scale urbanization construction. By the end of 2020, China's seventh national census data showed that 901991162 people lived in cities and towns, accounting for 63.89%, and the floating population of China's population migration reached 376 million (China Bulletin of the Seventh National Census, 2020). In this unprecedented wave of urbanization in human history, hundreds of millions of people in China quickly entered cities and towns, completing the leap from an agricultural society to an industrial society. By implementing the urbanization project, this large-scale population migration based on civilization transformation has driven the rapid narrowing of the gap between urban and rural areas in China and provided strong infrastructure support for China's comprehensive poverty eradication.

China's infrastructure construction practice has important reference value for the anti-poverty of developing countries worldwide.

Infrastructure construction is the foundation for developing a country or region. Without systematic infrastructure construction, the development of a country or region will fall into a dilemma. However, basic engineering is a highly sustainable intergenerational relay race, which needs a stable political core force from relevant countries and regions to lead. Looking back on the last decisive battle against poverty under the leadership of the Communist Party of China, perfect infrastructure is a very important basic support for poverty alleviation. On the road to anti-poverty in the future, it is unavoidable for developing countries to explore an infrastructure construction model in line with their national conditions.

In old China, the forest coverage rate was less than 9%, the mountains and rivers were broken, and the land was barren. After thousands of years of development, this ancient land has been exhausted. However, for more than 70 years after the founding of new China, eco-environmental governance has always been an important part of the Chinese people's war under the leadership of the Communist Party of China. In the course of this epic ecological marathon, the CPC led the people of the whole country to carry out a series of major ecological projects such as farmland water conservancy construction and vegetation greening [the Mu Us desert at the border between Northern Shaanxi and Inner Mongolia is the fourth largest desert in China. After 70 years of treatment, the 42000 square kilometers desert has been comprehensively controlled, with more than 95% vegetation coverage. For the first time in human history, a large area of the desert has been erased from the earth. It is a miracle of human governance of the desert, which the Communist Party of China founded. In the early days of the founding of the people's Republic of China, the Communist Party of China led the people of the whole country to carry out large-scale ecological environment governance actions with extremely simple agricultural production tools. These continuous intergenerational relay governance actions built a good ecological foundation for China's national anti-poverty. Such continuous efforts put into practice that "green water and green mountains are golden mountains and silver mountains." It is the simplest ecological concept put forward by the Communist Party of China in its long-term practice, which has brought China into the stage of ecological civilization. Today, this concept is deeply rooted in the people's hearts, points out the direction of China's ecological governance and national development, and shows a new picture of green development that benefits the people, benefits the people, and serves the people.

With the support of the scientific ecological concept, deserts on China's land have become fertile fields, and resource-exhausting mining areas have become scenic spots. They earn money by relying on trees and leaves, "hometown of Moso Bamboo" Not selling bamboo and ecological products has become a new way of life for the Chinese people in the era of ecological civilization. Satellite images show that about 1 / 4 of the new green area globally from 2000 to 2017 came from China, with the highest contribution rate. China's great practice shows that green water and green mountains and Jinshan and Yinshan are not antagonistic but unified. The leadership force to realize the unity of the two is officially established Since the 18th National Congress of the Communist Party of China, China has innovated the socialist development path: forming a green development mode and lifestyle, transforming ecological advantages into development advantages, planting evergreen trees into cash cows, and green rivers and mountains have become an inexhaustible source of wealth and a green bank that will always add value. Ecological civilization has become the value pursuit of China's transformation of the development model in the new era. The ecological environment governance action under the leadership of the Communist Party of China embodies the development concept of people first in nature.

China's concept of eco-environmental governance has important reference value for most developing countries. It is: eco-environmental governance should go from "survival" to "ecology," from "looking forward to food and clothing" to "looking forward to environmental protection" This road is universal for developing countries and has universal significance and value for developing China's ecological civilization. Xi Jinping pointed out, "environment is livelihood, green hills are beautiful, and blue sky is also happiness." A good ecological environment will become a new growth point for China's people in China.

Industrialization as the foundation for anti-poverty

More than 20 years before the reform and opening up, China implemented the planned economy model to mobilize national resources to speed industrialization. It forms a relatively complete national industrial system and necessary infrastructure conditions and reverses China's long backward situation since modern times. It also created necessary human capital and material capital conditions for the growth miracle achieved in the later reform and opening up. At the beginning of the founding of the People's Republic of China, China's industrial sector was single, only mining industry, textile industry, and simple processing industry, and many industrial products depended on imports. After founding new China, the curtain of national industrialization was opened. From the 1950s to the 1970s, China initially established an independent and relatively complete industrial system, which laid a valuable foundation for industrial development. Since the reform and opening-up, China's industrial development has entered a take-off period. The industrial added value in 2012 was 38.2 times higher than that in 1978. Since the 18th National Congress of the Communist Party of China, China's industrial production capacity has increased day by day and has gradually moved towards the middle and high-end. From 2013 to 2018, China's high-tech industry and equipment manufacturing industry's added value increased by 11.7% and 9.5%, respectively. China has become a country with all industrial categories in the United Nations Industrial Classification. The output of more than 200 kinds of industrial products ranks first globally, and the manufacturing industry's added value has ranked first in the world since 2010. In 2018, China's raw coal output was 3.68 billion tons, an increase of 114 times over 1949; The output of steel was 1.11 billion tons, an increase of 8503 times; The output of cement was 2.21 billion tons, an increase of 3344 times. The electronic information industry came into being and achieved rapid development. In 2018, mobile communication handset and microcomputer equipment output reached 1.8 billion and 310 million, respectively 12. As a result, China has become the world's largest industrial country. Industrial civilization has been deeply rooted in China. The Chinese nation has fully realized the transformation from agricultural to industrial civilization. For the first time in human history, it has realized the industrialization case of a single population of 1 billion, which is the most solid and powerful economic foundation for China's anti-poverty.

The historical experience of China from a poor and backward agricultural country to the world's largest industrial country after more than 70 years of construction shows that the only way for underdeveloped countries to get rid of poverty is to transition from agricultural civilization to industrial civilization. It is important to promote their country out of the trap of poverty through the great practice of industrial civilization, Instead of rushing to find the way out of poverty through metaphysical models such as democratic elections. China entered the new era of socialism to actively promote the "one belt and one road" strategy. The construction of the China Pakistan Economic Corridor is a typical successful project in China's industrialization spillover. Only when most developing countries have completed national industrialization can they provide strong economic support for anti-poverty.

Conclusion

China is a large developing country with nearly one-fifth of the world's population. She is the only country in the world with the continuous evolution of civilization and a large socialist country under the leadership of the Communist Party. China's great success and accumulated useful experience in anti-poverty will certainly have important enlightenment value for the continuous promotion of the anti-poverty cause of all humankind. Especially for developing countries, China's experience will be a new source of ideas to get rid of poverty.

First, there is no universal development model in the world. Eradicating poverty and promoting development can only proceed from our national conditions and reality. In addition to learning from the excellent civilization achievements of human society, China's anti-poverty cause is more about exploring an anti-poverty model matching China's national system. Its historical background, cultural tradition, and social nature from China's national conditions is an anti-poverty road of seeking truth from facts, adapting to local conditions, classified guidance, and targeted poverty alleviation.

Second, the anti-poverty cause can only proceed from the people's actual needs of all countries. China's anti-poverty practice shows that poverty is the product of specific historical conditions, and it will continue to improve with the development of human history. The development model is not the best, only better; When development is not completed, it is only in progress; Problems in development can only be solved through development. The development model is not an abstract concept but a concrete cause for protecting and realizing everyone's specific rights.

Third, socialist China under the leadership of the Communist Party of China has great institutional advantages in respecting and protecting civil rights. In China, the leadership of the Communist Party, the socialist system, and the respect and protection of civil rights are inseparable. Adhering to the unshakable leadership of the Communist Party of China ensures that China's socialist road advances in a scientific direction and adheres to the protection of civil rights with the people first. It is the basic experience for the continuous enrichment and development of China's civil rights cause.

Fourth, build a new model of human industrial civilization. From the perspective of the evolutionary history of human civilization, the Communist Party of China adheres to the basic principles of historical materialism and dialectical materialism, creates a new model of industrial civilization in human society, enriches the basic connotation of industrial civilization, improves the choice of all humankind to industrial civilization, and helps to form a new world industrial civilization based on the community of human destiny.

Chapter 2
Modernization and Pioneer Economic Anthropologists

In China, economic anthropology started relatively later compared with that in the West; however, under the guidance of Marxist theory and based on the needs of China's economic development, it gradually formed unique advantages in its development process. In China's economic and social development practice, Fei Xiaotong and Shi Zhengyi, among other pioneers, creatively applied the economic anthropological paradigm to solve the specific issues, starting from the local characteristics, and completed some excellent academic results. This chapter probes and analyzes the scholarly contributions of the pioneers of Chinese economic anthropology; especially, it takes Marxist economics as the starting point to examine Professor Shi Zhengyi's theoretical contributions to the development of Chinese economic anthropology and its practical significance.

Introduction

Anthropology is an interdisciplinary subject that spans natural and social sciences. It takes human beings and their culture as the object of study. Because of its unique and practical research methods, anthropology has developed rapidly in western developed countries. As a branch of anthropology, applied anthropology is gradually becoming a new favorite of anthropology (Gunn, Otto, and Smith, 2015). As an essential branch of applied anthropology, economic anthropology is an interdisciplinary subject of economics and anthropology.

On the one hand, it involves the research paradigm of anthropology to solve some critical issues that were solved by economics research. On the other hand, it can also apply the research paradigm of economics and analytical tools to the problems addressed by anthropology research. Especially after Marxist anthropology effectively docks Darwin's theory of biological evolution with the theory of human historical development from the perspective of historical materialism, the development prospect of anthropology and economic anthropology is broader and worthy of in-depth study (Yang and Tian, 2018).

In recent years, in the western developed countries, especially in the United States, economic anthropology, as an interdisciplinary subject of economic and social development, economic management, and anthropology, has become an important part of the applied anthropology discipline. It has received the collective attention of academia and economic management circles. Economic anthropology started relatively late in China. Professors Fei Xiaotong and Shi Zhengyi were the early founders and promoters of Chinese anthropology and ethnology. Both of them had devoted their lives to the study of anthropology, ethnology, and ethnic economics. They had successfully applied their research results in various fields of society, including the development of ethnic regions, the economic construction of backward areas, the management of industrial and commercial enterprises. Their theoretical thoughts, works, and methods of thinking had made significant contributions to the discipline construction of Chinese anthropology; they pointed out the direction for the development of economic anthropology and even the further development of anthropology (Tian, 2014).

Professor Fei Xiaotong, based on the background of social changes in China, conducted anthropological fieldwork in different communities and villages to study the influence of culture and cultural differences on the cultural and economic life of human society. Fie is the author of *Peasant Life in China* and put forward the theory of "cultural consciousness." This book makes a highly concentrated theoretical summary of the formation of the Chinese nation, emphasizing anthropological theories and concepts such as the relationship between man and nature, man and society, and between man and culture. It lays a theoretical foundation for the development of economic anthropology. It is of considerable significance to the construction of ecological civilization and the practice of the scientific concept of development.

Professor Shi Zhengyi adhered to the basic principles of Marxism and devoted his whole life to the study of ethnology. His general contribution mainly lies in establishing the discipline of ethnic economics, broadly putting forward the concept of ethnology, and pointing out that China should strengthen the four modernizations of ethnic areas. In comparison, his outstanding contribution is commonly recognized in putting forward the "strategic guideline of accelerating development" to take western development as the task and attach importance to the economic development of ethnic areas.

To achieve balanced growth of the overall economy, Shi Zhengyi conducted a study of Shaman and other minority cultures, religious and cultural morphology, and comprehensively enriched the scope and content of China's economic anthropology. Professor Shi Zhengyi put forward a scientific thinking method, "concrete-abstract-concrete." His academic contribution inspires Chinese anthropologists and ethnologists to continuously expand research in new fields. His theories have cross-era significance for the development of economic anthropology has made contributions to the national economic construction.

Guided by the academic thoughts of Fei Xiaotong and Shi Zhengyi, some famous contemporary anthropologists, such as Professor Chen Qingde, Professor Zhou Daming, Professor Luo Kanglong, Professor Zhang Jijiao, Professor Chen Gang, and Professor Shi Lin, have studied economic anthropology from different perspectives and promoted the indigenization of economic anthropology in China. For example, Professor Zhou Daming devotes himself to the study of urban anthropology, applies anthropological research methods to the study of cultural and social processes in urban areas, and tries to find new ideas for the operation of urban-rural harmony through the study of the migration, integration, and reconstruction of the civic society of Chinese migrant workers (Zhou and Yang, 2014). Professor Zhang Jijiao devotes himself to the study of corporate anthropology (Zhang, 2014). He indicates that the commercial value of the cultural heritage of the "old brand" should be excavated to maintain the city's vitality (Zhang, 2016).

Professor Chen Gang conducts an economic anthropological study on the cultural tourism market of Lugu Lake, finding that the development of cultural tourism has a far-reaching impact on the relationship between local ethnic groups and traditional culture (Chen, 2012). He tries to find solutions for many social problems by studying market and group behavior in economic anthropology, such as the case study of Kunming taxi drivers through an economic anthropology perspective (Li and Chen, 2014). In her review of ethnicity in Ethiopia, Shi Lin points out that when ethnology and anthropology are used to do fieldwork, it will be more useful to research ethnic governance through a comprehensive understanding of the historical context and ethnic composition of racial relations. She insists on realizing the multi-dimensional and systematic research methods of panorama and close-range dimensions, vertical and horizontal, and the combination of theory and description (Shi, 2016). In her monograph *Economic anthropology*, she elaborates on the theoretical sources of early economic anthropology-the academic contributions made by Malinowski, Polanyi, and others in the field of economic anthropology (Shi, 2002).

Besides, as the leading promoters of economic anthropology in China, a group of scholars has tried their best to explain the importance of anthropological research to the academia of China's economic management discipline. The representative works include *Economic anthropology* (Tian and Luo, 2013), *General Theory of Business Anthropology* (Tian and Zhou, 2013), *Environmental Anthropology* (Wang and Tian, 2012), *Marketing Anthropology* (Tian, Feng, and Wang, 2017), *Management and Business Anthropology* (Tian, Zhou, and Ma, 2018), *Management Anthropology* (Tian, Tao, and Lv, 2019). Their works emphasize the importance of anthropological research methods such as fieldwork, observation, and interview in the economic sectors. Their works, such as Economic anthropology, elaborate on the research content, research object, and method system of economic anthropology in detail. Using the relevant theories and methods of anthropology, they make a study of cross-cultural marketing (Tian, 2014), consumer behavior (Tian and Zhou, 2013), dietary culture (Li and Tian, 2014), and anthropology and economic management education (Lan and Tian, 2011). Some of these scholars are Professor Shi Zhengyi's students and have made remarkable contributions to the promotion and development of economic anthropology in China.

From Fei Xiaotong to Shi Zhengyi

With the ongoing efforts of the pioneers and leaders, all the progress has been made to develop China's economic anthropology. Fei Xiaotong's *Peasant Life in China* and Shi Zhengyi's *Ethnic Economy and the Four Modernizations in Ethnic Regions* occupy a unique historical position. They are the essential achievement of the pioneer academic thoughts of China's economic anthropology. Therefore, it is necessary to conduct an in-depth comparative study of these two masterpieces to sort out and understand the early development of economic anthropology in China.

As one of the founders of sociology and anthropology in China, Mr. Fei Xiaotong constantly calls for attention to the issue of "cultural consciousness" and emphasizes that anthropologists should have their historical responsibility (Fei, 2004). The birth of *Peasant Life in China*, a famous work of Chinese rural society, started anthropology research in China and is a milestone in developing anthropological theory and field investigation (Fei and Dai, 2012). *Peasant Life in China* provides a reference model for studying China's indigenization of economic anthropology. It highlights a practical methodology for the anthropological research of Chinese rural communities (Quan and Cui, 2013). The formation of this literary masterpiece is attributed to Fei Xiaotong's field investigation of Kaixiangong village by the anthropological method. In this book, he pointed out that under the condition of unbalanced land and other resources, balancing the relationship between agriculture, animal husbandry, and forestry to develop the rural economy is very important, thus putting forward the theory of rural economic development earlier. In his works, the "Jiang Village" is a miniature transformation from an agricultural society to an industrial society in China, reflecting Chinese farmers' local economic development model and characteristics. It is the germination of early economic anthropology research in China.

For the development of Chinese anthropology, Professor Fei Xiaotong's significant theoretical contributions can be broadly summarized in the following aspects (Huang, 2007): scientifically analyzed and summarized the historical process of the formation of the Chinese nation, the national system structure and its evolution law, and the self-cognition of the Chinese society. Utilizing anthropological research, the author re-examines Chinese traditional culture and makes a lot of original ideas, which dramatically develops his teacher Malinowski's theory of functional school. Put forward the philosophy of "cultural consciousness," that is, people should have "self-knowledge" of the culture they live in to have a clear self-awareness of their cultural environment. People should understand what it has done, how it works, and how it may evolve in the future. Still, it does not mean "cultural return," nor advocate "wholesale westernization" or "wholesale otherness." In other words, the purpose of "cultural consciousness" is to understand better and develop human beings themselves, rather than to fight for the sphere of influence and domination in various specific cultural forms. He believes that every intellectual in China should take the initiative to understand the culture itself and its position, appreciate different lifestyles, and actively participate in cross-cultural dialogues (Fei, 2003). At the same time, he advocates that culture has the characteristics of mobility, expansion, change, and innovation. Paying attention to the community research theory, in the book "*Peasant Life in China*," Fei

Xiaotong put forward the development of local industry, the realization of local reconstruction theory, and established its anthropological status internationally. Professor Fei Xiaotong, as a pioneer in the field of Chinese anthropology, had made considerable academic contributions to the discipline construction of Chinese sociology and anthropology and left much precious educational wealth for the academic development of Chinese economic anthropology, social anthropology, and even the entire anthropology.

Professor Shi Zhengyi studied many classic works of economics and ethnology both at home and abroad with the stand, viewpoint, and method of Marxism from his unique perspective. In the process, he developed his ways of thinking and research methods. First, he insisted on the concrete abstract-concrete way of doing academic works (Shi, 1983). Professor Shi Zhengyi put forward the four modernizations and the Strategy for Accelerated Development in Ethnic Minority Areas by emphasizing the importance of theoretical thinking, adhering to the principle of the relationship between understanding and practice of Marxism, and in the field of economic anthropology. He pointed out that the scientific method of theoretical thinking has the characteristics of indirect, abstract, and conscious, which is a trinity organic unity process of "practice-cognition-practice," "individual-general-individual," and "concrete-abstract-concrete." Based on this theory, he founded the discipline of Ethnic Minority Economics. He defined it as an interdisciplinary discipline with distinct ethnic characteristics, which means to study the aspects and laws of the interweaving and interaction between economic factors and social factors in different social forms (Shi, 2001).

Secondly, based on absorbing the essence of the methodology of Marxism, Professor Shi Zhengyi summarized the relevant theories of the former Soviet Union and Chinese economists, constructing the unity of history and logic and other critical theoretical principles to guide the development of the economy in ethnic areas. The facts have increasingly reflected its unique value and should become one of the academic resources for developing the Ethnic minority economies of socialism with Chinese characteristics (Shi, 2001).

Thirdly, Shi Zhengyi studied, challenged the traditional view of theoretical thinking and cognitive process on Karl Marx's *Das Kapital* dialectically. He argued that the process of cognition includes not only the process from concrete to abstract but also consists of the process of "abstraction to concreteness." He put forward the tracing and reduction methods of irrational thinking based on this point. He believed it is important to ask questions, trace back to the source, and find the answers. It is also important to dialectically treat the existing conclusions, inspect the causes, find out the problems and establish new theories and viewpoints (Yang, 2006).

In his book *Ethnic Economics and the Four Modernizations in Ethnic Regions*, Professor Shi Zhengyi pointed out that the main task in the new period for China is to realize the four modernizations in ethnic areas. He indicated that in developing modern society, the state should proceed from the country's actual conditions and carry forward the glorious traditions of all ethnic groups, give full play to their strengths and avoid their weaknesses. At the same time, the state also should adhere to the correct direction to consolidate, develop and constantly improve the public ownership of the means of production. The realization of the four modernizations in ethnic areas, especially the accomplishment of industrial modernization in ethnic regions, is the basis for consolidating and developing the great unity of all ethnic groups in China. It is necessary for the development and prosperity of all ethnic groups in the country. The four modernizations must be realized to improve the Ethnic minority economies. Today's practice increasingly bears out these insights, but it is precise because he has been criticized by some people who believe too much in western neoliberal ideas (Shi,1992 c).

Professor Shi Zhengyi's theoretical elaboration on industrial modernization is highly consistent with the early branch of American economic anthropology, "Industrial Anthropology." Before the 1980s,

American anthropologists referred to the study and practice of business-related phenomena as "industrial anthropology," which studied workers and managers. The 1930s were the most glorious period of American Industrial Anthropology. From the 1940s to the 1950s, industrial anthropologists identify the factors and forces that balance the organizational system by studying workers and managers (Baba, 1986). After the Second World War, with the decline of business enterprises, the school of interpersonal relationships and its practitioners slowly fell behind. The academic environment changed, industrial anthropology began to decline, and many industrial anthropologists gradually became professors of business schools. Then, as a sub-branch of economic anthropology, business anthropology steadily rose.

As a Marxist economist, ethnologist, and anthropologist, Professor Shi Zhengyi's theoretical thoughts are similar to that of Professor Fei Xiaotong's and have some noticeable differences. First of all, Professor Fei Xiaotong is the proponent of the topic of "Research on the Socioeconomic Development of Ethnic Minority Areas in Border Regions." After inspecting the ethnic minority areas in Inner Mongolia, Gansu, and other provinces and regions, he noticed the unbalanced development between the east and the west. He actively advocated the research on the development of the Border Regions. For several years, Professor Fei Xiaotong pointed out the significance of ethnic studies by his research achievements in this field. The shared prosperity and progress of all nationalities based on equality is the fundamental national policy of the country and can affect the overall situation of the construction of the "four modernizations" of the entire country. It is related to China's long-term stability and prosperity (Fei, 1997).

It is very much in line with Professor Shi Zhengyi's view. They all believe that in a socialist country like China with special national conditions, it is necessary to research ethnic minorities. At the same time, narrowing the gap between the east and the west and equally treating the people of all ethnic minorities are the crucial ways to realize the four modernizations of the country. However, there are differences between the two professors' research perspectives. Influenced by his early academic thoughts, Professor Fei Xiaotong explained the need to balance the development of the east and the west from the perspective of demography and biology (Sun, 2017), while Professor Shi Zhengyi explained the problem from the standpoint of Marxist economics, ethnology, and anthropology.

Professor Shi Zhengyi once pointed out that the economy of minority nationalities is an indispensable part of the Ethnic minority economies of the country, and the economy without animal husbandry is an incomplete Ethnic minority economy. To narrow the gap between the east and the west, it is necessary to develop the economy of minority nationality areas faster than that of the general areas (Shi, 1991). Minority people generally live in mountainous regions or vast grasslands. Their living space is several times more than that of the Han people, very suitable for the development of animal husbandry. Therefore, the animal husbandry economy in the minority economy occupies a considerable proportion; attention must be paid to it. While Professor Fei Xiaotong pointed out: Northwest China occupies one-third of China's land area. Animal husbandry is the economic foundation of Northwest China and has excellent potential. Most of the people engaged in animal husbandry are ethnic minorities. Therefore, from the perspective of developing the economy of ethnic minorities, Professor Fei Xiaotong believed that the modernization of animal husbandry is essential to accelerate the development of the border areas, and it should start from the pastoral areas (Fei, 1993). Professor Shi Zhengyi and Professor Fei Xiaotong regard the rural economy as a breakthrough in the development of the economy in minority areas and emphasize that in minority areas, China must combine the characteristics of minority areas and vigorously realize modernization of the pastoral regions. These similar views are related to the particular national conditions of the country and the same experiences of the two scholars in the minority areas in their early years.

During the fieldwork in the countryside of south China, Professor Fei Xiaotong thought that the development and perfection of the rural financial market should be given full attention and support to revitalize the rural economy. Urban funds should be returned to rural areas, and domestic and foreign aid should be given according to local conditions. Rural areas should be domestic and urban as foreign aid (Fei, 1996). Professor Shi Zhengyi believed that to develop the economy of minority areas, China must develop "two markets," namely, the market of means of production and the financial market in western minority areas (Shi, 1998). Therefore, from the two scholars' similar academic points of view, to invigorate the enterprises in minority areas, the government must invest more in them and make up for their capital defects.

Shi Zhengyi used Stalin's interpretation in 1913 to define ethnic groups in his book *Ethnic Minority Economics and the Four Modernizations of Ethnic Regions*. He considered that in historical development, ethnic groups are a stable community formed by the people who have a common language, region, economic life and show a common psychological quality to the prevailing culture (Shi, 1985). Professor Fei Xiaotong also thinks that an ethnic group has four common elements: the common region, the common language, the common economy, and the common psychological quality. The two scholars agreed with Stalin's definition of an ethnic group, showing their common understanding of social attributes and similar theoretical ideas.

Professors Shi Zhengyi and Fei Xiaotong attach great importance to developing the Great Northwest. Professor Fei Xiaotong said: To speed up the development of the western region, to positively and adequately develop the township enterprises is a meaningful way, apart from increasing domestic and foreign investment, improving infrastructure construction, developing high-tech industries, and implementing water-saving agriculture. To this end, he also proposed a "business-to-work" start-up strategy (Fei, 2000). Professor Shi Zhengyi put forward the procedure of developing the western region at the beginning of establishing Ethnic Minority Economics and pointed out that, to a certain extent, Ethnic Minority Economics and the development of the west region co-exist and grow together. It also emphasizes that in developing the western region, China should unite all nationalities to realize socialist industrialization, the same as Professor Fei Xiaotong's strategy of taking business as a guide to work.

However, in developing the Northwest, Professor Fei Xiaotong paid more attention to developing, protecting, and utilizing human resources in the western region. Professor Shi Zhengyi studied the fundamental problems of the development of the west region from the angle of Ethnic minority economies research. Professor Shi Zhengyi indicated that China needs to pay more attention to handling the relations between ethnic and economic factors in the western region and among all ethnic groups and between ethnic minorities and the state. He stressed that it is necessary to draw lessons from the widening gap between the east and the west caused by prioritizing the east's development. He suggested the government must pay attention to the development of the west and ethnic regions in the future and find ways to narrow the gap between the east and the west, and eliminate the polarization between the rich and the poor. From Fei Xiaotong's *Peasant Life in China* to Shi Zhengyi's *Ethnic Economy and the Four Modernizations of Ethnic Regions*, and then to the contemporary anthropological research in the economy, society, culture, and education demonstrate that in the long historical development of Chinese economic anthropology, it has not only its historical height but also has its unique practical significance.

From Economic anthropology to Ethnic Economics

With the accelerated process of socialist modernization in China, ethnology has appeared in many academic disciplines and is forming into an independent, substantial new group of subjects. If ethnological research is limited to the scope of traditional research, it will undoubtedly affect its development and is not conducive to the economic development of ethnic areas (Li, 2008). Shi Zhengyi started the construction of broad ethnology in the journal of *Ethnic Minority Economics* in 1991. Later, he published "Broad Ethnology" (Shi, 1992). The book systematically introduced broad ethnology's research object, method, and content. Professor Shi explained that ethnology refers to ethnology with Chinese characteristics in a broad sense. It was initiated by Chinese ethnologists under the guidance of Marxist theory and expanded the scope of ethnic studies to the entire world. The emergence of broad ethnology has added important content to ethnology. It is significant in the development of ethnology. In particular, the research methods involved in the broad sense of ethnology provide a handy reference for the development of economic anthropology in recent years (Shi, 1992).

According to Shi, any subject has its specific research methods. As a comprehensive subject, broad ethnology has three main research methods: guiding, basic, and specific application methods. The guiding method is the fundamental guiding principle in the methodology, which is mainly based on the viewpoint of Marx's practice, development, and dialectical materialism. The so-called primary method refers to the subject's most important or commonly used approach in the specific research process. The fundamental techniques of ethnological research include fieldwork, participatory observation, historical narration, cultural auditing, and subject-object analysis. Most of the research methods used in Chinese economic anthropology come from the primary research methods of broad ethnology and have been developed to a certain extent. The specific methods refer to generally applied methods. In other words, the specific methods or unique methods adopted according to the actual needs of tasks in the research process can be divided into general techniques in general scientific research and specialized research methods related to broad ethnology (Shi, 1992).

The broad sense of ethnology takes the worldwide "nation" as its object of study. It studies the history of the nation's formation, development, and extinction. It focuses on the various characteristics of the nation and its various forms of expression, the material culture and spiritual culture, the economic structure and social formation and the psychological quality of each nation, and so on, to reveal how each nation develops, changes, and influences each other (Shi, 1990). From the founding of Ethnic Minority Economics to the proposition of broad ethnology, Chinese scholars have made significant progress in the practice and theory of economic development in minority areas. As an interdisciplinary subject of economics and anthropology, the research scope of western economic anthropology is relatively narrow. The birth of Ethnic Minority Economics in China was 30 or 40 years later than that of western economic anthropology, with different theoretical bases and backgrounds. Economic anthropology in the West focuses on various trivial human cultural and economic phenomena (Wilk and Liggett, 2007).

Ethnic Minority Economics in China focuses on the position and function of each ethnic group in the process of economic activities, revealing the relationship between different ethnic groups and the relationship between economic changes and economic development in minority areas (Shi, 1993). The study of ethnic economics in China is from the perspective of ethnology to study the economy. It is the specific application of the unique value and subject advantages of economic anthropology, which is worthy of careful study and reference in the practice of the scientific concept of development and the construction of ecological civilization today. In other words, to study nationalities from the perspective of economics, to achieve the cross-integration of the two significant issues of ethnicity and economy is worthy of careful study and reference in the practice of the scientific concept of development and the construction of ecological civilization.

Since the beginning of the development of western economic anthropology, there have been many different definitions in its discipline. As a product of the Second World War, economic anthropology takes the realization of human concern and the reflection on human development as its research content. The study of human heterosexuality can understand society and the times of its own life. According to Herskovits (1936), Economic anthropology is a study of "the economic life and behavior of primitive people." Stuart M. Plattner (1974) holds that economic anthropology is a subject that studies the economic system and economic behavior of human society from the perspective of anthropologists, using ethnography and other methods. Keith Hart (1996) emphasizes that economic anthropology can be regarded as a science concerning the material evolution of human society, that is, the interaction between human beings and the natural environment. It is difficult for scholars in other fields to understand the essence of economic anthropology with different definitions of discipline. Since the founding of Ethnic Minority Economics, Professor Shi Zhengyi had made clear that its subject is to study the characteristics and laws of the development and change of Ethnic minority economies, which is authoritative.

The research fields of Ethnic Minority Economics in China are similar to those of western economic anthropology, both of which are devoted to studying different groups of people (Shi, 2002). In recent years, many anthropologists in China have introduced western economic anthropology into China and written books, such as *Economic anthropology* by Professor Chen Qingde (2012), by Professor Shi Lin (2002), and by Professors Tian Guang and Luo Kanglong (2014). When Chinese scholars introduce western anthropology, they combine western economic anthropology with China's unique national conditions to a certain extent and inject vitality into it. It can be predicted that in future research, the indigenization of economic anthropology and Ethnic Minority Economics in China will complement each other, absorb each other, and develop together.

One of the subjects of ethnology is to study the religious beliefs of ethnic minorities. Here, Professor Shi Zhengyi regarded religion as a cultural form and put forward a new concept of "religious-cultural morphology." The original theory put forward by Professor Shi Zhengyi involves many subjects such as anthropology, ethnology, culture, religion. It is noteworthy that economic anthropologists have conducted specialized studies of shamans and change consultants. They point out that Shamanism is a culture-centered religion. A Shaman's resource is the cultural resource itself. A Shaman's knowledge is the content of culture, which coincides with the focus of religion, cultural morphology (Tian and Dai, 2013). Therefore, the development of religious and cultural morphology also promotes economic anthropology to a certain extent.

To develop the economy of ethnic minority areas rapidly, China must actively adjust the industrial structure of ethnic minority areas, vigorously promote the commodity economy and increase the wealth of ethnic minorities. The development of township enterprises is necessary to develop the commodity economy. However, in remote ethnic minority areas, people's thoughts are conservative and backward because of the long-term semi-closed living environment. People in these areas tend to wait for the government, rely on the government, and want help from the government. They pay attention to agriculture and despise commerce, and this ideology severely hampered the development of industry and business in ethnic minority areas. Therefore, Professor Shi Zhengyi pointed out that emancipating the mind and renewing ideas through various channels and ways is the first step in adjusting the industrial structure of ethnic minority areas. They are developing industry and commerce in ethnic minority areas (Shi, 1993). At the same time, the government should attach importance to the development of commodity production, give full play to the advantages of human resources, and promote the transfer of labor force from the primary industry to the secondary and tertiary sectors in planned way minority areas. Also, it is important to increase the proportion of industry and commerce in the economic sector and vigorously develop such advantageous industries as the fur industry and construction industry in the minority areas (Shi, 1988).

Recently, supply-side reform has been a hot topic in China's academic circles (Tian and Wang, 2016). Many industrial and commercial enterprises have urgently needed supply-side reform as early as the 1980s. In the last century, the industry has been the leading sector of the Ethnic minority economies; the development of the industry can provide funds for the economic development of ethnic regions, improve their productivity level, and narrow the gap with the developed areas. However, the efficiency of many industrial productions is extremely low in these areas, and the waste of resources is dangerous. Therefore, the key to improving the minority industry is strengthening the production's technical transformation and management optimization (Shi, 1986).

"Acceleration strategy" and the Development Economic anthropology

In recent years, with the increase of poverty alleviation efforts of the Chinese government, the issue of accelerating the economic development of ethnic minority areas is becoming more critical. It has gradually risen to the national strategic position. The imbalance between minority areas and developed areas has become increasingly prominent due to historical development, geographical conditions, and national economic policies. It is not conducive to the healthy and coordinated development of the Ethnic minority economies; it will affect the country's national unity and long-term stability in the long run.

It is believed that the western minority areas have many advantages in resources and huge development potential. If the state can give them enough policy support, then the minority of the west areas may catch up with or even surpass the developed regions. The two-step theory is to improve the eastern coastal areas actively, regard the east coastal areas as the strategic focus of economic development, and return to the development of the western ethnic areas after completing the task of developing the eastern coastal regions. Synergetic theory, namely synchronous development, advocates that the economic development of the East and western regions or the three major zones should advance at the same speed and in coordination with each other. The strategy of accelerating development emphasizes giving special attention to the western minority areas and accelerating the economic development of the minority areas, which is the most active development strategy for the development of the minority economy, put forward by Professor Shi Zhengyi (Shi, 1986). Later, Professor Shi Zhengyi pointed out that the strategic policy of accelerating modernization in ethnic minority areas should take accelerated steps to narrow the gap with the developed regions in the shortest possible time. This strategy will finally wholly eliminate the backward predicament and enter the ranks of advanced nationalities (Shi, 1993). Of course, for various reasons, this development strategy has not become the dominant strategy, but its theoretical significance is undoubtedly paramount, worthy of our study today.

Instead of merely unrealistically and unilaterally pursuing high speed, the so-called Accelerated Strategic Approach is a systematic project that fully considers the functions and conditions of the system and is most conducive to the scientific acceleration of the overall long-term development of the system. It mainly includes the following contents:

First, "acceleration strategy" is a guiding ideology, and the governments at all levels must attach importance to its important strategic significance to the development of the western minority areas. Second, to carry out the "accelerating strategy" in ethnic minority areas is not to increase the speed of their economic development blindly, but to realize the four modernizations in ethnic minority areas in combination with the pace of the modernization of the country, to take "economic construction as the center" and to speed up the construction of political, educational and spiritual civilization in ethnic minority areas in an all-round way. Third, the acceleration is not a high speed divorced from reality, but a seizing of favorable opportunities to make full use of various favorable conditions to carry out modernization. It will help the minority areas to catch up with or surpass the development speed of the developed regions as far as possible and narrow the economic gap between the eastern and western regions.

Fourth, while speeding up economic development, we should also speed up the reform of the economic system in ethnic minority areas and speed up the process of building two civilizations in the western ethnic minority areas within the overall national system.

Implementing the strategic approach to acceleration is not a departure from the broader context of national policy. On the contrary, it must adhere to the central government's primary line of "one central task and two basic points," subscribe to the Four Cardinal Principles, comply with the reunification of the motherland and national unity. China should adopt local and social conditions in minority areas, speed the transition from a natural economy to a commodity economy, and promote the modernization process in minority areas. At the same time, it is necessary to firmly implement an opening-up policy in minority areas. It should be open to the outside world, not only to the border countries but also to other countries globally. Based on resource development, the development of border trade should be accompanied by the development of international trade (Shi, 1989). It can be said that the accelerated development strategy is a concrete way of opening up the country's significant policies of reform and opening up, and they are internally unified.

However, the "accelerated strategic approach" must also face certain historical limitations. Because of the restriction of the social environment and productivity level, our country mainly regarded the industry as the pillar industry of ethnic minority economies. It emphasized that the advanced sector was the primary way to realize the four modernizations. With the rapid development of the economy in the 21st century, the proportion of industrial output value in developed economies' national economic output value is becoming smaller and smaller, and the dimension of tertiary industry is significantly increased. In China, while ignoring the tertiary sector, a vigorously growing sector cannot better meet the growing needs of people for a better life, and today's world ecological civilization and green development requirements also have a particular gap.

Since the 1980s, Professor Shi Zhengyi first discussed the economic development of the western region based on general abstraction and put forward the strategic policy of the overall development of the west minority areas earlier. Subsequently, the actual situation of the western region, including geographical conditions, regional characteristics, and the concept of ethnic status and the level of economic development, were investigated and studied in detail. A large number of first-hand data were mastered. It was found that the western ethnic regions were far behind most parts of China, including the central area, than initially expected (Shi, 2002).

Professor Shi Zhengyi was fully aware of the extreme importance of developing the western ethnic areas to develop the whole country. He spent much effort studying it. First of all, he particularly stressed that ethnic minority areas are exceptional in terms of geographical location, local conditions, and customs and that the characteristics of different ethnic minorities are different. Therefore, to speed up the development of the economy in ethnic minority areas, China must grasp the specific "regional conditions." Secondly, in line with Fei Xiaotong's (Fei, 2001) view, Shi Zhengyi believed that when developing the economy in the western minority areas, the protection of human resources should be taken as a prerequisite for economic development. Third, Professor Shi Zhengyi repeatedly stressed that the development of the commodity economy is the only way for the economic development of the western ethnic areas. With the development of the economy and the acceleration of the four modernizations in ethnic minority areas, the small-scale peasant economy has been entirely unable to adapt to the development of the times and social progress. Therefore, it is necessary to speed up the transformation from a small-scale peasant economy to a commodity economy to speed up the development of the economy in minority areas. Fourthly, China should properly handle the relationship between "rich countries," "rich people," and "rich areas" (Shi, 2000). Not only to improve the national economic tasks, community economic tasks as a strategic starting point but also to improve people's living standards and quality, pay attention to people's livelihood construction.

Economic anthropology is a collection of anthropology, management, economics, ethnology and psychology, and other multi-disciplinary knowledge of interdisciplinary disciplines (Tian, 2012). Ethnic economics and economic anthropology are different in their development history and discipline definition. Still, they are similar in their research fields, so they will complement each other and merge in the discipline construction in the future. Comparing with economic anthropology, we can also find the commonness between them.

Firstly, in methodology, ethnic economics follows ethnological field investigation, comparative study, ethnological narrative, abstract economic analysis, and model analysis. In contrast, economic anthropology takes anthropological methods as the main method and emphasizes observing and studying people's behavior. Moreover, economic anthropology uses ethnographic methods and is good at combining remote areas with local areas to study farmers' economic life and pays attention to the role of the human network. As a branch of economic anthropology, business anthropology creatively studies industrial and commercial administration. It emphatically probes into the cultural differences and the influence of cultural change on management practice (Shi, 2011).

Secondly, in the research object, Ethnic Minority Economics and economic anthropology are based on studying people’s behavior and life in a specific cultural background. Influenced by the history of the times, China’s early society was predominantly rural. Therefore, the observation objects of new ethnic economics and economic anthropology are mainly farmers and rural life. In recent years, China's comprehensive national strength has been dramatically improved. The service-oriented tertiary industry formed by industrial and commercial enterprises has gradually become a pillar of the Ethnic minority economies. Given this, economic anthropologists will inevitably bring various business practices into the study object more and more. However, both explain the cultural essence and the root cause behind the behavior by observing and studying the different tones and guiding the economic activities. Their subject nature is the same.

Thirdly, Professor Shi Zhengyi realized the limitation of traditional ethnology. He developed ethnology in a broad sense in keeping with the trend of the times. This pioneering research idea brings the global ethnic, cultural, and social issues into the Chinese scholars' scope of the study. Moreover, it opens the way for the early reviews of ethnic economics and economic anthropology to expand to a global extent and, as such, makes the economic anthropology discipline construction like the confluence of hundreds of rivers into the blue sea. The reality also confirms the development trend of this discipline. Today, many Chinese economic anthropologists gradually shift their research focus from local enterprises to multinational firms due to the accelerated process of economic globalization and cultural globalization. It shows that the research and development direction of Ethnic Minority Economics and economic anthropology is very consistent. This pioneering thinking of Professor Shi Zhengyi extends the research scope of China's economic anthropology and points out the correct direction for the future development of China's economic anthropology (Tian and Luo, 2013).

Conclusion

Professors Fei Xiaotong and Shi Zhengyi, the forerunners of Chinese economic anthropology and Ethnic Minority Economics, devoted their whole lives to academic research and made indelible contributions to social sciences in China. Professor Shi Zhengyi, guided by Marxist economic theory, established the "Ethnic Minority Economics," which serves to develop economic construction in ethnic minority areas and has been highly apprised by the Chinese people. Shi Zhengyi was a Marxist ethnologist with Chinese characteristics. He constructed broad ethnology theories and accelerated strategic policy suggestions. His contribution helped the government narrow the gap between the East and the West in China. His academic achievement is innovative and significantly impacts ethnology and anthropology. With his unique perspective and deep theoretical foundation and experience, Professor Shi Zhengyi has put forward many constructive meanings, including "accelerating strategy," "two-way circulation," and "four modernizations in minority areas." Historical practice has proved that these pioneering policy recommendations benefited the economic development of minority areas and have practical significance for developing the western region, constructing ecological civilization, and implementing the scientific concept of development. In the final analysis, they are conducive to the development of the whole country, the revitalization of the nation, and the progress of humankind.

Economic anthropology has a history of nearly one hundred years since the rise of the West, focusing on the market and consumers and the organization and operation of companies. One of the missions of economic anthropology is to highlight the humanistic value of business practice; that is, economic development should ultimately serve the overall development of society (Liu and Zhang, 2017). It is also the academic value of Professor Shi Zhengyi, the establishment of Ethnic Minority Economics, "accelerated strategy," western development, and other strategic principles to serve the community, accelerate the economic growth of minority areas, and promote the implementation of the overall national strategy.

Western economic anthropology was formally formed in the 1940s in the American academic circles, and its foothold is to explore the processes of production, distribution, and consumption in different societies (Tian, 2015). The starting point of the discipline of Ethnic Economics lies in developing the economy of ethnic minority areas in China, narrowing the gap between the east and the west, and paying attention to the all-around development of humanities and economy. Although there are many differences between western economic anthropology and Chinese Ethnic Minority Economics, Professor Shi Zhengyi's "two-way circulation" and other academic theories inspired the localization of Chinese economic anthropology. China's economic anthropology combines western economic anthropology with ethnic ethnology and other ethnic economics. It considers China's unique national conditions, especially the particularity of minority areas, conducive to the integration of economic anthropology into China and the accurate positioning of China's economic anthropology.

Professor Shi Zhengyi has made remarkable academic contributions to Chinese ethnology. It can be considered that Chinese ethnology without Professor Shi Zhengyi is incomplete ethnology. The indigenization of China's economic anthropology is inseparable from the continuous development of Chinese ethnology. Professor Shi Zhengyi's academic contribution is of fundamental significance to China's economic anthropology. It will continue to promote the development of China's economic anthropology in future academic research.

Chapter 3
Modernization and Social Governance in Minority Regions

The modernization of the Minority Regions in Western China (the MRIWC) plays a vital role in the country's overall modernization progress. In recent years, the MRIWC has made remarkable achievements in improving the social governance system and enhancing the governance capacity. As the modernization process continues, the MRIWC can adequately deal with social governance issues by drawing lessons from typical cases like the Western Hunan Zila Tribute Rice trademark registration case. The anthropological theory and method, including but not limited to the holistic concept, emic-etic view, and ethnographic skills, are recommended in dealing with these issues. The MRIWC must construct cooperation governance patterns through the multiple subjects and adjust measures to local conditions by flexible governance means that are "lawful, rational, and affectional." It will accelerate the modernization of the MRIWC and help China build itself into a more advanced country.

Introduction

China is a multi-ethnic country enjoying shared prosperity. The modernization of China cannot be separated from the modernization of all ethnic groups and regions in the country. The modernization of the Minority Regions in Western China (MRIWC) is unique due to the combination of many factors such as natural conditions, ecological environment, social structure, and ethnic culture. It is somewhat biased to guide the study of this issue with economic theories alone. Widespread research combining ideas and methods from anthropology, sociology, and other related disciplines is needed to comprehensively analyze the current situation and responses to the MRIWC's modernization and social governance.

While previous studies have focused on theoretical discussions, the MRIWC urgently needs development experiences drawn on and applied. Based on an ethnographic case, this chapter aims to provide a reference model and inspiration for the modernization of minority regions in China and other multi-ethnic countries through an in-depth analysis of a typical case and theoretical discussions. It is expected to make a theoretical contribution to the existing literature on social governance by providing an operational new model of comprehensive approaches. The proposed model can be globally applied to most ethnic groups and minority regions and is significant in theoretical and practical levels.

Anthropology is a people-centered and culture-based social science that studies the laws of human social development (Lassiter, 2014). Social governance is a necessary activity for human survival and development. It can only be carried out under certain production relations and social environments and is bound to be restricted by production relations and influenced by social culture. Therefore, studying social governance in a specific environment and culture is one of the functions of anthropology. Anthropology emphasizes individual human adaptation to society, holistic research, and cross-cultural research. In social governance practice, applying anthropology's fundamental theories and methods can effectively expand the path of governance and improve its effectiveness. Therefore, anthropology has a substantial and unique role in practicing and researching social governance (Keesing 1981).

For Anthropologists, fieldwork is an essential manifestation of ethnographic research methods (Rowe, 2012), and ethnography is as essential to the cultural or social anthropologist as laboratory research is to the biologist, archival research is to the historian, or surveys are to the sociologist (Monaghan Just, 2000). Social governance workers should be familiar with ethnographic methods and tools to deeply grasp the essence of culture, different cultural characteristics, and their expressions.

Moreover, they should take the economic and social life of the grassroots as the field research object and collect an abundance of first-hand information through participatory observation, in-depth interviews, questionnaires, and other standard ethnographic research methods. In this way, they can grasp the basic situation of an aspect of a particular community in an all-around way and lay a solid foundation for subsequent analysis of social governance, thus effectively reducing social governance costs and improving governance efficiency (Tian and Yu, 2017).

In the process of social governance in minority regions, the anthropological emic-etic approach is of great practical value (Triandis et al., 1993). Social governance practitioners should think differently, go to the grassroots level, and put themselves in the people's shoes to understand their social and cultural backgrounds and discover and record their realities and needs. They should think from the standpoint of the public about how social governance guidelines and measures meet grassroots social demands and how the policies and standards work. And they should identify the fundamental problems and shortcomings to propose widely acceptable and practical improvements.

Social governance practitioners should apply the holistic concept of anthropology to specific governance practices. Any grassroots social organization has its particular self-organizing system, a subsystem of the social system (Thompson, 1944). Improving the social system starts with each subsystem. Nevertheless, the overall interests can be achieved at the price of local interests from the social system status in a specific period. In terms of the governance of a particular grassroots organization, it is the governance of a group of interrelated and mutually constrained groups with clear goals. There are inevitably different groups and interests (Jiggins and Röling, 2000). When addressing the problem of any part, the governor must consider how it affects the rest of the overall organizational system and the surrounding environment. The governor should take the situation into complete account based on thorough investigation and research and solve it in batches according to the priority (Tian and Yu, 2017).

Based on the above considerations, it is necessary to explore the modernization strategy of the MRIWC based on the analysis of typical cases to find feasible ideas for the organic integration of theory and practice. Xiangxi Tujia and Miao Autonomous Prefecture is a typical representative of the MRIWC. In the modernization of Xiangxi Prefecture, Zila Tribute Rice Trademark Squatting has led to many social problems in the Miao settlement, which the local government has resolved with means that are lawful, rational, and affectional. Its transformed social governance concept, sound governance system, and enhanced governance capacity can be regarded as a microcosm of the modernization and social governance of the MRIWC. It is a valuable reference for the modernization and handling of social problems in similar regions in the world.

After the instruction, it will present an in-depth discussion on the social governance of the MRIWC in China's modernization and a theoretical examination of the importance and specificity of social governance in the MRIWC. It then provides an ethnographic narration of Xiangxi Zila tribute rice trademark squatting, followed by an analysis on MRIWC modernization and social governance based on the case of Zila tribute rice trademark squatting, and finally outlines a conclusion.

Social Governance of the MRIWC in China's Modernization

Since the reform and opening up, China has achieved many remarkable achievements in its overall economic and social development. The modernization of China is closely associated with the effectiveness of social governance. The correct management of the relationship between the two embodies the essential characteristics of Chinese modernization and is an effective measure to boost China's rapid development. The modernization of the MRIWC is an integral part of China's modernization.

Social Structural Characteristics of the MRIWC

Intercultural patterns and governance cultural barriers. The social governance of the MRIWC has to implement the national policy and spirit of the mainstream Chinese culture while considering the characteristics of the ethnic culture that has been passed down to the present. In a multi-ethnic region, intercultural interaction is pronounced, and social governance is mostly cross-cultural. In Xiangxi Prefecture, 43.33%, 33.40%, and 22.53% of the residents are Tujia, Miao, and Han. The differences in language, beliefs, and customs among ethnic groups are significant. The foremost leaders of the autonomous prefecture have been composed of Tujia and Miao cadres to balance forces and achieve shared development. The selection of essential leaders at the prefecture-level must focus on the ethnic pattern. The guidelines must be interpreted and relayed by the relevant departments at the provincial, prefectural, and county levels to promote national policies from the central government to the grassroots. Subject to the influence of the mixture of provincial-level Han culture and prefecture-level Tujia and Miao cultures, policy effectiveness varies among Tujia villages, Miao settlements, and other ethnic groups due to ethnic, cultural barriers (Chen, 2018).

The plurality of governance subjects and the complexity of the counterbalancing forces. Social governance in minority regions involves various governors, including government, market, social organizations, and citizens, mostly with ethnic characteristics and regional orientations. Local governments and institutions assume the grassroots functions of national governance and play a significant role in ethnic autonomy. The market includes various companies and cooperatives, which influence regional development, employment, and social stability through investment and consumption. Social organizations have not only grassroots organizations, industry associations, societies, and other formally registered organizations, but also "family branches" (Wang and Wang, 2015), "village elders," and "wedding and funeral organizing committee," and other traditional organizations. Citizens refer to all citizens of minority regions, such as the Xiangxi Prefecture, which embraces 43 ethnic groups. The MRIWC has a wide range of social governors, and there are more combinations of them because of the different ethnic cultures attached to them. The forces with different natures, levels, functions, and cultures develop into a plurality of governance subjects, which determines the complexity of the composition of local governors and the governance process.

Variety of traditional means of livelihoods and differences in governance units. The diversity of ecological and natural conditions in the west determines the differences in traditional livelihoods of various ethnic groups. The Miao people in Xiangxi have developed a fixed farming livelihood suitable for fixed-point management through paving trees for fields. However, the nomadic livelihood of the Inner Mongolian people, who live by water and grass, is not suitable for fixed management. The Tibetan farming and herding livelihoods on the Qinghai-Tibetan plateau vary (Luo and He, 2019). The diversity of livelihoods with regional orientations and racial characteristics, resulting in various governance units and scopes, has led to the complexity and difficulty of social governance in the MRIWC.

Multiple resource owners and weak local governance bodies. Multi-ethnic groups often create and maintain cultural resources in the western China region during long-term interaction, exchange, and integration. The diversity of parties to whom the resources belong can easily lead to interest disputes and group conflicts over value transformation. The Hunan-Guizhou-Chongqing border area has a considerable value of ethnic medicine culture, but the interests are complicated. Guizhou has more than 4,800 traditional Chinese medicine resources, with obvious advantages such as supporting policies and ample funds, but the systematic theory of Miao medicine lags. Ethnic, cultural resources are attributed to many parties with complexity. The small number and weak capacity of local governors in Xiangxi Prefecture have led to regional conflicts and ethnic disputes over cultural resources, which have tested social governance.

Specificity of the MRIWC's Modernization Path

The primary goal of the MRIWC's modernization is to modernize individual residents of all ethnic groups, which requires that its modernization path prioritize people's livelihood (Yang, 2016). People's well-being is the sum of the needs of countless individuals, which requires social governance to be oriented toward maintaining and maximizing the public interest. Therefore its modernization process is involved in overall people's well-being. Currently, the MRIWC has abundant resource endowment. However, due to the lagging social management and local forces, it is not sticky enough to return benefits to the local community. It is likely to fall into the vicious circle of "capital injection - resource development - benefit export - environmental decline." Huayuan County in Xiangxi Prefecture once ranked second in the country in manganese resources, but after years of heavy mining, the resources are drying up. Most of the mine owners left with their money, leaving behind a flawed legacy of severe ecological pollution and multiple cancers among the residents. Only a few receive short-term gains in this approach, but the public suffers long-term losses. It runs counter to the principle of prioritizing people's well-being.

In 2008, the problem caught the attention of the central government, which ordered the county's mines to stop production for rectification, resulting in a rapid decline in the county's economy and a severe hindrance to modernization. Given this, the MRIWC's modernization must prioritize the people's livelihood and public interest. The wealth gained from resource development should be used for the overall development of the people to improve the people's livelihood, enhance the people's wisdom and increase their wealth, and thus enhance its sustainable development capacity.

The modernization of the MRIWC should mainly focus on social modernization, and regional orientations characterize its modernization path. The rice industry in the Northeast Plain is modernized based on mechanized and technological means on a large scale of fields. However, the industrial modernization in the farming area of Honghe Hani and Yi Autonomous Prefecture in Yunnan should be an organic combination of terraced farming wisdom and a modern marketing model. With the industrial modernization of the Dong and Miao artificial forestry in Jinping, Guizhou cannot abandon the slash-and-burn farming and forest-food intercropping culture in the mountains. The industrial modernization of the Yugur people in the Qilian Mountains cannot be separated from the nomadic livelihood tradition of the grasslands. Therefore, "modernization" is a fluid concept with different connotations in each era, and there is no fixed model of modernization. Society is modernized by integrating and balancing livelihood adapted to the ecosystem and contemporary technological standards rather than high-tech approaches. Building a social governance system according to local conditions is necessary instead of rigidly applying the governance model of first-tier cities or coastal areas to achieve a high level of social governance development.

The modernization of the MRIWC is to realize the modernization of each ethnic group, so its modernization path has distinct ethnic characteristics. For example, about 3/4 of the traditional food of the Dulong people in Yunnan is wild plants. Still, outsiders regard eating wild food as poverty, mistakenly thinking that March-August is the "hunger month" when the Dulong people pick wild vegetables. Since the 1950s, the government relief rice has become a staple food. Still, many Dulong people think: "The food now is flimsy, and we do not feel energetic when eating it, unlike the ragi, barnyard grass, and Tartary buckwheat before. It tastes good and gives people energy (Du and Chen, 2016)." The relief rice provided by the government with a large amount of human, financial, and material resources seems to eradicate the "hunger month" of the Dulong people. However, it is worth reflecting on the misjudgment of the etic cultural values, the misunderstanding of the governance target, and the actual effect of governance.

Theory and Practice of Social Governance in the MRIWC

To better promote the modernization of the MRIWC and its social governance, the Chinese central government and the MRIWC governments at all levels are actively engaged in practical exploration and theoretical research. The relevant academic research findings mainly include the following aspects:

First is the holistic research on the modernization of social governance in China. Scholars have concluded from Chinese practice that the fundamental purpose of state governance modernization is to build a community with a shared future for humankind and other views different from Western modernization. Also, scholars have explored the modernization path of China's national governance and proposed policy recommendations such as improving national governance capacity such as grassroots penetration capacity (Zheng, 2019) and establishing the concept of adjusting measures to local conditions (Gao, 2020). They focus on the connotations, features (Gu and Wu, 2017), and system building (Lu and Zhu, 2021) of social governance in the Chinese context and make a helpful exploration of China's modernization and social governance issues from a holistic view. However, the above studies are not very specific to the MRIWC, and although they are essential inspirations, detailed analyses are needed for particular issues.

Second, it is the doctrinal study on the modernization of the MRIWC. Scholars systematically studied the modernization of the MRIWC from the perspectives of the concept of social governance in minority regions (Chen and Zhao, 2014), pattern evolution (Qi, 2019), and theoretical sorting (Fang, 2017). They argued that social governance in minority regions had ethnic characteristics (Shi, 2019) and particular dilemmas (Yun, 2017), so that they conducted in-depth studies from the perspectives of governance mechanism (Li and Zhang, 2021), legal security (Wang, 2020) and realistic path (Yang, 2016). The results of this category are closely related to the modernization of the MRIWC, which has important implications for the top-level design, institutional improvement, and the rule of law of social governance in China. However, there is still some room for combining theory and practice, and it is worth referring to typical cases for further research.

The third is the research on the economic development of the MRIWC. Earlier studies were closely integrated with national policies such as the Western Development (Zhan, 2001), focusing on the development in line with the regional reality (Wang, 2001) and prioritizing the acceleration of social development (Wen and Hu, 2003) in line with the development concept for economic construction. Recent studies have balanced macroscopic and microscopic perspectives, focusing on essential issues such as the preservation of cultural resources in the modernization process (Yuan, 2021). They have conducted in-depth studies in the context of national policies and other practical experiences (Wan, 2018), which are of high reference value in guiding the MRIWC's economic development and modernization. However, modernization is not only to build a modern economic model, and social governance does not solve economic problems merely. Hence, the study of modernization in other fields needs to be added.

In recent years, with the formulation and implementation of national strategies such as western development and targeted poverty alleviation, the MRIWC has achieved rapid progress economically and socially. However, the region is still lagging in various fields. The MRIWC is subject to harsh natural conditions, a fragile ecological environment, weak economic foundation, diverse and complex governors, and far-reaching ethnic culture. So it is still poverty-stricken, accompanied by difficulties and problems in social governance (Yun, 2017).

Just as the MRIWC's absolute poverty must be eradicated as a priority for China to make a moderately prosperous society in all aspects, the

MRIWC's social governance system and governance capacity must be improved simultaneously for pushing forward China's modernization. Social stability and ethnic unity are the foundation for the sustainable development of a community for the Chinese nation and an essential condition for comprehensive modernization. Due to various issues and reasons outlined above, the social governance of MRIWC is very complicated and needs a better institutional system and wiser governance tools to create a stable environment for modernization. In this context, China should build a replicable model of social governance in the MRIWC to overcome the bottlenecks and accelerate its modernization.

Ethnographic Narratives of Xiangxi Zila Tribute Rice Case

The village of Zila in Xiangxi Prefecture is a vital field site for the authors' anthropological research. The authors have conducted several surveys in this field site for five years. During the field research, they focused on and profoundly examined the Zila Tribute Rice Trademark Squatting, arguing that it is a localized reflection of the complexity of the modernization process of social governance in minority regions and all its related aspects.

Historical Background and Case Details

In Huayuan County of Xiangxi Prefecture, Hunan Province, a brand of regional orientations passed down for about 200 years--Zila Tribute Rice (Chen and Huang, 2020). During the Daoguang Reign (1782-1850) of the Qing Dynasty, the rice became a tribute to the court when Ma Guoxiang was an official of Linwu County. The unique name of the rice, such as Fragrant Rice, was recorded in the county annals during the Tongzhi Reign (1856-1875) of the Qing Dynasty, indicating that the rice had already become a brand name and had a considerable scale of cultivation during the Tongzhi Reign. Zila Tribute Rice is not a brand created by a single family because of the long-standing tradition of tributes from seven or eight farmers. It referred to the rice produced in the "paved fields from forests" of Zila Village in the early days. Still, it refers to the high-quality rice produced in Zila Village, one of the brands with geographical indications.

Due to insufficient awareness of local protection, the trademark was registered in 2015 by a lotus planting cooperative in Longtan Town, Huayuan County. In 2016, the Huayuan County government launched the targeted poverty alleviation project of Zila Tribute Rice. It cooperated with Jishou University to declare Zila Tribute Rice as China's Important Agricultural Cultural Heritage. In June 2017, the Complex Zila Tribute Rice Farming System in Huayuan County, Hunan Province, was officially recognized by the Ministry of Agriculture and Rural Development as the fourth batch of China's important agricultural cultural heritage and had a brand foundation for developing high-end agriculture. However, it met strong resistance when the county government wanted to promote brand building and the poverty alleviation industry through products with geographical indications. The relevant leaders of the County Food, Drug, Industry, Commerce, and Quality Supervision Bureau firstly attempted to touch the trademark registrant emotionally. They took the initiative to interview the trademark registrant several times. Still, the registrant replied that he was neither willing to sell the trademark nor authorize or cooperate with relevant government departments to develop it.

Moreover, there was no such action as an emotional investment in the development of the industry alone, as he claimed. After several unsuccessful negotiations, the county government asked the former Hunan Provincial Bureau of Quality and Technical Supervision for permission to list "Huayuan Zila Tribute Rice" as national products with geographical indications to be protected and to designate a larger area such as Shilan Town as the origin of Huayuan Zila Tribute Rice as a product with geographical indications. In October of the same year, "Huayuan Zila Tribute Rice" was declared a product with geographical indications for protection. However, the final approval at the national level could not bypass the issue of trademark squatting.

The county government abandoned the conventional "purchase by cash + policy subsidy" approach to solve the economic development problems and calm the villagers' conflicts. It took an exemplary step in the history of public interest rights protection. Given insufficient social governors for trademark protection in Huayuan Country, the Huayuan County Brand Protection and Development Society was established. In December 2017, the Society commissioned Jishou Wuling Intellectual Property Agency Co., Ltd. to file a request for invalidation of the trademark Zila Tribute Rice based on a large amount of supporting information. The notice of defense sent to the applicant was returned and later served through the Trademark Gazette, and the respondent failed to defend within the specified period. Hence, the Trademark Review and Adjudication Board of the State Administration for Industry and Commerce ruled in early 2019 that the disputed trademark should be declared invalid.

Due to dissatisfaction with the decision, the lotus planting cooperative changed its registered domicile to Zila Village, Shilan Town, and appealed to the Beijing High People's Court. After careful consideration, the Beijing High People's Court found that the facts of the original judgment were clear, the applicable law was correct, and the conclusion was correct, and issued a final decision in April 2021, which "rejected the appeal and affirmed the original judgment. At this point, the ownership of the Zila Tribute Rice trademark has been decided. The government of Huayuan County has legally defended the public interest and included the original registrant as a user of the geographical indication and will establish production procedures after the geographical indication is approved. In addition, the county government has encouraged relevant cooperatives, villagers, and companies to protect and develop Zila Tribute Rice cultural resources in an orderly manner through supporting policies with different levels and focuses.

Substantive Points of the Conflict

The case appears to be a trademark dispute, but the essence of the conflict is between individual interests and public interests. When the trademark snatcher obtained the monopoly right of the famous local specialty products, the general interests of the Miao people, who have long been working together to maintain the brand with regional orientations, were infringed. Therefore, the trademark protects the whole county's public interest, preserves cultural resources for regional development, and promotes the balanced and joint development of all ethnic groups in the county. It is the objective requirement of the holistic concept of social governance.

Zila Tribute Rice is neither a new term nor an exclusive product, but a term for the unique rice produced in a specific region under natural conditions. There are 308 households in the village with close blood and marriage ties, and their Miao ancestors collectively created and long maintained this agricultural brand and cultural resource. In addition, four cooperatives registered by Zila villagers and domiciled in the village have been producing and selling Zila Tribute Rice for a long time. After the trademark was squat, other cooperatives or individuals were prohibited by law from selling "Zila Tribute Rice" without permission, and the law enforcement agencies received reports of infringement and seized infringing packaging and other materials. The government and other cooperatives warned and complained about promoting the "Hunan Huayuan Complex Zila Tribute Rice Farming System" as an agricultural cultural heritage.

Although it had been freely traded for hundreds of years, the law-ignorant Zila villagers were afraid to sell Zila Tribute Rice. Not only was "Zila Tribute Rice" prohibited from appearing on the packaging, but when buyers asked if it was "Zila Tribute Rice," the villagers dared only reply, "Zila Tribute Rice is others' trademark! We are selling Zila rice with another trademark." Otherwise, the villagers involved would face legal disputes or family conflicts. According to the government's arrangement, a cooperative supporting the declaration of agricultural cultural heritage developed a poverty alleviation industry. The trademark registrant also challenged it at the door. The people said: "I do not dare to ask for support policies even if they are good! When they came to my house, it was big trouble!" Township cadres often went to the village to regulate the conflict but could not do anything.

Conflicts between the trademark registrant and other cooperatives gradually intensified due to insufficient resources, cultural differences, and family rivalry. First, C, a relative of registrant A, was unsuccessful in electing the secretary of Zila village. By mistake, D, a corporate member of another cooperative that had long protected the agricultural cultural heritage of Zila Tribute Rice, was later elected as village secretary. Then, someone repeatedly went to the Discipline Inspection Commission to make an anonymous complaint, trying to get D to resign from his position as village secretary so that he could compete for the right to make decisions and have a voice in the village. After the Discipline Inspection Commission investigated the report and confirmed that it was false, two factions were formed in the village cadre group. C, a relative of the registrant, was not working, either because he was not interested in working or because he wanted weak D to resign from his position as a village official.

After the first instance judgment, registrant A took the initiative to negotiate with D to claim that his cooperative had been operating the rice industry under A's trademark license for many years. After D refused, A could only use the rice purchase and sale contract with his relatives in Zila Village to respond to the lawsuit. In addition, registrant A also had disputes on interests with other rice cooperatives in his village and Dongma Village Rice Cooperative. As the dispute over the trademark intensified, the relationship between the families representing different interest groups became more and more complicated and gradually accumulated mutual resentment. When there are other conflicts such as disrespectful words and land disputes, it is prone to group fights.

Due to the trademark squatting incident and the unique characteristics of the MRIWC, it has severe impacts on the cultivation and cooperation of industrial development actors, branding and product sales, agricultural cultural heritage protection and resource development, the establishment and promotion of related poverty alleviation projects, villagers' conflicts and family conflicts, resulting in the unfavorable situation of grassroots government governance. There are four main reasons for the outbreak of conflicts and problems in the early stage of the incident:

First, the concept of governance is lagging, and the protection measures are not effective. Previously, the Xiangxi Prefecture and county governments positioned themselves as managers and decision-makers. It was not until 2017 that the Governor of Xiangxi Prefecture promoted the prefectural level declaration of Zila Tribute Rice as a product with geographical indications.

Second, the governance system is imperfect, and the division of authority and responsibility is obscure. Firstly, three departments, such as the industry and commerce department and agricultural commission, can approve or manage geographical trademarks, leading to project collisions and institutional contradictions. Secondly, the rights and responsibilities of the registrant are not detailed, which may lead to the registrant being unwilling to invest in the development and only desiring to resell the trademark at a high price. Finally, trademark registration should regulate the improper profit-making behavior of others. However, the registrant firmly believes in the right to monopolize all activities such as production, sales, and publicity, including public welfare publicity and development projects for poverty alleviation, which eventually led to foreign capital concerns and hair-trigger conflicts.

Third, the governor and the filer are not made clear. Trademark registration regulations only impose restrictions on the county level and above administrative divisions. If specific protection agencies, funding, and exceptional protection activities are not implemented, similar trademarks named after villages or towns are vulnerable to squatting.

Fourth, there are single governance approaches, and it is affected by national cultures. Zila Village is inhabited by Miao people alone. It has a traditional custom to declare ownership by placing a straw mark on cow dung and other objects on the road. The first-come-first-served convention has led to misunderstandings about the rights and interests of the collective trademark among the villagers, making them perceive that they have no chance to win a lawsuit. The whole village is blood relatives, in-laws, close neighbors, and other relations, so no one is willing to stand up for the public interest or pay to offend others. Misconduct should not be pursued if the person concerned does not request the authorities' prosecution. And then, minor conflicts should be handled by the grassroots bodies. If the conflict is amplified, the government will attract investment to buy the trademark or send cadres to the grassroots to regulate the conflict. Nevertheless, in this case, the local government's conventional approach serves as a mere palliative and cannot resolve the fundamental conflict.

Key Elements and Results for Resolving Conflicts

In the case of Zila Tribute Rice Trademark Squatting, the key to resolving the conflict lies in the government's dominant role and the flexible use of "lawful, rational, and affectional" game strategies. The primary key element in resolving the conflict is the timely replacement of the government body. In May 2017, the local government launched a door-to-door survey and included Zila Tribute Rice in the list of items under protection. Still, it failed to communicate with the trademark registrant through several negotiations. Given this, the local government prepared the application for Zila Tribute Rice as a product with geographical indication and submitted it to the Hunan Provincial Quality and Technical Supervision Administration for approval.

The whole process took only half a year. The change of the local government from the "etic" position to avoid involvement in the conflict to the "emic" position of appropriate and proactive governance is a vital sign of the modernization of the governance of minority regions. After the trademark was infringed and the conflict between the parties quickly intensified, the Zila Village Committee was not in a position to file a complaint to defend its rights. The county government made a sensible decision and promptly set up the Huayuan County Brand Protection and Development Society as the governor and used the Society as the applicant to invalidate the trademark. In this way, the geographical trademark and public interest were effectively protected. The registrant competed with the Society instead of conflicting with the cooperative and other villagers. Through a long game, the feud was worn down, and after the final judgment, it was emotionally recognized by the majority of villagers. Ultimately, it thoroughly eliminated the social conflict.

The second key element is the pluralism of governance subjects, the rule of law, and the team's professionalism. In the past, local governments primarily purchased the trademark by cash and granted policy subsidies when dealing with similar conflicts. "Shibadong" was originally the name of a village in Huayuan County, famous for being the first place where General Secretary Xi Jinping advocated the concept of targeted poverty alleviation. After the trademark "Shibadong" was squat, the trademark was eventually resold to BBK Group for about 100,000 RMB after the government's matchmaking and negotiation. The government also provided the original registrant with specific projects and policy preferences. However, the Zila Tribute Rice trademark has definite regional orientations. Its transfer price was much higher than "Shibadong," and the local government failed to communicate with the registrant. Thus, the government set up the Huayuan County Brand Protection and Development Society to resolve the conflict by employing legal means in a planned way and entrusting a professional team to protect public interests. After the final judgment, the trademark was recovered permanently from the legal point of view and legally clarified as a geographical brand and cultural resource involving seven townships. It provided a solid foundation for the county government to break the restrictions of 1,000 acres of paddy fields in Zila Village, develop the industry on a larger scale in the future, and gain a more expansive development space and public support than in Zila Village. At the same time, the Huayuan county government took this opportunity to improve the public interest protection mechanism represented by geographical trademark and the social governance system.

The third key element in enhancing governance capacity is the wisdom and flexibility of gaming strategy. Huayuan County Brand Protection and Development Society put forward three main reasons at the preliminary stage. Firstly, Zila Tribute Rice is a geographical indication and a piece of China's important agricultural cultural heritage and has been included in the scope of protection by the county government. Secondly, the registrant's residence is not located in Zila Village and within the range of protection of the geographical indication, and its business scope does not involve rice. Thirdly, the registration was considered improper use of public resources, which damaged the rights and interests of the actual producers of Zila Tribute Rice and the brand reputation of the geographical indication. In the game process, the local government used anthropological theories and methods.

On the one hand, the materials for the declaration of agricultural cultural heritage and the geographical trademark are mainly based on field research by anthropologists in Zila Village. On the other hand, the local government entered Zila Village to investigate the facts and needs of the people and put forward the overall demands and governance measures from the public viewpoint by replacing the etic position with the emic position. In the final instance, the original registrant changed its domicile to Zila village and provided the "Rice Purchase Contract" with several farmers in Zila village. The county government then changed its game strategy. Since four cooperatives in Zila Village have been producing and marketing Zila Tribute Rice for a long time, the county government insisted that Zila Tribute Rice is a public agricultural product brand. To protect the public interest of the entire county, the county government argued that the critical project of targeted poverty alleviation has been supported by the government for many years and benefited a large number of residents. Finally, the county government's arguments were accepted by the judiciary. Beijing High People's Court held that Zila Tribute Rice involves public interests for all residents. If the cooperative obtained exclusive trademark rights and monopolized the trademark rights of the "rice" in question, it would undermine the public interest and shared prosperity for all residents.

In this case, public interests outweighed individual interests. Finally, the county government won the lawsuit, and shared interests were protected, effectively resolving the conflict between villagers. Immediately after the final judgment, the county government issued a press release about "Zila Tribute Rice" through the media, which not only extensively publicized the dispute over the trademark and sought the emotional recognition of the people in the county but also took the initiative to guide public opinion to avoid conflicts afterward. Finally, the county government planned and managed this agricultural cultural heritage industry. And it established a development model involving farmers, local cooperatives, foreign capital, and local universities to achieve a win-win outcome between public interest, ethnic culture, and market capital. This case reflects that the modernization of the MRIWC and social governance is changing to a rule-of-law, intelligent and information-based model, and the social governance of local governments is becoming more proactive and service-oriented.

What Can Be Learned from the Zila Tribute Rice Case

The case of Xiangxi Zila Tribute Rice Trademark Squatting is just a drop in the ocean in the modernization of the MRIWC and social governance, reflecting the social conflicts arising from different interest orientations and the role of local governments in resolving disputes. This case is an inspiration for the MRIWC and other similar regions to deal with similar problems effectively in modernization and social governance.

Correct Perceptions of Social conflicts Caused by Different Interest Orientations

The modernization of the MRIWC means modernizing individuals in ethnic groups, the regional society, and the ethnic groups. Different interest orientations may lead to many social contradictions and conflicts in this process. In this regard, the case of Zila Tribute Rice Trademark Squatting in Xiangxi is typical. Once an individual registers a trademark, the relevant law protects the exclusive rights of the registrant, which are possessive and monopolistic. The right of individual residents to develop and modernize is the priority for protection, so the interests of the trademark registrant should be protected. It is also the fundamental reason the county government cannot privately and arbitrarily deprive the registrant of the relevant rights. However, Zila Tribute Rice itself is a geographical trademark created by a group of people and jointly maintained for a long time, a public interest enjoyed by the residents of a specific area. The registered trademark Zila Tribute Rice has infringed upon the individual development rights of many residents in the county.

Suppose the law only protects the registrant's rights. In that case, it indicates that the law recognizes the individual interest over the public interest and allows the public interest to be appropriated by the individual for a long time. Once this concept is widely accepted, the adverse impact of individual interests overriding public interests will arise. As a result, the contradiction between personal and public interests and the dichotomy between different stakeholders is not alleviated. However, it may lead to the wave of a few "competent" persons to seize the public interests by pre-emptively registering the regional brands, which will lead to the deepened confrontation and intensified contradiction between such individual registrants and the public. Therefore, different interests and governmental protection ideas may lead to other social governance effects and varying degrees of modernization of the population, whether the priority is given to individual modernization or public interest and overall modernization of the people.

In addition to the conflict between individual interests and public interests, it is also necessary to pay attention to the problems arising from the orientation of interests between regions and ethnic groups. In terms of regional interests, the core farming technology of the Complex Zila Tribute Rice Farming System is the "paving trees for fields" technology. After field research, the "paving trees for fields" technology is best protected and most famous in Zila village. Similar technologies were found in the neighboring Miao villages, such as Liaoqiu village and La'e village, and even in Mayang, Huaihua, Qiandongnan, Guizhou. It suggests that the core technology may be a multi-point shared technology within the Hunan-Guizhou-Chongqing border area. Therefore, as Zila Village in Huayuan County pre-emptively declared Zila Tribute Rice as an essential agricultural cultural heritage of China, other regions could not apply their rice products as national agricultural cultural heritage. It is a conflict of interests between regions. In June 2018, Dongma Village in Huayuan County hosted the Xiangxi Farming Folk Culture Festival. Since the cadres of Zila Village did not participate in the event, the golden signboard of agricultural cultural heritage was given to a village adjacent to Zila Village. Some people in the village thought that the village was included in the core protection area in the protection plan, and even if the village was not called Zila Village, it had the right to use the signboard of Zila Tribute Rice. The person in charge of the agricultural cultural heritage application project called several times to communicate with the village leaders but to no avail, and the signboard had excellent resistance to return to Zila Village. Some of the villagers in Zila Village were outraged when hearing of this. Fortunately, after several months of mediation by the head of the county agricultural bureau, the signboard was finally returned to the village, thus avoiding a group conflict between the two villages over the brand.

In terms of ethnic interests, Zila Village is inhabited by Miao people alone. The Zila Tribute Rice brand created and operated by the Miao ancestors of Zila Village is a cultural asset passed down from the Miao ancestors. However, there were no rice fields in Zila Village more than 700 years ago. Still, it resulted from the wisdom of the multi-ethnic ancestors during the Ming and Qing dynasties, when the Miao, Han, Tujia, and Manchu ethnic groups exchanged, interacted, and mingled. If the scope of the geographical trademark is only within the narrow range of Zila Village, or if the public interest is only attributed to the Miao group, it is a slightly narrow view in terms of the origin and history of the technology. From the holistic concept of building a community for the Chinese nation, the Huayuan County government-protected Zila Tribute Rice as a trademark shared by local ethnic groups based on cross-cultural governance concepts and means. And the county government also supported Zila Tribute Rice production and marketing as a critical county-level industry. It contributes to economic growth, social development, and national unity. Similar conflicts between geographical trademarks and public interests should also consider individual interests and general interests and pay attention to the balance of regional interests and the sharing of national interests. Such social governance, which takes overall livelihood as the priority and social equity as the orientation, can better promote the modernization of the MRIWC.

The Role of Local Governments in Resolving Social Conflicts

From the 1950s to the 1980s, the Chinese government was the leading player in resolving social conflicts, playing a decisive role in economic, social, and cultural aspects. In the following 40 years, China has been building a modernized market economy. The government has shifted from an "emic" athlete taking on everything to an "etic" referee and supervisor.

However, when it comes to protecting public interests and resolving related social conflicts, local governments cannot and should not be completely free to do so but should play an active role in different situations.

Local governments construct the social governance system and have a decisive role in formulating and implementing social governance rules. Since the founding of the People's Republic of China, China's minority regions have consistently implemented the policy of regional ethnic autonomy, and local governments in minority regions have significant freedom in terms of local laws, economic policies, social management, and ethnic customs. Therefore, we can build social governance system with national and regional characteristics according to local conditions. In early 2017, the People's Congress of Huayuan County approved the Protection and Development Plan of the Complex Zila Tribute Rice Farming System. And the County People's Government agreed on the plan and issued several documents to regular and guide its implementation. In response to the realities of Zila Village and other areas, a core agricultural cultural heritage protection zone and an industrial radiation zone were designated. With the launch of these initiatives, a governance mechanism for the protection and development of Zila Tribute Rice as agricultural cultural heritage resources were initially established.

Local governments govern social undertakings and assume the primary responsibility for social management and supervision. Government management can serve as a resource and play an essential role in accelerating economic development (Tian et al., 2017). Because of the enormous economic value of Zila Tribute Rice, there were fierce competition and frequent conflicts among cooperatives, enterprises, villagers, and different ethnic villages. The government of Huayuan County took the geographical trademark into its possession by legal means and then discussed with the agricultural cultural heritage team of Jishou University to establish an agricultural cultural heritage protection and development zone with Zila Village as the core demonstration point and seven surrounding townships. It adopts an ecological industry development model with one brand, several varieties, multiple points for diversified and differentiated development, and complementary sub-brand positioning. This global development concept and the establishment of the intercultural system allow different stakeholders, regions, and ethnic groups to have their interests and benefits. In this way, it resolves the conflicts and disputes between various stakeholders and the problem that village industries are challenging to develop on a large scale to lay the foundation for the orderly development of Miao cultural resources.

Moreover, the county government has set some rules for overall regional development. It provides an institutional guarantee for creating a benign environment of targeted protection, orderly development, and win-win cooperation. These rules manifest the local government's "moderate emic" governance concept and strong governance capacity. The local government protects people's well-being and plays a vital role in protecting public interests and maintaining social justice. In the court, although the leading player is Huayuan County Brand Protection and Development Society, it is coordinated by Huayuan County Government. The relevant departments fully exercise protecting people's well-being and maintaining public interests. At the same time, the Huayuan County government supported several non-profit cooperatives of the village. It cooperated with enterprises such as BBK Group and Jishou University's Jinsui Public Service Organization for the protection and development of the project. The government established an industry-university-research development model centered on agricultural cultural heritage and a benefit-sharing mechanism for multiple subjects. As the Chinese government continues to streamline administration and delegate power to the lower levels and various social conflicts still exist, this idea of fostering pluralistic subjects to complement the social governance function of the government has some implications for the MRIWC to resolve similar disputes.

Inspirations of Zila Tribute Rice Case to Social Governance in the MRIWC

The MRIWC's social governance system construction is fundamental to protect people's well-being and public interests. The social governance reform prioritizes diversified governance subjects, a systematic governance system, orderly governance objects, and intelligent governance means. It involves twists and turns to protect the Zila Tribute Rice trademark. Local governments, especially the MRIWC governments and related departments with abundant cultural resources, should work together to preserve local resources, national cultural resources, and public resources as quickly, comprehensively, and effectively as possible. Geographical trademarks and other resources are closely related to people's well-being. The geographical trademark was created by unidentifiable parties and involves multiple resources. It could be pre-emptively registered by an individual. As such, the public interests might be monopolized.

The best way to control the situation is to have the local government register and protect it unified, which requires more attention from administrative agencies such as industry and commerce quality supervision administration, agriculture, forestry, and animal husbandry departments. Relevant government departments must work with local scientific research institutions to discover and organize geographical trademarks under protection. Moreover, the county government should provide sufficient essential protection in terms of human, financial, and material resources and support several conservation subjects with clear rights and responsibilities and law-abiding and compliant governors. In this way, we can continuously improve the relevant laws and regulations, policies, supervision systems, rewards, and punishments from top to bottom and establish a mechanism for various governors' joint participation and benefit-sharing.

Social governance in the MRIWC should pay attention to the complexity of the local social structure and the specificity of the modernization path. The MRIWC has specific cultural barriers to social governance and involves a complex game of multiple parties, and governmental governance capacity needs to be improved. The modernization path has pronounced ethnic characteristics and regional orientations. However, practice proves that we should uphold the holistic concept of social governance with a sense of national community and mutual benefit for all ethnic groups. We should protect and scientifically develop people's well-being projects in an integrated manner. Thus, the people can effectively enjoy the many dividends of modernization and stimulate the initiative and sense of achievements of all ethnic groups, regions, and subjects in social governance. As long as we can do so, we can be motivated in difficult situations, and crisis also contains great opportunities

Social governance in the MRIWC needs to improve the governance capacity of local governments. In today's rapidly developing market economy, conflicts arising from disputes over interests cannot be entirely avoided but need to be resolved by improving the social governance capacity of local governments. Local governments should flexibly use lawful, rational, and affectional governance to safeguard public interests. They should take advantage of modern media and other information technology to promote the government's measures and social governance concepts for people's well-being. And the grassroots disputes and conflicts of interest should be resolved by fostering new governors. In short, the law-based, information-based, and intelligent mode of social governance is a primary sign of modernization and an essential way to advance modernization.

Conclusion

China's modernization is faced with complex domestic and international situations and uneven regional development patterns. More attention needs to be paid to the MRIWC, which is relatively lagging in development. The MRIWC is characterized by cultural barriers to governance, diverse governance subjects, a lagging governance system, and governance capacity that need to be improved. In addition, local social governance modernization features ethnic characteristics, regional orientations, and overall people's well-being. Therefore, the local governments of the MRIWC should build a social governance system suitable for the region according to local conditions and promote local modernization by designating diversified governors to adopt systematic governance systems and intelligent governance means or orderly governance targets.

The anthropological theories and methods have some guiding significance for the modernization of the MRIWC and its social governance. The ethnographic case of Zila Tribute Rice shows that the MRIWC's local government must observe various economic and social phenomena from the grassroots perspective as the "subject" in the process of modernization reflects on multiple issues related to them. Thus, it can reinforce the holistic concept while maintaining people's well-being. With the steadily improved social governance system and enhanced governance capacity, local governments should proactively obey the law when it is appropriate to intervene directly and cultivate relevant governors when it is not fair to intervene directly. Also, local governments should introduce regulatory mechanisms and incentives for social governance with diversified, multi-level, and multi-faceted forces and in a traditional manner. Inspired by the numerous cases of "Zila Tribute Rice," the modernization of the MRIWC is bound to act as a propeller of China's overall modernization and a vital booster to China's integration with the world and its overall development.

Chapter 4
Unique Path and Process of Urbanization in Old Shiyang Town

Urbanization is a significant process in present China's history. Although rural characteristics primarily dominate the traditional Chinese society, the Chinese people are keen on the urbanization of their hometown. Due to the long history and large territory associated with various cultures, the urbanization path and process differ from place to place. Taking old Shiyang (stone sheep) town in Dayao County of Yunnan Province as an example, this study probes a unique urbanization process and pattern in rural Southern China by examining the role salt resources played from a historical perspective.

Introduction

Traditional Chinese society can be interpreted as a single rural society. In the Chinese view of rural society, the system and attributes of the traditional urban society in China are obscured (Chen, 2012: 424). Because of the absence of urbanity in the traditional Chinese view, cities are deliberately or unintentionally classified into Western modernity. At the same time, they are also regarded as the implanted non-native culture in China's modernity (Chen, 2012: 429). The attention to traditional Chinese towns can also deepen the recognition of traditional Chinese society. Of course, to have a deeper understanding of the status quo of the city, we must go through the diachronic skyline to inspect those faint traces, to understand the more ancient structure and more primitive functions of the city, which should become the primary task for us to study cities (Mumford, 2005:2). The author aimed to extract the key factors that influence the urbanization process of Shiyang Town. Shiyang old town is a salt industry production base located in Dayao County, Yunnan province.

Its radius is less than two kilometers, can accommodate more than 10000 residents. The author attempts to study urbanization as a systematic project, pays close attention to its complexity, and explores how to seize the key and the practical part of the outline of the development background. The factors of resources, the market, the flow of people and the state's role are the concentration points of the core and conclusion by the authors in this chapter.

Urbanization is a process of transformation of the mode of production, the way of life and values, a microcosm of the development of human society, and the reflection of the phenomena in multiple dimensions of material, space, economy, population, system and social characteristics (Li, 2013: 2-3). To understand the complex system of urbanization itself, it is necessary to have a comprehensive grasp of these dimensions. Therefore, the study on the urbanization of the old Shiyang town involves a dynamic dimension. Urbanization is a dynamic integral structure composed of geographical, population, economic, social, conceptual and behavioral factors and a dynamic operation process driven by the "historical resultant forces" where these factors affect each other. Many factors influence the urbanization of the old Shiyang Town, and on this basis, it presents a clear context of urban development. The unique resource endowment for local development has been formed because of salt. The old Shiyang Town's urbanization process is full of salt flavor. It shows the urbanization stage of "thriving because of salt, declining because of salt, and reviving."

Resources: Congenital Endowment of Urbanization

The salt production of Shiyang Town can be traced back to the Han Dynasty with documents, and the local salt production industry has a history of more than 2,000 years. Significantly since the Ming Dynasty, the salt industry in the old Shiyang Town has been improving day by day. The history of the salt industry formed in the old Shiyang Town constitutes a history of the old Shiyang Town. The history of the rise and fall of salt resources is also a history of urbanization in Shiyang Town.

Just as the sweetness of sugar studied by Sidney Wilfred Mintz is an overall taste experience in human nature, the saltiness of salt is also a pervasive taste experience in human nature, as well as a necessary experience. The local salt resources have played a significant role in the old Shiyang Town's urbanization process. It acted as different resource superiorities in various stages of urbanization while presenting the characteristics of resource superiority. Since the discovery and exploitation of salt resources symbolized by the legend of the Daughter of the Dragon King Tending Sheep in the old Shiyang Town, the local salt resources began to transform from purely natural resources to economic resources. Salt brings about the aggregation effect of crowds, the integration of pluralistic cultures, and the continually expanding market as an economic resource. As an economic resource, Salt creates value for national taxation and national construction and participates in the urbanization of the old Shiyang Town.

After the late Qing Dynasty, the old Shiyang Town's salt resources gradually fell into the trap of resource superiority. In contrast, the economic value of salt resources declined, and the old Shiyang Town also showed a declining state with the decline of the salt industry. In the declining stage of local urbanization, the local authorities were also looking for a new way out of value. Until the 1990s, the local urbanization moved towards a road of tourism development with the development of the local salt industry's social, historical and cultural resources as the dominant factor. In contrast, salt was regarded as the brand of local cultural resources. In transforming cultural resources into economic resources through tourism, the economic and cultural advantages have been realized in local urbanization. Local salt can be used as cultural resource because the local salt culture has been formed and developed with salt resources development. Over time, it has been solidified into the resource endowment and cultural characteristics in local urbanization, which is also the precious wealth the local salt community has left to the later generations for their survival and development.

The transformation from Natural Resources to Economic Resources

As a valuable resource of exceptional national control for a long time in history, salt has entered the vision of national control earlier. The state's superior control towards salt also brought the old Shiyang Town into the scope of state control earlier. The superior control made the old Shiyang Town, an insignificant part of the southwest, enter the state's vision. General Gazetteer of the Great Ming Dynasty, General Gazetteer of the Great Qing Dynasty and other national multiple-volume historical records all paid attention to the old Shiyang Town. The state's control of the old Shiyang Town is accompanied by the strategy against Yunnan, or earlier than Yunnan's strategy. In the oral history of the local people, the most vivid feeling is that the value and significance of the old Shiyang Town in the minds of local people lie in the fact that such a narrow area has brought a lot of tax revenue to the country and participated in the national construction. Simultaneously, due to the closure of geographical location, the old Shiyang Town presents the openness of its culture, especially the absorption and continuation of the Han culture.

In the fifth year of the Jiaqing period (1800), for example, after the salt in Yunnan was changed to the mode of "cooking and selling on the stove, and civil transportation and marketing," salt tax was levied by three items of regular taxation, tax on salary for public officials and tax on the funds for well affairs. At that time, the annual amount of salt decocted in Baiyanjing was 8,739,300 jin (1 jin equals 500g), and the amount of regular tax levied as in silver was 61,622.811 liang (about 0.7051 liang levied as the regular tax on per 100 kg of salt, 1 liang equals 1.76 ounces). The tax on salary for public officials was 13,374.549 liang (about 0.1531 liang levied as the tax on salary for public officials) per 100 kg of salt.

The amount of tax on the funds for well affairs was 12,331.91 liang (about 0.1411 liang levied as the tax on the funds for well affairs), and a total of 87,329.27 liang was levied on the tax on the funds for well workers. It can be calculated that the salt tax of the Baiyanjing during the Jiaqing period is about 0.9993 liang per 100 kg of salt.

As an economic resource, Salt provides a lot of tax revenue for the country, contributes to the development of local society in Baiyanjing and provides sufficient economic basis and sources for local urbanization construction. In Baiyanjing's urban construction, three main forces are involved: local officials represented by Ti Ju (提举), salt-maker production organizations represented by well and stove offices, and individuals represented by the clans in local society. Some of the income from salt production is reserved for local urban development funds and allocated by the local officials represented by Ti Ju (提举) and salt-maker production organizations. Simultaneously, the clans represented by individuals who do not have the right to control the funds for urban development will also actively devote themselves to urban construction to obtain a specific social identity and status. The three forces of local officials, salt-maker production organizations and clans form the demand for common interests between salt production and the development of local society, between the subjects of salt production and the local society and the people.

Firstly, the three forces have realized the standardized construction of urban public space, including Confucian temples, academies, schools and free private schools and other educational spaces, as well as religious public Spaces such as "seven temples, eight pavilions and nine courtyards" religious space events and other public spaces, such as roads and Bridges. The investment of funds completes the presentation of the physical state of public space and realizes the continuation of public space as a living form.

Secondly, it realizes the joint participation of urban festival culture represented by urban culture. It presents the typical cultural prosperity of “a festival every day” in the memories of the elderly.

Thirdly, it achieves the joint development of urban charitable undertakings. There are a variety of charitable organizations and sites, such as local public granary, ever-normal granary, State Refuge for the Care of Ill and the Poor, nursing homes, the burial ground for the needy, coffin house, skeleton burial, water almsgiving and foundling hospitals, presenting a complete form of charitable undertakings under the joint promotion of the three forces in Baiyanjing and the strong support of the salt economy.

The Transformation from Economic Resources to Cultural Resources

The above elaborates on the salt industry in Baiyanjing as a presentation of economic resources. In contrast, in the salt industry's long development process in Baiyanjing, salt resources were also precipitated in the form of cultural resources. Salt is a commodity, but it is more than a commodity. “The concept of material culture coincides with commodity culture and spills over the field of commodity culture (Meng, 2008: 2).” Changes in cultural behavior create material and material culture itself. “Since it is a material form created by the change of cultural behavior, the material has the nature similar to words, symbols, narratives and even history (Meng, 2008: 3) .” The authors' concern for salt is based on material culture's cognition as the object to be narrated. The transformation of salt resources from economic to cultural resources has the following conditions.

First, it is because of the particularity of salt as an essential national resource. The state and local governments have been making every effort to exploit and utilize the salt resources, and Baiyanjing has not been forgotten by history because of salt. The development of salt resources by the state and the demand for sustained development in local areas form a common interest demand. The protective development of salt resources improves salt resources' life course, enabling salt resources to be formed and continue as cultural resources.

Second, it is because of the timeliness of the development of salt resources. The exploitation of salt in Baiyanjing has lasted since the Han Dynasty. It is documented in local historical records, especially in the Ming and Qing Dynasties when recorded in many documents, to the 1990s. This process of salt development is lasting. Because of the limited mineral resources, some resource-based production areas' exploitation only carries out temporary development. While the resources are developed, it mostly aims to develop and build simple buildings. With the exhaustion of resources, everything is gone. These areas remain deserted while leaving only the ecology, which is difficult to repair in the mining area, thus developing a “violent plunder.”

Because of the long-term development of salt resources, Baiyanjing has formed a unique salt society, continuing over time. Local cultural resources centered on salt have also become the expression of individuality in the local urban culture. Many legends in the salt industry have changed and have regularly endowed the times with the style, such as “the place where the Dragon King’s daughter herds sheep.” The local King of Brine Dragon (卤龙王), Infanta of the Dragon King(龙女郡主) and General Stone Sheep (石羊将军) have become the unique salt gods in the salt society. In contrast, definite and lasting belief concepts and ritual behaviors have been developed around the salt gods. Dragon King Fair, Salt Merchants Fair, Fire God Fair, and other fairs have become the salt industry's performance sites. In changing from economic resources to cultural resources, in the local society, salt has changed from a temporary exploitative resource to a sustainable resource available for the generations in local areas. The cultural resources represented by salt have the inheritance and continuity of history.

The Reversible and Irreversible Fate of Resources

When the old Shiyang Town transformed salt from natural resources to economic and cultural resources, salt resources adapted to the times' needs and kept pace. When the salt resources in Baiyanjing developed to the late Qing Dynasty, its inadaptability to the times gradually exposed. The constraints imposed by the local salt society in the face of transportation, technology and management cannot be avoided. Moreover, in promoting the development of things, the alternation and renewal of new and old things cannot be changed. The local salt resources will eventually withdraw from the market as an economic resource. It has historical inevitability and becomes a manifestation of resource development's irreversibility. However, on the other hand, the local society has realized the reversible expression of resource development. The cultural endowment and practice of salt resources have become an endogenous motive force to change local development and promote the development of local society. After the 1990s, the local government and local people jointly formed local society's cultural awareness and conscious practice. They intended to link the local development and prospects of the old Shiyang Town with the salt society in the old Shiyang Town history. They took the initiative to take the salt society in history as the basis for the town's future development to realize the production and reproduction of culture. In the new era, the salt industry's cultural form has realized the vivid expression in the form of tourism, which has become the local practice of breaking the "resource curse."

Above all, the authors' research on salt factors in the old Shiyang Town's urbanization process has injected the research findings on "the social life of things" and the studies related to food anthropology for reference. For the convenience of narration, the authors use "things" to cover them. During the development of the history of studies, the nature and role of material culture have varied. Whether it is the early theory of evolution, the theory of communication, the later theory of structure, or the new archaeology that emerged in the late 1960s, material culture has played a passive role as a new tool to achieve another goal. Until the rise of the theory of practice, during the late 1970s and the early 1980s, material culture was given an active and positive role. Material culture is again regarded as a bridge in integrating (social culture) anthropology and archaeology (Chen, 1996: 415-444). It has become an essential method of study on thing culture to trace the change and growth of things in time (Meng and Luo, 2008: 12-13). "Material culture is a place to stimulate new thinking and promote new dialogue (Meng, 2008: 4)." Then, taking care of things as the starting point, the transformation from the perspective of "people-centered" for "people looking at things" to the perspective of thing-centered "things looking at people" is a practical dimension to understand the relationship between people and things. "Any social change will manifest itself through the changes in the relationship between people and things (Waynes, 2008: 486)."

Things are not merely used by human beings, while things have their independence and play a dominant role on human beings. There are biographies, ups and downs, and unique historical narratives. The scale of things, nature, and the relationship between things and people become an essential symbol of consumer society. Represented by The Social Life of Things by Arjun Appadurai, the attention to the timeliness of commodities and the process of "de-commercialization" has begun to enter the vision of research. An article entitled "The Cultural Biography of Things" written by Igor Kopytoff in this book directly regards the change and growth of things in time as an essential method to study material culture (Kopytoff, 1986: 64-94). "Things" in "The Social Life of Things" refer to materiality. It is not merely the physical nature of things, namely, the expressive elements of materials and components that can be seen, but the physical, cultural and social nature of materials and their relations. It emphasizes the interaction between people and things and its impact on social practice (Miller, 2005).

The materiality of material culture refers to the interdependent and inseparable relationship between social practices and the attached material (or environment). Only when there is material can there be human activity, and material also restricts human behavior. Material qualities or properties (physicality) directly affect how people know, understand and utilize specific social practice materials. Physicality also determines how things run through people's social life, shape and influence people's thoughts, emotions, social relations and the people themselves. Materiality stresses the dynamic relationship between people and things, especially the relationship between the way, the approach of social practice and physicality (Boivin, 2008).

We understand things themselves. It is not only limited to the understanding of things themselves, but we are more willing to "see people through things," to see the people who create and utilize the things themselves through these things and understand the social generation of things based on these things. If we put things in the position of the whole social history, that is, the social life of things, we can better grasp this society's dimensions. Just as human beings have biological and social expressions, things also have physical and social expressions in the dimension of "the social life of things." Like human beings, things have initiative and activity (Gell, 1998). In almost all cultures, things are endowed with souls, values and symbols. The physicality and sources of material and its history directly affect the social and cultural values of the material. With material's social, cultural, and historical differences, material's social value and cultural connotation will also change (Appadurai, 1986: 3-63).

From the perspective of the social life of things, salt and human beings have been in continuous interaction. Salt is not only a necessity but is also scarce in the historical period. Salt is the source of nutrition for all people to maintain their lives and the source for a small number of people to gain wealth and power. In the long history of exceptional control over salt, salt has been not only a sort of commodity because of the intervention of state power, which is not merely marketed commodities but also a thing of state power and political empowerment. In the salt era, the price of one decalitre of rice is equivalent to that of one jin of salt, while it is not what ordinary people can afford. Salt has grades, and different groups purchase different grades of salt. It means that the population in the region is stratified. The fineness of classifying a thing in society can reflect its importance. For example, like the snow classification by Eskimos, there are also different classifications of salt in Baiyanjing, with different names for the salt utensils.

After that, salt descended from the noble identity that the price of one dekaliter of rice is equivalent to that of one jin of salt to a good "flying into the homes of common folks there." As a good "flying into the homes of common folks there," salt has been unable to reflect the grades of salt and the group stratification behind salt grades. The first stage thus developed is the decline and narrowing of symbolic value. The decline of salt's symbolic value is almost at the same stage as the technological change under the background of industrialization. Salt also enables the tiny area in the southwestern border to be tightly linked with the world system. Local salt does not just enter ordinary people's homes, but the decline and narrowing of symbolic values and the gradual decline of the cultural system accompanied by it come to an end or lose the expression of its meaning. The local salt is scarce in the regional space, and the lost salt here becomes the scarce resource for us to look back on history and restore the past. When salt changes into another form and is scarce again, it is in a clear and ordered pattern to take salt culture as the direction of tourism development in local urbanization. As a result, the local salt also formed a process from narrowing the symbolic value to reconstructing such value. "Reconstruction of symbolic value" is the preservation and performance of the salt society's memory by restoring the past salt society to develop a form of cultural resources of social urbanization in the local areas.

Even today, we admit that we are in an age of things. We are still inevitably in "an age of things bound by culture." "Culture is becoming an economy, a value in use, a living space for us, as well as tableware, clothing, living room and food for us (Meng, 2008: 4)." Given today's materialistic society, things' culture and vividness are not drowned by cold and physical nature. Still, the expression and expansion of culture are more prominent. Instead of being surrounded by things, we are surrounded by the culture represented by things. The tourism development of the old Shiyang Town is a process in which the original practicability of salt is no longer in existence but comes on the stage in cultural commodities. In this process, salt is culture, and culture is a commodity. Since salt exists as a cultural product, its past (reconstruction of the historical information of salt as a commodity) and present life (the process of value reappearance after its disappearance) are also entirely displayed.

Market: The Key to Urbanization

Salt production in Baiyanjing belongs to export-oriented production. The salt produced must be supported by a broad market. Therefore, the market has become the lifeline of the rise and fall of Baiyanjing. Just like Zigong, a city with a high homogeneity with Baiyanjing, "the market determines its formation and prosperity and decline (Wang, 1995: 2)." In urbanization, the market is the decisive driving force for developing the urban system (Ding, 2014: 89).

G. William Skinner summarized the factors that influence the urbanization process. First, it is the population density, while relocation is a process that will make each region close to its population potential. Second, it is the division of labor. Third, it is the application of technology. Fourth, it is commercialization and trade within the region. Fifth, it is foreign trade in the region. Sixth, it is administration. Skinner argues that the economy drives the occurrence of urbanization and that the economy's critical function is the city's primary function (Skinner, 2000: 267-271).

First, towns and commercial cities are their central nodes in exchanging goods and services, in the circulation of money and credit, in the flow of people for livelihood and other economic interests. Business centers attract other types of essential functions. Second, the extraction of the economic surplus is the key to enabling political institutions to function. Third, in terms of various aspects that constitute the urban systems, the trade seems to have outperformed administrative activities and outperformed any other forms of communication in cities (Skinner, 2000: 328). In this regard, G. William Skinner strengthened his understanding of cities from the economic level. We can define an economically developed region: within this region, production is divided by specialty according to the regions, with a different occupational structure and a credit hierarchy system, which supports a coordinated trade network within the region. In this region, the main technological level is converted into the public social utilities (roads, bridges, canals, dams and irrigation work) through accumulated investment. In the region's ascending cycle, these achievements are inextricably intertwined with the following developments: population growth and urban development (Skinner, 2000: 252).

John King Fairbank also pointed out the importance of the market to the local society in his research. "It is always a problem to transport agricultural products to the market. Thus, it is dominated by the type of decentralized market, and each village community exchanges its products on a barter basis in the local market towns. A market center and nearby villages within walking distance make up a unit. Of course, this unit is likely to be destroyed by natural disasters such as floods and droughts, but in contrast, if the natural conditions are good, it can almost live on its own (Fairbank and Reischauer, 1992: 14)."

Since 1988, Fei Xiaotong has been concerned about the relationship between market factors and regional systems. He believes that the market factor is a factor of great significance that he has neglected in his research work over the years. Although he was eighty years old, he still advocated making up lessons (Ding, 2014: 90). Throughout history, urbanization in the west has largely been based on market mechanisms' innovation (Zhang,

2011: 1-11). The classical urbanization theory suggests that urbanization, industrialization, and marketization have close internal and symbiotic relations. The subjects and contents that promote industrialized and urbanized development and the environment that restricts their development are based on the market mechanism. Thus urbanization itself is a market-oriented process. The government departments have repeatedly stressed that urbanization should be based on marketization (Chen, 2005: 23). Scholars who study farmers have also made some proposals concerning making the rural problems market-oriented and society-oriented, reducing the process of general problems being politics-oriented (Zhao, 2013: 69), and putting the market into the solution of the problems of the rural areas and farmers.

Based on the above existing studies, the authors consider the market factor as one of the crucial factors in the old Shiyang Town's urbanization process. The market factor occupies a prominent position in the urbanization process of the old Shiyang Town. The old Shiyang Town in the era of salt has a market every day, fully displaying the market prosperity driven by the country fairs. The salt trade dominates the country fairs in Baiyanjing, and the caravans to transport the salt come and go in a continuous stream. As the only fuel to boil salt in Baiyanjing, firewood also became a significant commodity in the fairs. Besides, the production necessities centered on the salt society, such as iron pots, horse gear and so on, have also become the primary constituent commodities of the fairs in Baiyanjing. In Baiyanjing, because of frequent market trade, the caravans, salt merchants, and other vendors gathered here because of the trade led to the local accommodation and catering industries' prosperity. Simultaneously, the unique way of livelihood of "replacing farming by brine" and no engagement in agriculture in Baiyanjing has also led to the commercialization of the surrounding areas of Baiyanjing. The surrounding areas solely supply the necessities for life except for salt. Baiyanjing and its surrounding area also develop aggregation and interaction through the fairs, and the salt in Baiyanjing forms a self-contained sales area. Simultaneously, the surrounding areas also supply the materials necessary for the production and life in Baiyanjing with its advantages.

With the decline of the salt industry in Baiyanjing, the salt industry's agglomeration effect is gradually lost. Also, the formation of closed markets after the PRC's founding has become a shackle for local markets' activity. Since 1953, when the state implemented the centralized purchase and marketing of grain, the active local market has gradually disappeared. The local commodities have been included in centralized purchase and marketing. The everyday fair in Baiyanjing was changed to the regular fair due to the shrinking market.

The local tourism industry, which was opened with the gradual revival of the urban energy and vitality in the old Shiyang Town since the 1980s, won the title as the historical and cultural site under local government protection. The acquisition of the honor of the first batch of historical and cultural towns at the provincial level has actively opened up the local towns' development market. With the formation and expansion of the tourism market, a series of markets have grown up, such as the local real estate market, consumer market (catering, accommodation, etc.). The tertiary service industry market has also been formed and developed in the local areas compared to the tourism market and then becomes an expanding market after the tourism industry. Compared with the historical period, the old Shiyang Town's existing market has been narrowed in quality and quantity. However, it is necessary to pay attention to the fact that markets have had relatively single materials for exchange, mostly because of the obstruction of transportation and other reasons. At the same time, the commodities are limited to limited areas. But at the present stage, the markets involve various materials for exchange, and there are infinite commodities from infinite regions. With the optimization of a transportation network, the acceleration of globalization, the sharing of modernity, and the Internet, the convergence of commodities from different origins in the old Shiyang Town has come true.

Every town must have the regions to support its development, while the rural areas mostly support these regions. It is relatively prominent in terms of the current administrative divisions, but the actual administrative divisions cannot represent the actual influence of cities. Almost all towns tend to cross the visible administrative boundaries due to the market's power from the market's perspective. The old Shiyang Town is a good example. As a famous historical and cultural town, the old Shiyang Town has been developed into a tourist town. Its popularity in tourism has reached that of Chuxiong, Kunming, Panzhihua in Sichuan and other places, a lot of tourists come here out of admiration. The local specialty products, such as walnut and chestnut, are transported to all parts of China through the market. The small towns represented by the old Shiyang Town are closely linked with rural areas. Some of the towns' materials come from the supply of higher-level cities, such as clothing, processed food and household appliances, which the Chuxiong and Kunming markets can almost meet. Some materials come from local rural areas, such as vegetables, grains, fruits and other daily necessities. According to the authors, the fresh agricultural and sideline products sold by local farmers' markets come from the surrounding rural areas. Part of the materials continues to flow to the market through the town's transit station, which mainly depends on the regular fares on Wednesday and the commodity trade in the town on weekdays. Next, there are also mobile markets in the countryside. Some merchants usually drive the truck to sell the electrical appliances through the loudspeaker in the countryside. Some people peddle tofu pudding, tofu and bean jelly in the countryside on a motorcycle. As a result, based on the town as a crucial point, its impact formed a network that has been continuously extending outward. The surrounding rural areas become the old Shiyang Town source, especially the agricultural product and labor markets.

As far as the market is concerned, the authors must respond that the market is not everything. Conservative economics firmly believes that the market is the panacea for all social and economic problems. In contrast, neoclassical economics and new institutional economics believe that market and private property rights can stimulate the driving force for corporate innovation and competition. They all regard the market mechanism as the decisive factor of development and advocate the rational pursuit of maximizing personal benefits and profits through the market mechanism. Faced with China's national conditions, more than 200 million irregular workers are deprived of social equity while making individual contributions. Removing the institutional barriers has transformed from a country of cumbersome control and absorption into a service-oriented country. Simultaneously, the government should be limited to a "development-oriented government" to participate in economic development properly. Then, in the face of such a large group, we cannot blindly be centered on the market but need to highlight the responsibility of a country. It may be the proper meaning of "socialist market economy" to provide these groups with "dignified working conditions (Huang, 2009: 51-74)." As a result, the urbanization process's market factors need to cooperate with the government and other factors. As for the role of government, the authors will elaborate on it in the following text.

In this regard, the authors attempt to eliminate the consideration of merely taking the market as a pure market of economic freedom but regard it as a complex field for exchanges, a place for the transformation and exchange of economic, political, cultural and social capital. In investigating the market of Shiyang Ancient Town, we will find that political, social, cultural, and symbolic markets dominate the trading of salt, and the economic market of the salt industry even becomes an appendage of the political market social market other markets. It is not difficult to find that pure market rules do not necessarily control the sales area and price of salt in the traditional salt era, but the balance result of various political demands such as national power and local interests. Salt is destined to be imperfect in its market growth mechanism with political commodities. Even the market of state power directly restricts the salt market, and the economic market of the salt industry has become the service platform of the power market. The gradually missing salt market also symbolizes the collapse of the state power market. In the tourism era, local salt plays its role again as cultural capital and symbolic capital.

Human Flow: Vitality and Individuality of Urbanization

The urban studies by Robert Ezra Park et al. have noticed the importance of mobility to vitality. "The process in which a city absorbs and integrates its local or external factors into its own body can be called the metabolism of urban life. Mobility is an index of metabolism (Park et al., 2012: 229). Gu Shengzu's book "Population Mobility and Urbanization in Contemporary China" reveals the relationship between urban population flow and urbanization. Many similar studies reveal that people are the main body of cities and towns. The rise and fall of cities and towns are mainly manifested by the attractiveness of cities and towns to the population. Therefore, the narration above talks about urbanization from human flow and heterogeneity in resource development. In other words, one of the clues of the study is resource development and human flow.

Human Flow and Urbanization

The profound adjustment of population and socioeconomic structure is the core content of urbanization in China. Its evolution path shows that urbanization in China has undergone two transitions. First, urbanization is based on population transfer, stressing the spatial transfer of population from rural areas to urban areas. It is a primary form of urbanization. Second, urbanization is based on structural transformation, which stresses transforming regional economic and social structure from traditional to modern society. It is an advanced form of urbanization. China's urbanization has entered a new stage of development and transformation. Population-based urbanization and structural transformation-based urbanization will inevitably take two different roads (Kong and Cheng,

2013: 25). Therefore, the city's real vitality should be the floating population who come to the city in a steady stream.

In the old Shiyang Town's urbanization process, "human flow" is essential for realizing local urbanization. Since the Ming Dynasty, "people gather here, some of whom come from various regions, some of whom are merchants living here for the time being in substantial numbers, while there are immigrants here frequently (Yang, 2005: 420)." Influenced by political and military immigration, the immigrants based on salt taxation officials, land reclamation by peasants without farmland, army units and salt merchants, and free immigration poured into Baiyanjing in a continuous stream, promoting the expansion in the scale of the urban population. The types of these immigrants and their development in the local area are well documented in their genealogy. Because of the considerable number of immigrants in local areas, the local urban culture reflects immigration's distinct characteristics. We can glimpse immigration characteristics in local society from the perspective of a diverse diet, multiple beliefs, and mixed customs and concepts. With the massive growth of the immigrant population, the Baiyanjing area's population was overly inflated, forming a narrow area but dense population. Under such circumstances, some original immigrant population in Baiyanjing moved to the settlements of ethnic minorities, thus developing a residential pattern was beyond the boundary of Baiyanjing. There are more mountains and less land; the land is secluded. In contrast, the mountains are scarce. With a distance of several li apart, the Han people and ethnic groups live together (Yang, 2005: 408), which further promotes the integration of immigrant culture and local culture and is another expanding form of urbanization.

As far as Shiyang Town's population, which declined because of salt at the urbanization stage, is concerned, liquidity is significantly weakened from liquidity intensity. By the flow direction of the population, it is dominated by outflow. First, the characteristics of the form and flow of people at this stage are influenced by the decline in salt society. It is accompanied by the decline of the salt industry in Baiyanjing. Second, it is influenced by the restrictions arising from the closed market and the household registration system based on national policy. During this period, the old Shiyang Town was dominated by the closed market and the strict household registration system, and its liquidity became almost impossible. Third, the local flood disaster was represented in 1961, making the local area almost an empty city.

In the urbanization stage of the revival of the old Shiyang Town, the total population of the area and the old Shiyang Town administrative region show a weak growth trend. Still, there is no significant increase or decrease in population. There were no noticeable visible changes in the old Shiyang Town population size. Still, behind the population size without apparent changes are the complex characteristics of population mobility. The mobility of the local population is manifested by the type of population inflow and outflow. The characteristics of population inflow and outflow have led to the old Shiyang Town population has not increased or decreased significantly for a long time. The flow of population in the old Shiyang Town has the form of both inflow and outflow. The local population's inflow mainly includes educational immigrants, business-based immigrants, and short-term tourists from surrounding areas. The population outflow can be roughly divided into migrant workers from local areas to other places and students. No matter the inflow or outflow of population, it has enhanced the mobility of the local population and become the vitality and individuality of the urbanization of the old Shiyang Town.

Throughout the urbanization process of Shiyang Ancient Town, whether long-term immigration, short-term market trade, tourism and other forms are conducive to information sharing and cultural exchange, and urban lifestyle is spread and absorbed in the process of people flow. At the same time, with the advancement of modernization and globalization, culture is realized through the flow of people as carriers. The emergence of various media is a form of cultural sharing compatible with the flow of people. Even though these new forms of cultural sharing in urbanization are not in the scope of this study, they are indeed new supplements to the status of "human flow."

Freedom of Migration and Urbanization

The intensity of human mobility is directly related to the development of urbanization. It promotes the mobility of people and becomes the choice to realize the vitality of urbanization. As for the promotion of human mobility, the authors introduce the current research results - "freedom of migration," which used to be a fundamental right of citizens. The first Constitution in 1954 expressly stipulated that citizen had freedom of migration and residence, which disappeared in the Constitution issued in 1972. Since then, the Constitution has been amended several times, but the freedom of migration has not been restored. (Jiang, 2008) From the historical perspective, China's freedom of migration has experienced a tortuous course from affirmation to negation and then to a certain degree of surrender in contemporary times. Taking urbanization as the value orientation of the household registration system reform in China treated symptoms and not the root cause. It was unable to solve equality of civil rights and identity. Therefore, it is necessary to establish the freedom of migration as the household registration system reform's value orientation as soon as possible (Huang, 2003: 26).

At present, people's flow has not undergone fundamental changes due to the dual system of urban and rural areas in China, resulting in the failure of synchrony between the "employment in cities" and "identity transformation" of many peasants. "The new generation of migrant workers" must choose to live in the way of "not leaving cities, not returning to their hometowns and not doing farm work." Simultaneously, the left-behind peasants become "decertified in spiritual life (Zhang, 2009: 16)." "Freedom of migration" is proposed to solve the obstacles of peasants entering cities. At present, the population migration in China shows a substantial growth momentum. From the actual scale perspective, population migration has developed from 21.45 million in 1978 to 62.99 million in 2000, while the scale of informal migration has increased rapidly from 3.15 million in 1978 to 43.91 million in 2000. Its proportion in total migration has exceeded household registration migration (Wang, 2013: 66).

At present, the household registration system's reform is an important means to carry out the state's urbanization. The household registration system is a legal system for the state's relevant authorities to collect, confirm, and register the basic population information about citizenship, kinship, legal address, and other aspects. The institutional system of an orderly flow of population and resource elements in urban and rural areas should be gradually established to guide and encourage the orderly transfer of agricultural population to cities and towns. During the 12th Five-Year Plan period, it is necessary to adopt policy guidance and scientific advancement to solve the stock problem and prioritize transferring critical groups of the qualified population for agricultural transfer to change the household registration to cities. During the 13th Five-Year Plan period, the transfer of household registration should be normalized so that the new generation of migrant workers can gradually be transformed into urban residents. Most of the qualified migrant workers can be transformed into urban residents. Rural graduates from junior colleges and technical secondary schools can almost settle in cities and towns and develop themselves. The migrant workers whose cultivated land has been fully or mostly appropriated but have not been transferred to the non-agricultural status have resolved their identity as urban residents properly. (Department of Housing and Urban-Rural Development of Chuxiong Yi Autonomous Prefecture, 2014)

In transferring the household registration, the cadres of town organs, village committees and Party committees took the lead in transferring the household registration for the entire household, playing a good exemplary role. The village committees have set up household registration agencies.

That is to say, based on the voluntary application of the masses for the formalities of transferring Agricultural Residents to Non-agricultural Residents, the village committees collect the household registration information and application forms of household registration transfer and submit them to the police station for centralized handling. As of August 20, 2012, a total of 1,532 residents transferred their household registration in Shiyang Town, thus completing the target of 1,390 residents transmitted by the Dayao County People's Government by 110.2%. (Zhang, 2012)

The above policy is the policy of "transfer of the agricultural to non-agricultural status." It was proposed and implemented based on the assumption that the peasants wanted to go into cities and change from agricultural to non-agricultural status. But in the authors' field survey, it seems to be the opposite of the assumption. Simultaneously, many people are unwilling to change their identity from rural to urban residents. In the transformation process, they will lose their land and the material basis for their survival. As far as peasant status is concerned, their most significant capital is that they own the land, continuously inputted and re-produced. Despite a small amount of income earned from agricultural production, their land ownership can enable their families to have the expenditure to maintain their basic livelihoods. The authors' field survey findings are consistent with the latest research.

According to the Report on China's Migrant Population Development, about 60% of the floating population in rural areas was unwilling to transfer to non-agricultural residents. 35% of those who said they were willing to change from agricultural to non-agricultural status were unwilling to return the contracted land. And 34% of those unwilling to transfer to non-agricultural residents wanted to retain their land. (Department of Floating Population of National Health and Family Planning Commission of the People's Republic of China, 2013) Simultaneously, according to the relevant statistical research, the elderly in need of support at home will make migrant workers tend to return to their hometown's rural areas and counties. The probability of migrant workers willing to stay in cities will be reduced by 7.3%. The first generation of migrant workers has lost their best age to work outside and lacks professional competitiveness. Because of their attachment to rural life, they have returned to their original land. The farmers' different realistic choices can also respond to the proposition of urban construction, which blindly pursues the metropolitan model in the existing studies of urbanization.

A paper on urban household registration cannot bring additional changes, and a paper on urban household registration cannot have a substantive explanation. In the final analysis, we should enable the rural residents to enjoy the same way of life as urban residents and enjoy the urban residents' cultural and public services. According to the survey, there have been tremendous changes in rural areas in recent years. Twenty years ago, the rice was insufficient to fill the stomach, and many families needed to mix with corn and other coarse cereals, commonly known as corn rice and coarse cereal rice. This year, for the same 20 households, three have bought mini cars or pickups, and two have bought houses in the county town.

Mou Fuli pointed out that China had not endowed typical urban activities with significant importance than other civilized countries. Chinese values do not support the view that the urban upper-class society is a component of the population. The urban population of the total population does not represent and dominate the tone of Chinese life. (Skinner, 2000: 113-114) He further concluded that China does not have a unique metropolitan center, the perfect realm of its citizens and the epitome of its civilization, which makes us feel that China is a rural China. It is not the urban factors but the rural factors that define China's way of life (Skinner, 2000: 117). As a result, the Chinese cities in history have not been prostrated in worship and scrambled for as they are now, which creates a certain space for cities to grow freely. In traditional Chinese society, the practice is in an open society.

The people have the opportunity and power to move freely, and there are channels for people to move in the geographical and social dimensions. "Find shelter in rural areas in case of tiny disasters and find shelter in urban areas in case of significant disasters." Cities become places where people move, especially when they choose the best shelter, which reflects the security of cities. In migration, the people who move do not realize the need to cross the obvious boundaries, and there is no dual division of the internal as urban areas and the external as rural areas. Second, the authors doubt that there are some problems in both the voluntariness of the people in the existing household registration system reform and the reform's thoroughness. In the urbanization process, the household registration system's reform mostly points to the passage from the rural population to the urban population. The ratio of the urban population constitutes the hard index of the urbanization rate.

The lack of a reverse channel for transforming urban to rural populations' shift without diversified channels has become a rigid and compulsory form of urbanization. It lacks the people's right to choose freely. The acceptance of the household registration system is not equivalent to social integration. Especially for the new generation of migrant workers, the non-integration here is "bilateral non-integration," they can neither integrate into the city nor into the countryside (Li et al., 2013: 307-326).

The freedom of population migration is considered when the net agglomeration effect of a place is not exhausted; there is no reason to stop population flow. It is really to stand out for the desire of farmers to enter the city. Freedom of migration provides a choice for farmers to enter the city or not to enter the city and provides a series of guarantees for them to enter the city. Some studies suggest that the household registration system reform's value orientation should not be urbanization but should be replaced with freedom of migration. Specifically, it establishes a unified household registration system. It replaces the planned indicators by the international standards for household registration, such as legal residence, stable occupation or income source, exercise control, and guaranteeing people's freedom of residence and migration. (Huang, 2002: 38) From the perspective of satisfying citizens' rights, the fundamental problem of the household registration system's reform is to realize citizens' freedom and rights of migration and residence. (Huang, 2002: 38) Giving citizens the freedom of migration does not result in a crazy rush into the city.

Therefore, the value orientation of the household registration system's reform should not be urbanization but should be redefined as freedom of migration. First, from the perspective of satisfying citizens' rights, the fundamental problem of the household registration system's reform is to realize citizens' freedom and rights of migration and residence. Second, from the perspective of adapting to the market economy, the household registration system's reform is to realize the freedom of migration and allow human resources to have logical flow following the requirements of allocating resources in the socialist market economy. The development of the market economy and the rational pricing and optimal allocation of labor resources need to be guaranteed by the freedom of population migration. Thirdly, the scope of urbanization is too narrow to cover the whole content of population migration. As such, it is not suitable to replace the freedom of migration with urbanization as the value orientation of the reform of the household registration system. Finally, from the perspective of the endogenous nature of the reform, the most attractive thing for the people is the freedom of migration rather than urbanization (Huang, 2002).

Back to the present, China presents various forms of migration: international and domestic migration, cross-provincial migration and intra-provincial migration, survival-oriented migration and development-oriented migration, 274 million migrant workers (Yang, 2015) and millions of college graduates, which shows the universality of migration at the present stage. Its large scale and frequent flow are unprecedented in Chinese history, marking the advent of "the era of mobility" in China (Wang, 2015). It is undeniable that "migration" is not a keyword accompanied by reform and opening but a natural social phenomenon accompanied by Chinese society's development. It is inevitable to have some contradictions in migration, but the long-term integration after conflicts and interest demand is also visible. We reflect on China's immigration strategies since the founding of the People's Republic of China from the perspective of the legitimacy of migration in the historical process and find that it is not thought or practiced based on migration's legitimacy.

The policy of migrant workers in China has gone from restriction to loosening. Then it was from the control over blind flow to regulation on flow, and then to the encouragement of flow and advocate of integration into the city. The overall migration strategy tends to slow down. However, the current problems are still not optimistic. It is undeniable that urban residents in China still enjoy many "urban privileges" in employment, housing and various social security systems. Simultaneously, the concept of human beings has regarded mobility as a legitimate existence, while the flow is acknowledged and put into practice. But what is lagging in the system, which has not yet fully recognized the legitimacy of migration. The governance of mobility increases the cost of social management. Simultaneously, the liberalization of governance and the formation of "governance by non-interference" may also lead to substantial social costs after institutional inertia. William Petersen regards the form of free population migration as a form of forced population migration, which is higher than the primitive migration in the period of human collection and nomadism and caused by the state's pressure. When free migration becomes a social fashion, it will form a larger and more universal mass migration (Duan, 1998: 12-16). At present, people's free migration has not been guaranteed by legality, and it is more difficult to refer to legitimacy. The idea of mass migration is also beset with difficulties. We cannot deny that there is a lack of legitimacy of migration at present and that there is still a long way to regard migration as the existence of legitimacy.

The Role of the State in Urbanization

In the process of studying the urbanization of the old Shiyang Town, the authors have sincerely felt that the state has become an unavoidable existence in the study. From the beginning of the study to its conclusion, it has been deeply intertwined with the state. Local towns' development context lies in the deep understanding of the state institution and the "state discourse." Suppose we neglect the existence of the state to speak of local urbanization. In that case, we will inevitably have the bias of "attempting an ineffective solution" and "applying others' experience mechanically." Thus the way of "seeing like a state" in the study is also revealed. James C. Scott proposed the concept of "seeing like a state." It means that the country tends to carry out social transformation through some grand modern social engineering or projects, remolds the society and environment simply and straightforwardly for its purposes and tries to conduct a rational design of the social order under the ideology of extreme modernity.

The way of "seeing like a state" has weakened society's growth and neglected the public opinion and demand because of the excessive emphasis on national action (Scott, 2012: 2-3). From a realistic point of view, "seeing like a state" is more evident in China's urbanization process. Alan Stott reveals the increasingly dominant role of the state in social life based on the state mode of production. He points out that state managers, bureaucrats, planners, professional consultants, and scholars have constituted a new class and become the primary embodiment of social authority and control in late-capitalist countries. In every place, the state apparatus manages social relations in one way or another (Stott, 1993: 5-13).

Faced with the influence of state power, some studies have put forward the concept of "embedded politics" specifically to refer to the negative impact of state power on the local economy in the era of collectivization based on the brute force and excessive intervention of local authorities (Lu, 2007). “Embeddedness” was first proposed by the economic anthropologist K. Polanyi. Embedded politics refers to the process and phenomenon in which political movements, political actions, and power are embedded into social and economic life and become constituent parts of people's lifestyle and economic activities (Lu, 2006: 118). Embedded politics deprives farmers of free space for development and deprives them of the opportunity to choose, resulting in stagnant social development in rural areas.

Looking at the existing studies, the discussion on the relationship between the state and the local of the South China School has become an unavoidable objective existence. Thus, understanding the state and the local relationship has become a classic research paradigm of the South China School. The Art of Not Being Governed: An Anarchist History of Upland Southeast Asia by James C. Scott can be called subversion of the relationship between the existing state and the local (Scott, 2009). Through the mobility of the internal society, the people in Zomia refuse the permanent internal hierarchy and state control. From his perspective, the relationship between people, people, and groups in such an institutional society is temporary and changeable, effectively preventing the emergence of hierarchy and centralization.

Traffic barriers, nomadic mode of livelihood, flexible social structures, oral cultural traditions, and heretical religious beliefs in mountainous societies are distinctive from transportation facilities between countries, settled agriculture, solidified social structures, writing traditions, and orthodox religious beliefs. But this is far from a natural objective existence. At the same time, it is the conscious “adaptation” and “design” of the people in mountainous areas who flee the country and prevent the country but must be neighbors of the country (Du, 2014: 98). It should be noted that such subversive studies as Scott's are still within the framework of the discussion on the relationship between the state and the local. The background of state rule covers the Art of Not Being Governed by James C. Scott, while “escaping” and “not being governed” are only typical and unconventional forms under the rule's framework by the dynastic state. Rule by the state is still the central theme. The strategies for rule by the state include market and tax, the marriage strategy of the royal court, the decentralization of royal power (the relationship between the royal court and gentry group), and the critical manipulation of state antenna in mountainous areas, such as the control of resources in mountainous areas, the formation of military cities and political cities, and so on. During the dynastic period, the state power's military and political cities were more than the economic cities developed spontaneously, which became a powerful portrayal of the state power reaching the local authorities.

The above studies by the South China School and James C. Scott have shown the two sides of understanding the relationship between the state and the local. The relationship between the local people and the state is like a game of cards, in which some people are willing to sit down and argue, negotiate and compromise (the focus of the South China School). Still, some people have no interest in playing cards and are unwilling to sit down, so they hide far away (the focus of the study is on zombies), while some people may throw the poker table out of anger. Just as Cheng Meibao assessed, "escaping" and "joining" are two sides of the process of national expansion. Since modern times, more and more people have joined in, while less and less space to get away (Cheng, 2010; Du, 2014: 99). At present, the distance between the state and the local will only get closer and closer. In the context of the development of modern technology, the popularization of "distance reduction" tools (such as railways, telephones and other modern communication tools) has dramatically changed the involvement of "autonomous groups" in the areas of not being governed.

The urbanization process in China is a process of natural generation of "agglomeration and diffusion." It is also a planned process of the government driven by policies (Dong and Wang, 2014: 8). One of the characteristics of modern cities is the straight marching of state power, which has become an independent force above the mode of social production and directly impacts urban development (Chen, 2012: 22). The existing urbanization in China has increasingly become an exogenous and human-made process dominated by the government (Wen, 2014: 84) but lacks endogenous power. The problem is that urbanization calls for the ideology that fits in with the state's goal, and then all kinds of problems in it are likely to be neglected and hidden consciously or unconsciously. Urbanization is also endowed with the overwhelming necessity and urgency, allowing people to turn a blind eye to many problems or abandon the essential judgment criteria when encountering many problems (Chen, 2004).

Under the political call, urban development in China has spread from big cities to small cities and villages and towns. We should discover spontaneous and conscious urbanization when urbanization was not the national ideology. It is more conducive for us to see clearly, to achieve the purpose of comparison and reflection. Fei Xiaotong indicated the importance of seeing a state to the urbanization process. He advocated that all regions should be market-oriented in the urbanization process while advocating the "support" of national policies and that the state's participation is necessary. Still, the most fundamental driving force derives from the local people (Ding, 2014: 90-91). It is impossible to eliminate the influence of national factors in the urbanization process. Under the state strength, the implementation of local government policies represented by the state policies is deeply embedded in urbanization in the old Shiyang Town.

Because of the state's superior control over salt as a unique resource, Baiyanjing has also been specially controlled from a national perspective. There is no doubt that the shadow of the state impact has been left on the production, circulation and sales of local salt, salt tax extraction, the reform and implementation of salt affairs. The heavy salt tax burden imposed from the administrative level and the salt affair administration of long-standing abuse has become obstacles in the urbanization process in

Shiyang Town. After the flood in 1961, due to the lack of administration, it was difficult for Shiyang Town to undertake post-disaster rehabilitation and reconstruction for a long time. In the 1980s, especially since the 1990s, the local government has taken advantage of the local advantages of historical and cultural resources to find a new way to develop the town. The old Shiyang Town is included in the historical and culturally famous towns of Yunnan Province. Under this opportunity, the People's Government of Chuxiong Yi Autonomous Prefecture has taken the initiative to promote the development of famous historical and cultural towns and villages and to explore the ways of combining protection with rational utilization and guided the development of the cultural and tourism industries of famous historical and cultural towns and villages. At the same time, it encourages the population of agricultural transfer to become urbanized in local and surrounding areas, engages in the tourism service industry, and achieves the sustainable development of the famous towns and villages.

Also, a scientific plan has been made to develop ancient villages and towns, ancient buildings, ruins and sites. The plan develops the sightseeing tour of cultural heritage and incorporates the protection and development of significant cultural heritage into economic and social development. The urban and rural construction, tourism development planning and attaches great importance to improving the living environment for the residents. The infrastructure construction has been developed to improve residents' living conditions, promote them to maintain the historical heritage on a conscious and willing basis. These works provide a guarantee and foundation for protecting history and culture (Department of Housing and Urban-Rural Development of Chuxiong Yi Autonomous Prefecture, 2014). These practices at the government level will undoubtedly provide an impetus for the old Shiyang Town's follow-up development.

Local urbanization is also springing up under the wave of urbanization throughout the country. The original office of Baolian Village in the town area of Shiyang Town has been changed to Shiyang

Community Residents' Committee. The government has the target of changing from agricultural to non-agricultural status issued by higher authorities, which is included in local governments' work objectives. A particular office changing from agricultural to non-agricultural status is set up in Shiyang Town Police Station to facilitate procedures. In recent years, the policy of changing from agricultural to non-agricultural status has affected the population of the town area in Shiyang and expanded the propaganda of this policy to the village level within the administrative region of the town. Each village committee has several special quotas for changing from agricultural to non-agricultural status every year. Only the influential people in the village can obtain the quota for changing from agricultural to non-agricultural status.

Yunnan Province government encourages building projects on mountains for urbanization to avoid the deprivation of land resources. This policy is based on the fact that more mountains sit in the province. The Department of Housing and Urban-Rural Development of Yunnan Province suggests that mountain urbanization is well-designed. It is based on the full investigation and demonstration by the government sectors and in line with the reality of Yunnan Province. It is the key to resolving the double pressure of more mountains and fewer dams in Yunnan, developing construction land, and protecting cultivated land. Building urban projects on mountains accelerate the construction of cities and towns on mountains. Yunnan has very prominent advantages of building cities and towns on mountains (Luo, 2014: 107). Building urban projects on mountains also have a local practical expression in the locality. The typical expression of the local implementation of building urban projects on mountains is to level Laoshu Mountain in the town to the ground and conduct infrastructure construction. Laoshu Mountain, located in the middle part of Shiyang Town, is an independent hill on the town area's edge. There are relevant records in local chronicles.

In the expression of history, too many memories of local people towards the mountain accumulated, resulting in the legendary stories of

Laoshu Mountain. The overall shape of Laoshu Mountain had not changed a lot as of 2003. In 2003, the old Shiyang Town cut half of Laoshu Mountain to build the road for the sake of developing traffic. In 2015, the government allocated the land on Laoshu Mountain to enterprises to build cold storage. In July of that year, Laoshu Mountain was gradually razed to the ground under the excavator's operation. The future Laoshu Mountain will be filled with buildings to reflect the speed of local urbanization. The geographic coordinates of Laoshu Mountain will be eliminated in the latest geographic signs, and the later generations will have no way to know about the legends of Laoshu Mountain. It has brought about profound changes in the spatial pattern of local areas, which is also the manifestation of the powerful administrative force to apply its force and form the tremoring process of local urbanization.

There are also some problems in local urbanization while some achievements have been made. Urban construction lays too much stress on something fancy, such as devoting significant attention to cultural performances, like the Confucius Ceremony by tens of thousands of people and students. These similar performances have also been popular in surrounding towns, such as selecting "the most beautiful Rhododendron delavayi" and creating "the first mutton hot pot. To our surprise, behind a prosperous festival, there is only desolation left and the ending that the government makes significant efforts but receives negligible effect. Even in daily affairs, the government's financial expenditure is excessively devoted to urban centers' expenditure. The old Shiyang Town has carried out a significant urban area renewal project to develop tourism. However, the authors argue that these strategies, which seem to promote tourism, will only make the town lose its unique flavor because of imitation, just like other tourist towns. The government does not know that it is just chasing after other similar towns and imitating blindly so that it just creates the town's appearance (all antique-style buildings with one white side of the walls) but falls into the trap of development.

For these issues above, we need to respond further that the national policy is merely a supporting role, rather than the leading force in the old Shiyang Town's urbanization process. At present, urbanization relies more on policy. The residents almost regarded urbanization as the same as agricultural to non-agricultural status. The change from agricultural to non-agricultural status is commonly believed to be urbanization. Based on the authors' studies, policy advocacy and efforts are only a part of the urbanization process instead of a critical factor. As the supporting role of urbanization, the state sometimes caters to the inevitable needs of urban development and becomes the promoter of urban development. Sometimes, it tries to "maliciously" break urban development's inherent needs and affect urbanization to a certain extent. For example, in a period, the government adopted robust policies, such as the regulatory measures on household registration, employment, commodity grain, housing and so on, to realize the population's attempt not to expand to cities. While gradually realizing that such measures have blindly broken the existing market rules, the government has gradually liberalized its policy to allow the rural population to flow to urban areas. It has gradually introduced relevant provisions to ensure that the floating population can obtain the rights to survive and develop in cities and towns.

There is no doubt that there is a noticeable color of government mobilization in China's current urbanization process policy, which is in the ascendant. The current development pattern of urbanization is based on government intervention. At the same time, the lack of individualized planning causes a waste of resources and makes the government's efforts challenging to get a return. Does the urbanization process a natural process in modernization or a process in which the government should take the initiative and intervene forcefully? The government-led urbanization is based on the logic of "being like a country." The effect of the pressure mechanism finally deviates from the core goal of "human urbanization." To solve this problem, based on the perspective of social construction, the government put forward the concept of "new urbanization." This new concept emphasizes the co-construction of state and society, city and countryside, to correct the traditional model of urbanization (Dong and Wang, 2014: 8-17). In the development of urbanization, "there is a situation that the transformation at the utensil level and the city's development," and even "the alienation tendency of seeing things but not people" becomes more and more prominent. Urbanization should emphasize "the urbanization of people," which can end people with subjectivity (Dong and Wang, 2014: 10).

As the government predominance restrains the market and society's role in effectively allocating resources and forming compatible incentives, eventually, it becomes the mode of blind expansion. It evolves into the urban construction movement of large-scale demolition and construction, which has played a negative role in speeding up urbanization. It is driven by the two driving mechanisms of the market and the government. The market is the fundamental driving force, and the government is the key driving force. Only by the effective combination of the two can the healthy development of urbanization be promoted. However, China's traditional urbanization mode presents a distinct government-led feature. It is the concrete embodiment of "policy-oriented governance" in the urbanization process. New urbanization puts forward a new orientation of the relationship between market and government, which is market-oriented and government-led. It requires us to give full play to the decisive role of the market in allocating urbanization resources. On the other hand, it optimizes the government's behavior in the urbanization process by innovating institutions and mechanisms (Zhang, 2014: 4-10).

The Chinese central government's strategic development goal of the new urbanization indicates that the government has begun to face the drawbacks of the traditional urban construction mode. It has been pursuing the urbanization of land unilaterally for a long time and neglecting the quality of urban construction. The governments from top to bottom tend to become the primary participants for the dominant force and strength of urbanization, making the government face the pressure and powerlessness to manage everything. Therefore, the development of urbanization should be promoted by multiple subjects. These objects include the governments, enterprises, individuals and other market subjects. Each should influence urbanization in unique ways and jointly promotes urbanization in China (Song, 2011: 122).

Urbanization of "Culture"

Old Shiyang Town's long-term urbanization process involves the relationship among resources, markets, human flow, and government role. The four will reach the same goal in the urbanization process: everything aims to retain the culture and lead to a better life in cities and towns.

As early as 2,000 years ago, Aristotle, an ancient Greek philosopher, wrote in his masterpiece Politics that "people come to the city for the sake of life and stay in the city for the sake of a better life." Ban Ki-moon, Secretary-General of the United Nations, once said in The World Cities Report that "Cities are one of the most complex works by humanity. It has never been completed and has no definite form, just like a journey without an end. It is the past, the present and the future." Over the past 20 years, the number of urban residents worldwide has increased from 1.5 billion to 3.6 billion. Urbanization has become the main driving force for poverty reduction and the achievement of the Millennium Development Goals. 80% of the world's economic activities are concentrated in cities (Li, 2013: 1). In 2000, Joseph Eugene Stiglitz, a recipient of the Nobel Memorial Prize in Economic Sciences, indicated that the two most profound things that affect the process of human society in the 21st century are the new technological revolution led by the United States and the urbanization of China (Wu, 2002).

Wen Guanzhong, a famous economist, also pointed out that urbanization is where China's hope to get out of the agriculture-oriented society that has lasted for more than two thousand years lies. Urbanization is an important phenomenon and form of social culture. Furthermore, the small towns represented by the old Shiyang Town are the nerve endings of the state power, and there are various micro-incidents at the grassroots level. Small towns play a fundamental role, as they can fuel economic growth soon and control the general direction of economic and social transformation in the long run. Urbanization means that the population will gather in big cities and transfer to small cities.

Returning to the current urbanization, the phenomenon of "semi-urbanization" has become an accurate and useful concept to describe current China. In fact, "semi-urbanization" is a kind of incomplete urbanization compared with "urbanization." In addition to the regional and urban landscape, it is more concentrated that the industrial structure and employment composition have had a relatively high non-agricultural level. Still, the urban society is disconnected from the administrative and cultural systems, lacking integration. It means that part of the national economic rights is incomplete, political rights are incomplete, and cultural rights are incomplete. It also means the inequality of enjoying national development achievements and participating in national civilization (Kong and Cheng, 2013: 28). For example, at present, the accumulation of the urbanized population is the accumulation of the labor force, which excludes the family members (the elderly and the children) behind the labor force. At the same time, there is a particularly prominent loss of culture in the urbanization process.

"In the past ten years, 80 villages have disappeared every day in China. In the past 30 years, more than 40 thousand immovable cultural relics have disappeared." They have been cut off from a period of history and the unique cultures and customs accumulated there from generation to generation. The inherent working habits, the relationship between heaven and man, the ancestors and their beliefs in the land, and the "root" of the Chinese national culture disappeared. More generally, urbanization has been alienated in many places as "numerous investments are made in large-scale demolition. The reconstruction of high-rise buildings is built from the ground, all kinds of parks are clustered, and CBDs contribute greatly to GDP." In contrast, the traditional culture has been marginalized repeatedly (Liu and Liu, 2014).

As a general rush action, the city construction movement is destroying the value of cities as cultural deposits and cultural carriers. Simultaneously, there is no force to block the urban development movement by the bulldozers in China. It is the poetic expression of public expectation in policy and the signal of the return of urbanization culture to retain the culture and call the nostalgia back to mind. The new urbanization process will become an unavoidable cultural proposition to find ways to maintain the inheritance of culture, the continuation of context and the memory of history (Bu and Qi, 2013: 119-123). The differences between traditional and new urbanization are manifested in the following aspects.

First, the background of the times is different. Traditional urbanization originates from the traditional economic system. The new urbanization is based on the economy's dual transformation.

Second, the emphasis is different. Traditional urbanization stresses the population and the expansion of cities' scale and quantity. In contrast, new urbanization lays more stress on optimizing the quality of cities and devotes itself to the coordinated development between economy and society, between urban and rural areas, and that between resources, environment and population.

Third, the subject is different. New urbanization involves pluralistic subjects, mainly governments, enterprises and residents. At the same time, the government dominates traditional urbanization at all levels.

Fourth, the way is different. Traditional urbanization is mainly based on the "top-down" approach, supplemented by the "bottom-up" approach. In contrast, new urbanization is mainly based on the "bottom-up" approach and supplemented by the "top-down" approach.

Fifth, the dynamic mechanism is different. The fundamental driving force of traditional urbanization mainly derives from industrialization. In contrast, the driving force of new urbanization mainly derives from developing the urban service industry. It also derives from the innovation of new industries and informatization (Wang et al., 2009: 89).

There is always a demand for cultural construction and continuity running slowly in urbanization in the old Shiyang Town. In the classic salt era, local salt resources were transformed into economic capital as natural resources. Still, the local towns did not come to a halt at this stage but accumulated in the name of culture. The flow of culture is brought about by salt and humanity, while the musical culture brings the local towns' genes to remain on the glory trail for long years. "There is a festival every day," and "there are seven temples, eight pavilions and nine Buddhist convents…." The unique culture shapes the style of the old Shiyang Town, which is particularly prominent. The local authorities regained salt society's cultural value at the urbanization stage of reviving because of salt. They shaped the individuality of local towns in the name of culture. With the advent of the tourism era at present, the proposal and practice of new urbanization, to a certain extent, are coupled with the cultural revival of the local salt society.

Conclusion

Urbanization is a tremendous social transformation process for the Chinese people from a historical perspective. The urbanization in China varies from place to place; the urbanization of old Shiyang Town is unique because of the salt. In the urbanization stage of "thriving because of salt," first, the old Shiyang Town formed a typical salt society of "replacing farming by brine" due to salt. In the old Shiyang Town salt society, salt officials, salt-maker groups, salt workers, and salt merchants performed their functions. They found their proper positions due to salt production's particular division of labor. Ti Ju Si (提举司), an official salt-based organization represented by the official will, cooperated with the salt-maker production organization as a folk salt-based organization represented by the folk will promote salt's benign production.

Simultaneously, the salt production organization was also involved in the urban construction of the old Shiyang Town. In the old Shiyang Town, the salt industry's featured legends came into being based on salt production, while these legends have changed in history. The historical processes have endowed the legends with different vitalities. A series of local beliefs in salt gods have developed around salt production. Daughter of the Dragon King (龙女), Blue Sheet (石羊), God of Fire (火神) and King of Brine Dragon (卤龙王), and there developed some space for the belief in local salt gods, such as Infanta Hall (郡主祠), Dragon King's Temple (龙王庙) and Zong Long Hall (总龙祠). It has also formed the ritual expression of salt gods' belief, such as Dragon King Fair, Salt Merchants Fair and Fire God Fair. In the old Shiyang Town, professional records on the local salt industry have been developed around salt production, such as Chronicles of Baiyanjing. In contrast, many literary creations in the records are developed based on salt production activities to display the hardships of salt production and the prosperity of the salt industry. Above all, the salt society's typical characteristics in the old Shiyang Town are manifested from the salt-oriented division of labor, the salt production organization, the legends and changes of salt production and the literary expressions of salt and emotions in the town.

Second, the old Shiyang Town develops the markets due to salt, while the markets drive the acquisition of regional economic, political and cultural centers. The salt of the old Shiyang Town has entered the vision of national control. It has been transferred from the purely natural resources to the economic resources that provide the state's tax revenue and promote the development of local towns. Salt production, transportation and sales have developed a salt-centered market network. The formation of the salt market has driven the firewood market and other commodity markets. The old Shiyang Town has further formed the regional economic center, while the old Shiyang Town is satisfied with acquiring an economic center. During urbanization, the old Shiyang Town has successfully obtained its regional political and cultural center position.

It promoted the comprehensive development of urban functions in the urbanization process of the old Shiyang Town.

Third, the old Shiyang Town has promoted the flow of human beings because of salt. Settlements were developed in the old Shiyang Town because of salt, and the aggregation effect of crowds was formed with the exploitation of salt. Especially during the Hongwu period of the Ming Dynasty, it was documented in such a way that immigrants from other places continued to pour into Baiyanjing to engage in salt production. With people gathering here, salt production led to migration, which allowed the local area to present a typical social characteristic of migration. There are distinct types of migrants for different causes, and the multiple geographical structures of migration are developed due to the different origins of the migrants. In the local area, multiple religious manifestations, various diets, and mixed customs and ideas have become migration expressions in the old Shiyang Town.

In the urbanization stage of "declining because of salt," the existing salt production declined in the old Shiyang Town. Then the sales circles were shrunk continuously, and the salt society showed a declining trend. Simultaneously, under the guidance of the national policies, the closed market was formed, and the previous markets of the old Shiyang Town gradually lost their charm. Faced with the declining trend of the salt society, the local authorities also intended to carry out the salt society's transformation. Still, after the incompleteness of "changing from brine to coal" and the struggle of "the era of salt plants," it was difficult to recover. The salt industry showed a declining trend. In 1961, a catastrophic flood disaster in the old Shiyang Town became a bitter memory for Shiyang Town's people, making the old Shiyang Town that had been weakly unable to get up again after the decline. Thus, it also reflects that it is difficult to recover and reconstruct the town because of the social decline arising from the salt industry's decline.

With the decline of the salt society, local society was also changing quietly. And the diversified livelihood pattern replaced the livelihood pattern of "replacing farming by brine," while the salt organizations had withdrawn, and human flow had been weakened. In terms of the obstacles to urbanization in the old Shiyang Town due to the decline of salt, some come from the resources themselves. The deterioration of the environment and the decline in salt resources' value lead to the "curse" of salt resources. The shortcomings of salt tax and salt administration as a burden and the separation and integration of local administration and salt administration eventually become obstacles to the old Shiyang Town's urbanization. Simultaneously, the restrictions of natural disasters and human-made calamities in the old Shiyang Town have exacerbated the urbanization crisis in the old Shiyang Town.

In the urbanization stage of "reviving because of salt," the old Shiyang Town regained salt society's cultural value. With the local town rated among the first batch of famous historical and cultural towns in Yunnan Province since 1995 as the thrust, the old Shiyang Town has embarked on a road of tourism development as "Millennium Salt Capital," "Holy Land of Confucius," and "Famous Cultural Town." On pursuing the value of the local salt society and developing tourism, local urbanization has also changed, and the old Shiyang Town has regained its vitality. It used to be submerged in the culture of the salt society to achieve production and reproduction. The Well Opening Festival and Confucius Ceremony began to revive, and the salt culture museum retained the historical remains in the local salt society. People's flow is gradually increasing, while the flow of culture is also achieved above the flow of people.

Chapter 5
Endogenous Power of Rural Economic Development in China

This chapter studies the relationship between cultural capital and the development of the rural economy in China during economic transformation. It argues that cultural capital is an essential endogenous power for developing a rural economy, which is mainly reflected in the effects of cultural capital in increasing the output level in rural areas, improving farmers' income, and helping them out of poverty. As many enterprises with intensive cultural capital and relatively high marginal product arising in China, cultural capital advances the development of the rural economy to promote the advanced organizational methods to allocate resources. It also upgrades human capital and increases the number of rural labor forces employed in the industries with a relatively high marginal product and abundant cultural capital. Moreover, the industries with intensive cultural capital expand the coordinated development of the markets and initiatives for the rural economy.

Introduction

In the process of economic transformation, significant accomplishments have been made in the development of China's rural economy. The output and income have a considerable increase compared to before the transformation. However, it is less optimistic in many aspects of the development of the rural economy in China. There is a massive gap in economic growth between urban and rural areas. According to the China Statistical Yearbook, rural residents' per capita disposable income in China was 13,432.4 yuan (1 yuan =0.141 US dollars) in 2017, while urban residents in China were 36,393.0 yuan. In the same year, the per capita disposable income of rural residents in Shanghai was 27,825.0 yuan, and that of rural residents in Guizhou province was 8,869.1 yuan. Some farmers in less developed regions have not been lifted out of poverty. Therefore, it is necessary to vigorously acquire the economy in China's rural areas. However, the traditional driving force of China's economic growth has gradually subsided, and the reform has entered the deep water zone.

In contrast, the global economy has not recovered from the impact of the financial crisis. As a result, China's rural economy is developing under a severe external environment, which significantly impacts the development of the rural economy. Therefore, it is vital to cultivate and tap the endogenous power of developing the rural economy.

The Chinese government and the academic world have carried many studies on the driving force for China's rural economy. Chinese President Xi Jinping proposed the rural revitalization strategy in 2017 to encourage the development of industries in rural areas and provide necessary policy support. Some studies explore the driving force for the development of rural economy in China from the aspects of technology, institution and policy, infrastructure, and urbanization (Huang and Rozelle, 1996; Fan and Zhang, 2004; Ding, Qin, and Shi, 2018; Feng, Liu and Qu, 2019; Tian, Holland and Brown, 2016). However, there has not yet been an excellent understanding of the driving force of developing the rural economy in China. Because China involves a variety of cultures and the Chinese government attaches great importance to the role of culture, this chapter attempts to explore the endogenous power of developing the rural economy in China from cultural capital.

Cultural capital refers to capital accumulated, transformed, and inherited through time operation and series of transmission actions in the social fields (Bourdieu, 1986). As far as the development of the rural economy is concerned, cultural capital plays a vital role because severe problems are arising in the exogenous forces such as the supply and diffusion of technology, institutional (policy) support, and even infrastructure. The supply is exogenous, thereby leading to the failure to meet rural development needs at any time. For instance, some institutions (policies) may distort the allocation of resources due to improper implementation or repeated changes; besides, it may be difficult to guarantee the development of the rural economy by introducing the technology since it is not appropriate. Since the cultural capital is accumulated, transformed, and inherited naturally, it highly matches the internal environment of the rural economy.

The relationship between culture and economic development has been one of the focuses of the research on development economics, which has been widely concerned by the academic fields. Culture not only has a significant impact on the economic development of the countries or between them but also plays a crucial role in the business development of enterprises (Johnson and Lenartowicz, 1998; Peng and Lin, 2009; Yeh and Lawrence, 1995; Shao, Kwok and Zhang, 2013; Dasgupta and Gupta, 2019; Hogan and Coote, 2014; Power et al., 2015; Tian et al., 2018). However, some studies also believe that culture poses a relatively limited impact on economic behavior and performance (Acemoglue and Robinson, 2013) or must play its due role under certain conditions (Uzkurt et al., 2013; Lee et al., 2019).

Because of the cultural diversity and the disparity in economic operations, many fields of cultural impact on economic development need to be systematically studied. First of all, the studies attach importance to understanding the economic function of civilization from the non-institutional perspectives (North, 1990) but less from the standpoint of capital. Some scholars hold that, as an informal institution, culture shapes the rules of the economic game, standardizes the behavior of economic subjects, and thus affects economic performance (North, 1990). Secondly, no studies have been carried out on the relationship between cultural capital and the endogenous power of the development of the rural economy for such transition economies as China. Thirdly, the studies attach less importance to the impact of industrial culture or cultural capital on industrial and regional economic development. The authors combine the above aspects to conduct an in-depth exploration into the influence of the cultural capital on the development of the rural economy and its endogenous power during the economic transformation.

As aforementioned, the authors study the endogenous power of the rural economy in China during the economic transformation from cultural capital. Cultural capital may lead to the constant flow of goods and services (Throsby, 1999) and affect economic activities. Given this, the authors specifically study two core questions. The first question is whether cultural capital promotes the development of the rural economy in China. To find out the answer to the question, the authors measure the development performance of the rural economy from three aspects: the output level of rural areas, the income level of farmers, and the poverty alleviation of farmers. Cultural capital can help increase production and income in rural areas, lifting farmers from poverty. In this regard, the positive role of cultural capital in boosting the development of the rural economy in China is supported in this study.

The second core question studied by the authors is the influence mechanism of cultural capital, boosting the development of the rural economy in China is. There are several difficulties in understanding the mechanism of cultural capital boosting the rural economy in China based on Dong brocade. One key point is to scientifically identify the root cause of the backwardness of the rural economy in China. To a large extent, the following aspects cause the backwardness of the rural economy in China. First of all, the market economy is not perfect in rural areas, mainly embodied in a small number of enterprises in the rural market and a weak foundation for the coordinated development of industries. Secondly, economic activities in rural areas are carried out within a relatively narrow market scope, with low participation in the division of labor in the market, thus leading to the difficulty in efficiently allocating factors. Thirdly, compared with other industries, agriculture has a lower level of marginal product. Moreover, due to the relatively low human capital of farmers, the farmers have a high rate of hidden unemployment. They have been continuously locked in the agricultural sector with a low marginal product.

Based on the root mentioned above causes for the backwardness of the rural economy in China, the authors study the mechanism of cultural capital, promoting the development of a rural economy based on Dong brocade. However, there are still some difficulties in understanding the mechanism of cultural capital promoting a rural economy based on Dong brocade. On the one hand, Dong brocade can be regarded as a technique to some extent, which means that it seems to be possible to understand the economic impact of Dong brocade from a technical point of view. On the other hand, it seems to be possible to understand the economic impact of the inheritance of Dong brocade from the perspective of informal institutions, which is because the inheritance of Dong brocade can be regarded as a kind of cultural inheritance. In contrast, the culture can be considered as an informal institution.

In terms of technology and informal system, there is little difference in rural economic development before and after dong Brocade was listed as intangible cultural heritage. The dramatic improvement in the rural economy is unlikely to find a suitable solution after the Dong brocade was listed as an intangible cultural heritage. Based on the dilemma of the explanation from the perspectives of both technology and informal institution, it is inspired that we need to seek a new theoretical perspective to understand the relationship between Dong brocade and the development or endogenous development impetus of rural economy in China. In contrast, we can better understand their relationship from the standpoint of cultural capital.

The root cause of the rural economy in China, that cultural capital of rural economic development to promote role in the following aspects: one is the cultural capital adequacy, the cultural capital for the promotion of rural economic development, may appear on the market a large number of cultural capital intensive, the marginal product of the relatively high enterprise. Secondly, cultural capital promotes the introduction of advanced organizational methods into rural areas to integrate and optimize the allocation of resources. Thirdly, the combination of cultural capital and labor forces in rural areas advances the upgrading of the human capital of the rural labor force and increases the number of rural workers engaged in the industries with the relatively high marginal product and abundant cultural capital. In addition, cultural capital intensive industries expand the market scope of economic activities and the range of coordinated development of industries in rural areas. These mechanisms are also supported by the authors based on their field investigation on the cultural capital of Dong brocade in China.

Taking the cultural capital of the intangible cultural heritage Dong brocade in Tongdao Dong Autonomous County, Huaihua City, China, as an example, the authors study the core questions, mainly for the following reasons. Firstly, Dong brocade has a long history in Tongdao County, but it has a relatively weak impact on the development of the rural economy in earlier days. Secondly, at present, the cultural capital of Dong brocade in Tongdao Dong Autonomous County is prevailing. Since the Dong brocade art of Tongdao Dong Autonomous County was included in the second batch of the national intangible cultural heritage list in 2008, Dong brocade in Tongdao County has successively been exhibited on various platforms such as the International Festival of the Intangible Cultural Heritage, Chengdu, China, and International Exposition of Intangible Cultural Heritage and Ancient Art Macao, China and Shanghai World Expo, etc., and made considerable progress, with the efforts of local governments at all levels. Thirdly, the impact of Dong brocade in Tongdao County on the rural economy in China provides a reference for other similar cases. In October 2017, Xi Jinping, General Secretary of the Communist Party of China Central Committee and President of China, proposed the rural revitalization strategy to call on the local governments at all levels to promote the prosperity of rural industries and realize the revitalization of rural areas. Since then, Dong brocade in Tongdao County, as an item as an intangible cultural heritage or a typical representative of cultural capital, has dramatically impacted local economic activities, which, to a large extent, applies to other similar cultural capital items. Fourthly, Tongdao County is an inland region in China, and its local government actively responds to the call of the Central People's Government of PRC to excavate the endogenous power for the growth of the rural economy to revitalize the rural economy in its jurisdiction. Therefore, the cultural capital of the intangible cultural heritage Dong brocade in Tongdao County offers an excellent quasi-natural experiment for this chapter.

The new insights of this chapter are reflected in the following three aspects. First, it enriches the understanding of the endogenous power of the development of the rural economy in China during economic transformation. This study explains the analysis of the endogenous power of the development of the rural economy in China during the economic transformation from the perspective of cultural capital. According to the authors, cultural capital is an essential endogenous power for developing and revitalizing China's rural economy during economic transformation. The authors argue that the scholars have highlighted the expansion of the driving forces of China's rural economic growth from external forces such as technology, institutional reform, education, and infrastructure to endogenous forces of cultural capital (Hawkins, 1988; Huang and Rozelle, 1996; Ding, Qin, and Shi, 2018).

Second, it enriches the literature on essential culture hypotheses (North, 1990; Swank, 1996). We think of culture as a special capital, not an informal institution. We assess the mechanism and influence of culture on rural economic development. We provide some evidence for further understanding the critical assumption of culture as capital for rural economic development (Bourdieu, 1986; North, 1990). Third, it expands research on the economic impact of intangible cultural heritage (e.g., del Barrio, Devesa, and Herrero, 2012; Alberti and Giusti, 2012). Despite the emphasis laid on the economic functions of intangible cultural heritage by the scholars (del Barrio, Devesa and Herrero, 2012; Rodzi, Zaki, Subli,

2013; Guccio et al., 2017; Petronela, 2016), there is still a lack of research on the systematic economic impact of intangible cultural heritage in the form of traditional crafts. Unlike previous studies, this chapter takes the traditional craft Dong brocade in China as the object of study. It systematically explores the economic functions of intangible cultural heritage in conventional crafts from cultural capital.

Mechanism of Cultural Capital as the Endogenous Power

The mechanism of cultural capital becoming the endogenous power of the development of the rural economy is explored by combining the economic transformation and the root causes of the backwardness of the rural economy in China. It is argued that cultural capital promotes the development of the rural economy through the following mechanisms in the aspects of the increase of output value in rural areas, the increase in farmers' income, and farmers' poverty alleviation, and then becomes the endogenous power of the development of the rural economy.

First, abundant cultural capital promotes enterprises with intensive cultural capital and relatively high marginal product in rural areas. Throsby (1999) pointed out that cultural capital may arouse the constant flow of goods and services. In the case of an abundance of cultural capital in an industry, the factors may flow to the industry to promote the emergence of new enterprises. Enterprises play a leading role in the market economy. The rise of new enterprises can advance the prosperity of the market and economies. Moreover, the high-margin product is directly related to economic prosperity. The marginal product of the enterprises with intensive cultural capital is higher than that of the agricultural sector to give more effective impetus to the development of the rural economy.

Second, cultural capital promotes introducing advanced organizational methods in rural areas. The traditional small-scale peasant economy involves the production organization with a relatively low degree of division of labor based on specialization and cooperation, which leads to the low efficiency of resource allocation. However, enterprises with intensive cultural capital involve a higher degree of division of labor and collaboration. It is more likely for these enterprises and the villages where they are located to adopt more advanced forms of organization for production and operation. Advanced organization structure can create a new combination of production conditions (Schumpeter, 1911) to enhance resource utilization efficiency.

Third, the combination of cultural capital and rural labor force not only improves the human capital of labor forces in rural areas but also reduces the hidden employment of the labor force and transfers the labor forces in rural areas from the agricultural sector with a low marginal product to the industries with higher marginal product and intensive cultural capital. On the one hand, with the emergence of enterprises with intensive cultural capital, more jobs will be available, thus lowering the hidden unemployment of labor forces in rural areas. On the other hand, when rural labor flows to cultural-capital intensive industries, it will increase the learning effect of human capital. It enables them to work in high-marginal product and culture-capital-intensive sectors, but not in low-marginal product agricultural sectors.

Fourth, cultural capital has expanded the market scope of the rural economy and the range of coordinated development of industries. The development of industries or enterprises with intensive cultural capital has actively promoted the rural economy to utilize domestic and international markets and expanded the market boundary and division of labor of the rural economy. In contrast, the expansion of market scope and division of labor is relatively beneficial to economic development (Smith, 1776).

For the above reasons, the authors believe that cultural capital is an essential endogenous power of the development of the rural economy. The following will verify the mechanism and effect of cultural capital in promoting the development of the rural economy in China by combining the field survey of the cultural capital of Dong brocade in China.

Growth of Rural Economy Based on Dong Brocade in China

Dong brocade in Tongdao Dong Autonomous County, China, is an exquisite national handicraft of Dong nationality with a long history. But before Dong brocade was listed in the intangible cultural heritage, few companies engaged in the protection and inheritance of Dong brocade. In 2008, Dong brocade in Tongdao Dong Autonomous County was included in the second batch of national intangible cultural heritage by the State Council of China. Since then, Dong brocade has played cultural capital and has been protected, inherited, and promoted by local governments. In this way, Dong brocade has been further inherited, with several inheritance projects arising at the national, provincial, and municipal levels. The inheritors have successively set up companies to inherit and develop the Dong brocade. After nearly ten years of effort, Tongdao County has owned a wider variety of Dong brocade handicrafts as cultural capital. In the Southwest Hunan market, the industrialization of Dong brocade is prevailing. Due to the economic function of the cultural capital of Dong brocade, outstanding achievements have been made in the economies of corresponding villages.

Table 5-1 Enterprise inherited and developed the Dong brocade in Tongdao Dong Autonomous County

Enterprise	Legal representative	Time of establishment	Enterprise-scale	Main achievements
Yaluoye Dong Brocade Weaving Art Development Co., Ltd.	Ou Ruifan	November 2009	With a registered capital of 2 million Yuan, the Company has set up the main store in the county town of Tongdao County and a branch store in Huangdu Dong Village Tourist Attraction.	With Ou Ruifan, chairman of the board of the Company, Dong brocade in Tongdao Dong Autonomous County has been exhibited in various expositions. The Company won the Demonstration Line Base for Production and Protection of National Intangible Cultural Heritage. It provides jobs for more than 300 female brocade-weaving workers in the Dong Village. The company's annual output

				value is over millions Yuan, and the annual sales volume in 2016 was nearly 20 million Yuan.
Tongdao County Jinxiu Wenpo Tourism Development Co., Ltd.	Su Tianmei	August 2017	The Company has two Cooperatives: Dong brocade professional cooperative and Fuyuan Chinese herbal medicine planting cooperative.	Under the leadership of Su Tianmei, the national inheritor and the Company board chairman, the Company has been committed to the inheritance and innovative development of Dong brocade. It has become a demonstration base for experts to alleviate poverty by science and technology in Tongdao Dong Autonomous County. At present, there are more than 20 permanent female brocade-weaving workers in the training base, with an annual output value of more than a million Yuan.
Nianji Weaving Crafts Store of Intangible Cultural Heritage Dong Brocade in Tongdao Dong Autonomous County	Wu Nianji	July 2012	The store exists in an individual business, with a registered capital of 20,000 Yuan.	The products are sold to Taiwan and other places, with an annual output value of more than 200,000 Yuan.

Notes: The information in this table comes from the author's field survey and Tang Hui's paper (2014).

Since Dong brocade was included in the intangible cultural heritage list, many enterprises engaged in the inheritance and sales of Dong brocade arising in the market. Among these companies, Yaluoye Dong Brocade Weaving Art Development Co., Ltd. led by Ou Ruifan, Tongdao County Jinxiu Wenpo Tourism Development Co., Ltd. led by Su Tianmei, and Nianji Weaving Crafts Store of Intangible Cultural Heritage Dong Brocade in Tongdao Dong Autonomous County led by Wu Nianji are the representative enterprises that are engaged in the protection, inheritance, and development of Dong brocade in Tongdao County. These enterprises have been contributing to the development of the rural market economy. Table 5-1 presents a brief overview of the development of the Dong brocade industry of these enterprises. The reasons and effects of these enterprises contributing to economic benefits are as follows:

After Ou Ruifan founded Yaluoye Dong Brocade Weaving Art Development Co., Ltd. in November 2009, she set up the Dong Brocade Production Base and Dong Brocade Weaving Art Base in the county town of Tongdao County. For many years, the Company adheres to the policy of "priority to protection, rescue first, rational utilization, inheritance, and development." Unlike the low-efficiency organization mode based on the production of a single peasant household in Tongdao County, the Company has initiated an efficient organization mode of "company + base + farmers." The Company also actively explores domestic and international markets, participates in the division of labor at home and abroad, and sells its products to major cities such as Shanghai in China and overseas regions such as South Korea and Russia. Due to business production and service needs, the Company also provides some jobs for local farmers. The Company has more than 300 rural permanent female brocade-weaving workers in rural areas. While inheriting and developing Dong brocade, the Company has also taken the initiative to establish the training programs of Dong brocade. As of the end of 2013, the Company has trained more than 2600 female brocade-weaving workers to enhance their human capital using concentrated training in training classes and the decentralized training of inheritors. Due to the improvement of human capital, female brocade-weaving workers can get rid of the limitation of agriculture to a certain extent and be more competent for the jobs in the Dong brocade industry with the higher marginal product. By 2016, the company's annual sales volume was nearly 20 million Yuan, which made an outstanding contribution to the economic output value of Tongdao County.

Since Tongdao County Jinxiu Wenpo Tourism Development Co., Ltd. by Su Tianmei in 2017, the Company has actively built an industrial development system centered on Dong brocade. The Company cooperates with Hunan Dongmai Cultural & Creative Development Co., Ltd. In contrast, the village company is responsible for base management and production organization. Hunan Dongmai Cultural & Creative Development Co., Ltd. is responsible for creative design, marketing, product sales, and technical training. Unlike the low-efficiency organization mode based on the production of a single peasant household in Tongdao County, the Company has created a coordinated development model involving the Company, universities, research institutes, and farmers and introduced the advanced organization mode with higher production efficiency for operation. Under the effects of the cultural capital of Dong brocade, the Company has contributed 4 million Yuan to the economic output value of the village on an annual basis and provided jobs for the women in the village.

The company has presently absorbed 24 permanent female brocade-weaving workers as permanent workers in the village and 256 home-based female brocade-weaving workers as temporary workers. By 2018, the village had had more than 700 female brocade-weaving workers. Because farmers can get more jobs and work in the Dong brocade industry with higher-margin products, they can obtain better economic income. Every female brocade-weaving worker can earn a monthly income between 2,500 and 4,000 Yuan, far higher than farmers engaged in traditional agricultural work. Under the leadership of Su Tianmei, the founder of the Company, Wenpo Village, has gradually changed from a poverty-stricken village. From 2014 to 2016, 526 residents in 119 households were lifted out of poverty in Wenpo Village. Up to now, Wenpo Village has been out of poverty as a whole.

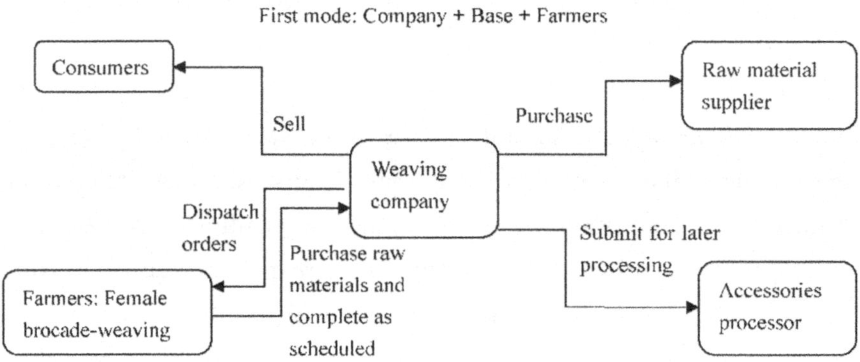

Figure 5-1 The development model established by Yaluoye Dong Brocade Weaving Art Development Co., Ltd. (Li, 2016)

Since its establishment in 2012, Nianji Weaving Crafts Store of Intangible Cultural Heritage Dong Brocade in Tongdao Dong Autonomous County, founded by Wu Nianji, has actively enhanced its ties with Taiwan and other regions based on the international market and made better economic achievements. The Company contributes more than 200000 Yuan to the economic output value of its village on an annual basis.

The following further explores the impact of the cultural capital of Dong brocade on the rural economy in combination with the employment situation. Table 5-2 shows the statistics of some female brocade-weaving workers in Wenpo Village. Although 75 percent of them are middle-aged and older women (41 years and older), 2.08 percent are young students, 6.25 percent are young women in their 20s returning home to work, and 16.67 percent are women in their 30s and 40s. These data further show that the inheritance of the Dong brocade industry can provide more jobs, especially for middle-aged and older women, who are less likely to find employment. By weaving Dong brocade, these female brocade-weaving workers can also earn about 2500-4000 Yuan at home per month, enabling them to take care of the elderly and children at home and get a reasonably good income.

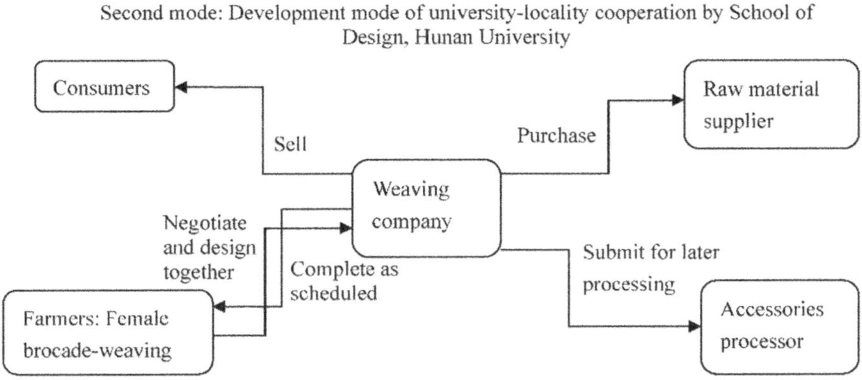

Figure 5-2 The development model established by Jinxiu Wenpo Tourism Development Co., Ltd. (Li, 2016)

Moreover, several poverty-stricken households can also get rid of poverty. According to the information of 14 poor households surveyed by the authors, ten families got out of poverty because they were engaged in the work relating to Dong brocade. The poverty alleviation rate reached 71.43%, indicating that the cultural capital of Dong brocade plays a vital role in helping the poverty-stricken households in rural areas out of poverty.

Table 5-2 Female brocade-weaving workers at Jinxiu Wenpo Tourism Development Co., Ltd.

Age	Below 20	21 - 25	26 - 30	31 - 35	36 - 40	41 - 45	46 - 50	51 - 55	Above 56
Total number of workers	1	0	3	5	3	5	18	10	3
Proportion of workers (%)	2.08	0	6.25	10.42	6.25	10.42	37.5	20.83	6.25

Notes: The data comes from the author's investigation.

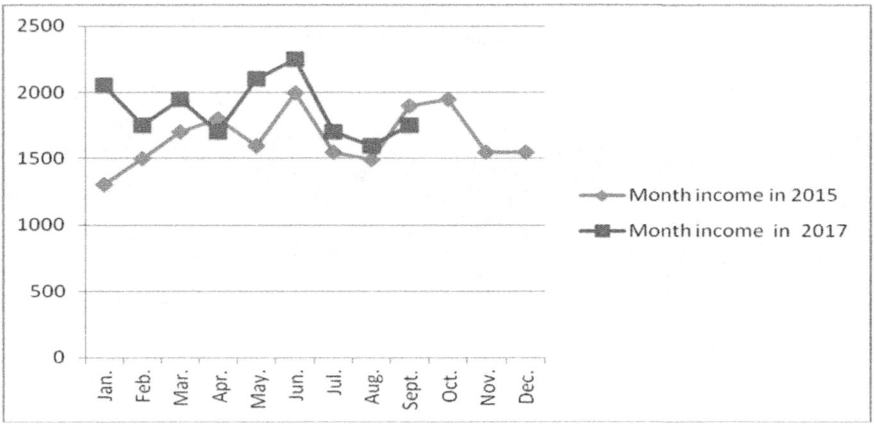

Notes: The data comes from the author's investigation.

Figure 5-3 Comparison of the average monthly income of female brocade-weaving workers in Yatunbao Town in 2015 and 2017

Table 5-3 Average annual income of female brocade-weaving workers in Yatunbao Town

Year	Average monthly income (Unit: Yuan)
2014	15,900
2015	19,500
2016	21,250
2017	16,750

Notes: The data comes from the author's investigation.

The following is a further analysis of the impact of the cultural capital of Dong brocade on the rural economy. Figure 5-3 shows the average monthly income of female brocade-weaving workers in Yatunbao Town in 2015 and 2017, which indicates that the payment of female brocade-weaving workers fluctuated in different months in 2015, the minimum value was 1,300 Yuan, and the maximum value was 2,000 Yuan. In 2017, the income of female brocade-weaving workers fluctuated in different months, with a minimum of 1,600 Yuan and a maximum of 2,250 Yuan. Table 5-3 shows the average annual income of female brocade-weaving workers in Yatunbao Town from 2014 to 2017. In 2014, the yearly income was the lowest, with 15,900 Yuan. In 2016, the annual revenue was the highest, with 21,250 Yuan.

These rural women, who have received little education, are traditionally dominated by their husbands and have minor economic status in the division of family labor. Now they work in the Dong brocade industry, becoming commodity producers with relatively regular income. Instead of relying on the agricultural work of low marginal products, they have become the leaders of local poverty eradication among the female residents. Considering the particularity of their home-based commodity production, their annual income ranges between 15000 and 21000 is quite considerable on the premise that they take good care of their family members. Meanwhile, according to China Statistical Yearbook, from 2014 to 2017, per capita disposable income of rural residents in Hunan Province, where Yatunbao Town is located, was about 10,060, 10,992, 11,930, and 12,936 Yuan, respectively. The results show that the per capita income of the female brocade-weaving workers in Yatunbao Town is higher than that of rural residents in Hunan Province in the same period. These statistical results provide a further basis for the effects of the cultural capital of Dong brocade in improving economic development.

In the preceding part, the authors pointed out that one mechanism of cultural capital to promote the development of the rural economy is to promote the coordinated development of industries, which will be analyzed below. The cultural capital of the intangible cultural heritage Dong brocade in Tongdao County has become a guarantee for expanding the industrial chain, cultivating more industries for the market economy, and leading to the coordinated development of industries. Dong Brocade cultural capital brings capital accumulation, makes the enterprise better recognized and supported by the public, and lowers legal barriers. It is conducive to the diversification of enterprise business and products and promotes the coordinated development of Dong Brocade and other related industries. The combined effect of cultural capital on Dong brocade is mainly reflected in two aspects.

On the one hand, it is necessary to build an industrial development system dominated by the Dong brocade industry and supplemented by the agricultural sector and folk tourism in rural areas. On the other hand, a Dong Brocade Museum and the franchise stores of Dong brocade should be set up in the Dong villages. Next, the authors will make further analysis in combination with the investigation.

Coordinated development mode in Tongdao County: The Company has built an industrial development system with one core and two wings, dominated by the Dong brocade industry and supplemented by the agricultural industry and folk tourism in rural areas. As shown in Table 5-4, the Jinxiu Wenpo Tourism Development Co., Ltd. has increased its investment in yellow peach, aquaculture, sweet potato, salvia miltiorrhiza, and camellia oleifera to achieve the multi-industry compound development. They made it under the premise of taking the Dong Brocade industry as the core business. This coordinated development mode strengthens the utilization of land elements, achieves good economic benefits, and contributes considerable output value to the local economy. In addition, the coordinated industrial development model provides local farmers with more employment opportunities and more income.

Table 5-4 The industrial and development planning of the coordinated development mode of Jinxiu Wenpo Tourism Development Co., Ltd.

Industrial project	Investment scale	Industrial status
Yellow peach industry	Investment of 970 thousand Yuan	The yellow peach base, located in Fengxiangzhai, Wenpo Village, has been built. In the first phase of 2018, 200 mu of yellow peach trees were planted, and additional 1,000 mu will be grown in three years. The annual income of yellow peach is 3 million Yuan after it enters the high-yield period.

Aquaculture industry	Investment of unknown funds	It mainly develops fish culture in rice fields. In 2018, 300 mu of standardized rice fields for fish culture were made, with an annual income of more than 180,000 Yuan.
Sweet potato industry	Investment of 330 thousand Yuan	The sweet potato planting base in Jiaoping Village, Shutuan Village, and Wenpo Village has been built.
Salvia miltiorrhiza industry	Investment of 451 thousand Yuan	The planting base, located in Sanbaitun, Wenpo Village, has been built. In 2017, 80 mu of Salvia miltiorrhiza was planted and harvested in December 2018, with an estimated profit of 160,000 Yuan.
Camellia oleifera industry	Investment of unknown funds	It is planned to plant 5000 mu of Camellia oleifera trees. It presently cooperates with Hunan Jinyueyun Company to produce 1,200 mu of Camellia oleifera trees. The annual rent of the mountains is 39,000 Yuan, the collective economic income is 20,000 Yuan. With 3,600 workers needed per year, the wage income is 330,000 Yuan.

Notes: The data comes from the author's investigation.

Coordinated development mode between Dong brocade and Dong village: The Pingtan River basin, as one of the two major producers of Dong brocade in Tongdao Dong Autonomous County, has not only the exquisite Dong brocade products woven by female brocade-weaving workers of Dong nationality but also has several Dong villages along the Pingtan River. Relying on Dong brocade and Dong villages, local governments and inheritors actively promote the coordinated development of Dong brocade and the Dong villages in the Pingtan River basin, which is mainly reflected in the establishment of the Dong Brocade Museum in Huangdu Dong Village and the establishment of the relevant franchise stores of Dong brocade in Huangdu Dong Village Tourist Attraction. By establishing Dong Brocade Museum and franchise stores of Dong brocade in the Dong villages, the industrial chain centered on the cultural capital of Dong brocade can be further expanded. Furthermore, such an industrial coordinated development model also guarantees economic benefits.

Conclusion

This chapter attempts to study the development of the rural economy in China during the economic transformation from the perspective of cultural capital. Moreover, this study is based on the relevant cases of the cultural capital of Dong brocade as the intangible cultural heritage in China. The authors pointed out and found that cultural capital promotes the development of rural economy, which is mainly embodied in the effects of cultural capital in increasing the output level of rural economy and farmers' income and helping the farmers out of poverty. This chapter further studies the internal mechanism of cultural capital promoting the development of the rural economy. And the authors found that cultural capital can advance the development of the rural economy by promoting the establishment of new enterprises. In addition, this study also shows that cultural capital induces rural areas to introduce advanced organizational methods to integrate the factors, which is also the mechanism of cultural capital promoting the development of the rural economy.

It proves that cultural capital promotes the development of the rural economy by increasing the human capital of the rural labor force. It provides more employment opportunities for rural residents and introduces farmers from agricultural production with low marginal products to industries with high cultural capital intensity and high marginal products. This study further indicates that cultural capital improves the rural economy by expanding the scope of the rural market and advancing the coordinated development of industries. Overall, this study shows and explains that cultural capital is an essential endogenous power of developing the rural economy in China.

By introducing cultural capital, this study provides a theoretical reference for exploring and cultivating the endogenous power of rural economic development in China and other similar economies during the economic transition period. It further enriches the understanding of the vital economic functions of culture and the endogenous dynamics of China's rural economic development. It should be emphasized that this study does not deny the crucial role of such external driving forces as technology and institutional reform in the development of the rural economy in China. The authors further believe that t is necessary to regard cultural capital, technology, and institutional reform as a complementary effect rather than a generational effect to understand the endogenous power of the development of the rural economy in China. In addition, by focusing on cultural capital rather than technology, this study also provides a new perspective to explore the economic function of traditional crafts. This chapter studies the specific cultural capital of Dong brocade, but the authors' explanation is also applicable to other similar cultural capital cases to some extent.

This chapter provides two critical implications for developing the rural economy in China. Firstly, during the period of economic transformation, it is necessary to excavate the economic functions of cultural capital in China's rural areas so that cultural capital can become a crucial endogenous power of the development of the rural economy. In particular, the authors need to emphasize that in revitalizing the rural economy, the parties concerned must integrate cultural capital with other elements, technologies, and institutions to better release the economic functions of cultural capital. Secondly, emphasis should be laid on cultivating, acquiring, and protecting cultural capital in China's rural areas. Villages with relatively scarce cultural capital need to strengthen cultural capital cultivation. In contrast, for villages rich in cultural capital, cultural capital's inheritance and protection should be maintained. In particular, for the items that are qualified for the application of intangible cultural heritage, the villages should take the initiative to strive to be included in the list of national or regional intangible cultural heritage and enhance the protection and inheritance of the existing intangible cultural heritage items.

However, this chapter still has some limitations, which provide direction for further research in the future. First of all, the empirical research in this chapter is only based on a small-sample case study and descriptive statistical analysis. Based on an extensive sample survey and multivariate regression, the subsequent studies can further verify the relationship between cultural capital and the development of the rural economy and the corresponding mechanism. Secondly, this chapter mainly studies the impact of cultural capital on the development of the rural economy from the perspectives of the output level in rural areas, the income level of farmers, and poverty alleviation. However, rural economic development also involves many other dimensions, such as growth quality and environment, and the above aspects. In the subsequent studies, it is necessary to explore the impact of cultural capital on other factors of the development of the rural economy. Thirdly, this study only considers the direct effects of cultural capital on the development of the rural economy but does not attach importance to the heterogeneity conditions of cultural capital. However, the heterogeneity of the impact of cultural capital on the development of the rural economy also deserves further research. Despite these limitations, this chapter is still reliable and valuable to some extent in terms of its research framework and core findings.

Chapter 6
Consumption Driving and Development in Post-Coronavirus China

The outbreak of Covid-19 has significantly impacted China's national economies. In Post-Coronavirus China, the macro-economic development situation must be undergone new and substantial changes with a trend from a production-driven economy to a consumption-driven economy. With the proposal of China's strategy of expanding domestic demand, endogenous consumption has become the main driving force of current economic growth. With the transformation and upgrading of the consumption structure and the continuous promotion of structural reforms on the supply side, the essential role of consumption in economic development will be more sustainable. The new model for China's economic and social development is to cultivate new consumer markets, continuously increase people's income level and consumption capacity, and accelerate the construction and growth of crucial consumptions. It should become a new and long-term policy for China's macro-economic development.

Introduction

The outbreak of Covid-19 has generated a significant negative impact on China's national economies. According to the China National Bureau of Statistics (CNBS) data, GDP growth in the first quarter of 2020 was slow. Compared with the first quarter in 2019, the industrial value-added above designated size down 13.5%, the service sector production index down 13.0%, fixed asset investment down 24.5%, and total retail sales of consumer goods down 20.5%. From the consumption side, the growth rate of consumption will be significantly reduced in the short term due to the need for epidemic prevention and control; residents have reduced their travel and significantly curbed their current demand for consumption.

Compared with previous years, the consumption growth rate will be slowed down considerably or even cut back, thus influencing the overall economic performance. Simultaneously, the serve pandemic would also negatively impact the environment due to increased medical scraps and logistical leftovers. Simultaneously, the serve pandemic would also cause some adverse effects due to the incased medical wastes and logistical scraps and worsen the country's pollution situations.

Nevertheless, China can effectively release this part of the suppressed consumer demand after the epidemic. Take the consumption changes in the period of "SARS" as an example; the peak of the SARS epidemic was from April to June 2003; the monthly growth rate of total retail sales of consumer goods was 7.7%, 4.3%, and 8.3%, respectively, 0.5%, 5% and 0.3% lower than that of the same period in 2002. However, after the epidemic subsided in July 2003, much previously suppressed consumer demand was released. That month's consumption growth rate rebounded to 9.8%, 1.2% higher than in 2002.

Since the epidemic outbreak, the Chinese government has issued policies to stabilize the economy, minimize the losses caused by the epidemic, restore normal economic and social order, and promote steady and healthy economic development. Accelerating endogenous consumption and raising the consumption level are critical policy decisions. Therefore, we expect the medium and long-term consumption potential release and consumption upgrading trends to remain unchanged if no other policies are implemented. However, because China's economic overcapacity and export growth will slow down due to the impact of the Covid-19 epidemic worldwide, we believe that China must work hard to increase its national aggregated consumption to maintain its economic growth vitality. At the same time, it is significant that China keeps its economic growth with a more substantial development strategy to protect the environment.

Chinese President Xi Jinping has repeatedly stressed that the Chinese Dream realizes the Chinese nation's great rejuvenation. It has been the greatest dream of the Chinese people since modern times. Its underlying connotation is national prosperity, national rejuvenation, and people's happiness (Xin 2018). From this perspective, vigorously developing the socialist market economy and accelerating the Chinese Dream's realization of the great rejuvenation of the Chinese nation is a concrete manifestation of socialist core values' formation and development. The Fourth Plenary Session of the 19th CPC Central Committee proposed improving the socialist basic economic system and promoting high-quality economic development (Zhou, 2011).

China needs to promote the healthy and substantial development of the macroeconomy by driving endogenous consumption (also known as internal consumption) characterized by environmentally-friendly consumer protection. This strategy will help the country cope with the difficulties and interferences of international trade conflicts. By so doing, China can maintain sound and rapid economic development momentum, and enhancing endogenous consumption would become the central task of China's macro-economic management. According to the mainstream western macroeconomics theory, national economic growth's driving force comes from three components: consumption, investment, and export. The growth of consumer demand and the change in consumption structure will lead to economic structure and industrial structure adjustment. Thus, it forms new consumption hot spots and economic growth points (Onaran, Stockhammer, and Grafl 2011). The driving effect of consumption on economic growth is the most stable and lasting. It is the internal factor for sustained, steady, and rapid growth of the national economy. It becomes the inner driving force of economic development (Kim, Setterfield, and Yuan 2014; Kongsamut, Rebelo, and Xie 2001).

The Chinese scholars' theoretical model of the three components of GDP termed "troika" of pulling forces for macro economies is a deformation of the Keynesian short-term analysis framework (Shen 2009). Keynes put forward the "effective demand" theory in "General Theory of Employment, Interest, and Money," when the aggregate demand can pay the aggregate supply and the total demand reaches equilibrium. The overall economic volume consists of four aspects: total residents' consumption, total investment, government expenditure, and net exports, while the proportion of government expenditure is limited (Keynes 2018). Therefore, consumption, investment, and export are the three components of GDP compared to the "troika" driving economic development. In different periods of economic development, various aspects of the "troika" play different roles in driving economic development, and the resulting "troika" theory of economic growth naturally reflects consumer demand, investment demand, and export demand (Muellbauer and Lattimore 1995). The short-term analysis framework of the three GDP components can represent the driving force of traditional economic growth.

This chapter argues that in the Post-Coronavirus, China should enlarge consumption's contribution to transforming economic development mode toward harmony contribution of consumption, investment, and export. In other words, China should vigorously construct the operation system of the consumer economy and pave the way for cultivating a consumer economy society (Wang 2016). New consumption concepts and unique patterns are taking shape with the overall development of China's economy and society, especially the rapid growth of e-commerce and online shopping. Consumers' demand is increasingly developing in a personalized and diversified form, reflecting the vast potential of China's consumption market and its increasing economic development role. During this period, the contribution rate of consumption to China's economic growth increased from 50% in 2013 to 76.2% in 2018 (Li 2019).

The Chinese leadership realized that it is necessary to rely on investment and export to endogenous consumption to drive economic development and continuously strengthen endogenous consumption in driving economic development. As a result, the consumption demand of urban and rural residents in China has increased rapidly. To shift from primarily relying on investment to consumption to stimulate economic growth is a new strategic choice for China's economic and social development. The new strategy requires the innovation of production and service and the diversification of consumption modes (Hong 2013).

The Endogenous Consumer Market and the Macroeconomic Development

Since the reform and opening up, China has made significant achievements in its development. These achievements have changed China's economic and social outlook and made tremendous contributions to China's peace and development in the world. China's economic growth continues to strengthen, with its gross domestic product exceeding 90 trillion yuan in 2018, equivalent to 13.4 trillion US dollars. In the 2018 GDP ranking of relevant countries globally, China firmly ranks second globally, 67% of the United States, and 16% of the world's total GDP (see Table 6-1).

Table 6-1. GDP Ranking of Relevant Countries in the World in 2018

Ranking	Country	Billion (USD)
1	United States	20529.049
2	China	13894.817
3	Japan	4954.806
4	Germany	3949.548
5	Britain	2860.667
6	France	2787.863
7	India	2713.165
8	Italy	2085.764
9	Brazil	1885.482
10	Canada	1716.262

The data comes from the IMF official website.

However, under the new development situation, China's social economy's further development is bound to face new constraints and different choices. The facts of China's economic expansion in recent years fully demonstrated that enhancing the internal consumption and market-oriented distribution of production factors is the best choice for transforming China's economic development model. It is not difficult to find that consumption plays an increasingly important role in economic growth by analyzing the contribution rate of consumption in recent years.

Since 2014, the contribution rate of consumption to economic growth has exceeded that of investment for five consecutive years, becoming the first driving force for economic growth. From 2013 to 2018, China's consumption to economic growth rose from 55.3% to 76.2%. Such significant changes have occurred in a few short years, showing that China's consumption mechanism continuously improves and innovates. Moreover, consumption has become an endogenous new driving force for national economic growth and development. Therefore, a correct understanding and analysis of consumer culture, excellent handling of the relationship between production and consumption, the cultivation of endogenous consumption power, and the development of endogenous consumption economy play an important guiding role in China's economic growth (see Figure 6-1).

Therefore, increasing sufficient consumer demand and further expanding the domestic market have promoted economic development (Peng and Shi 2014). After the 2008 financial crisis, countries actively implemented loose fiscal and monetary policies to drive economic growth. Keynes believed that economic crises were often caused by insufficient effective demand, emphasizing expansionary policies, which would affect investment and cause further production surplus.

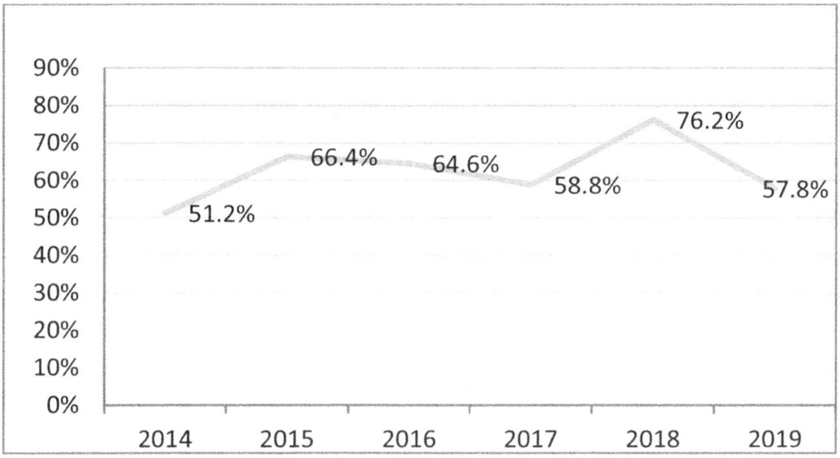

Figure 6-1 Contribution Rate of Final Consumption Expenditure to Economic Growth from 2013 to 2019 Source: Official Website of China National Bureau of Statistics

Marx believed that the development of consumption is the development of productive forces. Marxist political economics has comprehensively and profoundly explained the basic principles of the operation of the socialist system. In criticizing the bourgeois economic theory, Marx formed the ideological content of "consumption produces production." Further study of this exposition is conducive to a better examination of the endogenous new impetus of China's economic and social development and great practical significance to the rapid growth of China's socialist market economy (Zhang 2019).

Marx's production and consumption theories also illustrate consumer demand for economic growth (Hong 2013). The scale of China's domestic market is at the forefront of the world. Actively developing the consumer economy and meeting increasing consumer demand play an important role in improving China's economic development. Diversifications of consumption demand and consumption patterns are also ways to develop a consumption economy. It can meet the needs of consumption upgrading, contribute to poverty alleviation, and promote the sustainable economic and social development of the areas under assistance (Lin 2019).

The Chinese leadership claimed to continuously deepen their understanding of Marxist theory on the world market, more accurately comprehend its essence, promote the construction of "the Belt and Road Initiative," and guide the development direction of economic globalization. Under the new normal economy, Xi Jinping has put forward such theoretical discussions on consumer economy as "new normal of economy," "five development concepts," and "structural reform on the supply side." With the deepening and development of economic globalization, the government must correctly understand that consumer culture plays an essential guiding role in China's economic growth. Good consumer culture will speed up the adjustment of industrial structure, form a healthy and efficient economic development model, and promote the healthy and harmonious development of the social economy (Zha 2019).

Endogenous Consumption-Driven and Macroeconomic Development

After 70 years of development, China has consolidated its significant economic and trade country. The high-quality development of commerce has been steadily promoted, making outstanding contributions to economic and social development. The consumption level has been dramatically improved, and the endogenous consumption scale has been continuously expanded. The total retail sales of social consumer goods have increased from 27.7 billion yuan in 1952 to 38 trillion yuan in 2018. China has become the world's second-largest consumer market. At the same time, China's economic development plays a vital role in developing the world economy. China's total import and export volume increased from \$1.13 billion in 1950 to \$4.6 trillion in 2018, making China the world's largest trading nation. Under China's initiative to build a "the belt and road initiative," the scale of foreign capital has continued to expand. In 2014, China overtook the United States to become the world's largest trading country. In 2018, China absorbed $138.3 billion of foreign capital, ranking second globally (China National Bureau of Statistics 2019).

GDP per capita is the most important macroeconomic indicator to reflect economic development. In 2018, China's GDP per capita was $9,633, ranking 72nd globally. The actual increase of 174 times indicates that China has significantly improved its overall national strength and social productivity. In the same year, the per capita GDP of the United States was $62,600, nearly seven times that of China. In the past 30 years, although China's economic growth rate was the highest among the world's major economies. There is still a big gap between China's GDP per capita and developed countries by analyzing the top ten countries in the world GDP. Therefore, it is worth China's continued efforts (see Table 6-2).

China has a population of nearly 1.4 billion, with the most significant middle-income group globally, huge market size, huge potential, and unlimited prospects. China's enormous consumption potential promotes China's high-quality economic development and contributes consumption dividends to the world. While the entire Western world is worried about China's growing competitive advantage and manufacturing and energy demand growth, it ignores an important issue. China's rapidly developing American consumer culture will bring revolutionary changes to the lives of more than 1.4 billion Chinese and potentially change the world (Tian, Liu, and Wang 2014).

Table 6-2. Per Capita GDP of Relevant Countries in the World in 2018

Ranking	Country	GDP per capita (USD)
1	United States	62840.0
2	China	9976.7
3	Japan	39159.4
4	Germany	47639.0
5	Britain	43043.2
6	France	41631.1

7	India	2005.9
8	Italy	34520.1
9	Brazil	9001.2
10	Canada	46313.2

The data comes from the IMF official website.

China's economic growth has been mainly driven by investment and export in the past. This growth model can no longer meet sustained economic development needs and must be changed into a new model driven by consumption. This new monetary policy, which focuses on expanding domestic demand, is undoubtedly an economic decision that fully conforms to China's reality and international reality. It will create a vast market with a market capacity equal to the United States and Europe.

According to the data of the CNBS, Engel's coefficient has been declining in recent years. At the beginning of the reform and opening up, this index was as high as 60%. Significant changes have taken place in this indicator in the past 40 years of reform and opening up. According to relevant data, Engel's coefficient of urban and rural residents in China dropped to 29.3% in 2017, which was the first time it fell below 30%. In 2018, Engel's coefficient dropped to 28.4%, a new low. It shows that China's economic development level and living standards continuously improve. It also reflects the process of China's economy from rapid development to high-quality development. Simultaneously, this phenomenon reflects the continuous improvement of residents' income level and the change of consumption concept, the constant improvement of consumption structure, and the shift of residents' consumption from focusing on quantity satisfaction to pursuing quality improvement. It also shows that China's economic strength has improved significantly, resulting from sustained economic growth.

China's decision-makers have realized that to promote economic growth, they must adjust and change the structure of economic growth. In economic decision-making, they adhere to the guidance of new development concepts, take supply-side structural reforms as the mainline, and have made remarkable achievements in expanding the scale of consumption and improving the consumption level. It is necessary to improve the system and mechanism to promote consumption and enhance primary economic development. In recent years, consumption in economic development has become more and more apparent. In 2018, the contribution rate of consumption to economic growth was already 2.35 times that of investment (total capital formation).

China has the most potential consumer market in the world. China can form an active internal market by increasing residents' income, improving the consumer environment, and improving product quality. According to relevant scholars' research, every one percentage point increase in residents' consumption rate is equivalent to a 1.5 percentage point increase in the investment rate. It can drive the GDP growth by 0.6 percentage points. Suppose China's consumption rate can grow at an average annual rate of 5 percentage points in the future. In that case, the contribution rate of consumption to GDP growth will significantly exceed the international average consumption rate. This growth is sufficient to make up for the decline in economic pull caused by the decline in investment or foreign trade. Therefore, endogenous consumption is the primary internal driving force for China's economic growth in the future.

Chinese leaders agreed that in the face of the complicated and changeable international situation, the arduous task of domestic reform, development, and stability is to develop the economy, continue to deepen reforms, and further improve people's standard of living. The most important way to achieve this goal is to unite and lead the Chinese people of all ethnic groups to deepen reform and maintain steady and sound economic development, thus creating favorable conditions for high-quality economic development.

Manufacturing and agricultural labor have a high degree of substitution in China's labor market, constituting a feature of China's labor market. The growth rate of the minimum wage for migrant workers is about 15% per year. Suppose they stay in the countryside and work in agriculture. In that case, they hope to benefit from this growth rate. A "characteristic" phenomenon formed in the reform and opening up, especially in recent years. Many migrant workers went to work in cities, and the remaining migrant workers still had surplus land. Therefore, wages could not rise at that time, and agricultural products' prices could not raise much. However, after all, there is the so-called Lewis turning point, and it is difficult for the labor supply to be as sufficient as before (Tang and Ren 2018).

In recent years, the Chinese government has stressed the need to narrow the income gap, encourage the increase of the minimum wage standard, and at the same time, drive the rise of farmers' income and the price of agricultural products to rise. This phenomenon will cause both positive and negative aspects. The rapid growth of farmers' income can promote China's consumption growth as a whole. On the other hand, China is a developing country, and China's Engel coefficient remains about 40%.

Simultaneously, the per capita disposable income of urban and rural residents in China increases (see Table 6-3). Years ago, scholars (Tian, Liu, and Wang 2014) predicted that if the income of Chinese residents keeps at an average annual growth rate of 12% (higher than the growth of GDP), assuming a marginal consumption rate of 80%, China's average annual total retail sales of social consumption will grow by 12% and will become 42.6 trillion yuan in 2019, accounting for 44.1% of the total GDP (assuming a 7.5% growth rate) in the same period (excluding inflation factors). In 2023, the whole social consumption will reach 67.1 trillion yuan, accounting for 51.94% of the total national GDP (assuming a 7.5% growth rate) in the same period (excluding inflation factors). This growth model will undoubtedly fundamentally reduce China's GDP growth dependence on investment and exports. It aligns with China's national conditions and the changing international economic development trend. It is more in line with the theme spirit of China's economic and social development and the wishes of the people of the whole country.

Table 6-3 Disposable Income in China from 2013 to 2018

Urban vs. Rural/Year	2013	2014	2015	2016	2017	2018
Per Capita Disposable Income of Urban Residents (RMB)	26955	28844	31195	33616	36396	39251
Per capita disposable income of rural residents (yuan)	8896	10489	11422	12363	13432	14617
Per Capita Disposable Income Difference between Urban and Rural Residents (RMB)	18059	18355	19773	21253	22964	24634

The data are all from the CNBS

Cultivate Endogenous Consumption and Develop Key Consumer Markets

China's market capacity is enormous, and its growth potential is full. The contribution of consumption to China's economic growth is continuously expanding. Per capita consumption expenditure continues to grow (see Figure 6-2). The driving force for future growth will mainly come from consumption. The rapid consumption growth is bound to stimulate the national economy's growth strongly. Therefore, China must focus on developing the consumer market and continuously improving the national consumption capacity as the starting point, accelerating China's economy and society. China should further enhance and fulfill the total consumption system and mechanism. An accurate positioning start from the supply side stimulates a new round of consumption vitality, promotes commodity consumption and service consumption as a whole, and actively promotes high-quality intelligence. Personalized household electrical appliances with solid demand to meet the people's needs for a diversified and high-quality life enable the constant upgrading of commodity consumption and promote continuous improvement and expansion of service consumption.

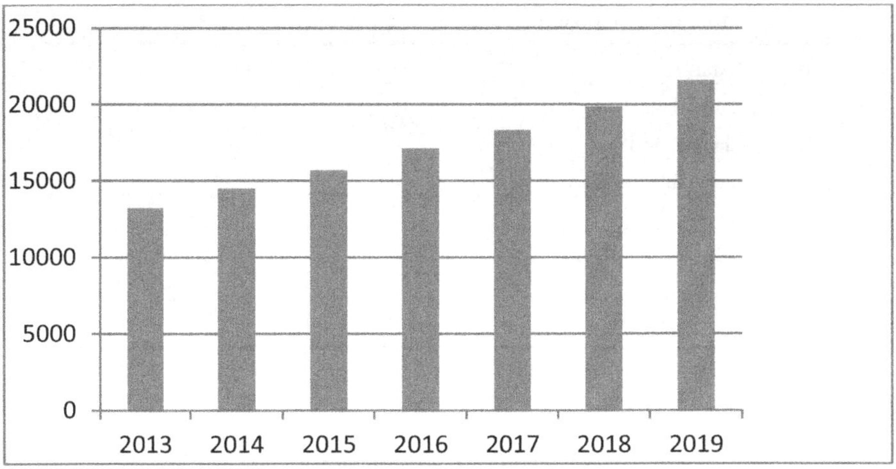

Figure 6-2 Per Capital Consumption Expenditure Levels of Chinese Residents from 2013 to 2019

Source: Official Website of China National Bureau of Statistics

The consumption scale has steadily expanded in recent years, and the consumption pattern has been continuously innovated. The contribution rate of consumption to the growth of GDP has continually increased (see Figure 6-3). Consumption growth shows the following characteristics: Consumers have diversified consumption demand, online retail continuously expands, and physical retail keeps warming up. In 2018, the national online retail sales of physical commodities increased by 25.4%, accounting for 18.4% of the total social zero, up to 3.5 percentage points from the previous year. According to State Post Office data, the national express delivery volume totaled 50.71 billion pieces, up 26.6%.

On the other hand, the retail industry actively uses new technologies and integrates online and offline, showing a steady development trend. It is necessary to actively promote upgrading consumption structure, with solid sales of new energy vehicles. Moreover, the service consumption multiplied, and entertainment consumption improved and expanded. The quality of service consumption and supply has been continuously improved, and service consumption in tourism, culture, education, and old-age care has developed rapidly.

The following aspects deserve special attention when discussing consumption growth in promoting the economy and determining the corresponding macroeconomic decisions and policy formulation.

First, China should speed up the information industry's development, give full play to market advantages, and actively promote the digital economy's development. China will use new technologies such as big data and blockchains to explore the innovation of digital economic models, create a pleasant business environment, and provide support for promoting structural reforms on the supply side. Actively promote the development of e-commerce to rural markets and rural markets.

Second, China should use the state's policies to reduce taxes and fees and expand opening up to promote consumption transformation and upgrading. With the continuous improvement of institutional reform on the consumer market's supply side, the consumer structure is bound to upgrade. Therefore, the supply-side reform must be strengthened to meet the consumer market's diversified demands for different qualities and structures. China needs to promote a better match between the supply and consumption structures and increase consumption momentum. Through innovation, drive to tap potential, stimulate consumption potential. China's market capacity is enormous, with an immense scale on average daily retail sales of about 100 billion yuan. China has an active consumer market. With the promotion of measures such as the increase of residents' income, the improvement of consumption environment, and the improvement of product quality, it is found that the consumption demand is active, the total consumption is increasing, and the consumption potential will be further released.

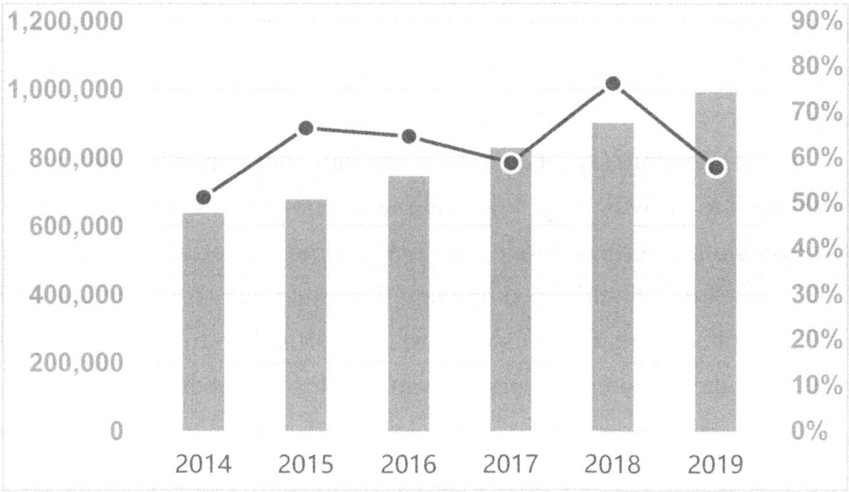

Figure 6-3 Contributions of Final Consumption Expenditure and GDP Growth from 2014 to 2019

Source: Official Website of China National Bureau of Statistics

Third, China should cultivate critical endogenous consumer markets and focus on supporting and developing industries and departments closely related to daily life. Accurately, special attention should be paid to the following aspects:

1. Consumption of green agricultural products as an effective means of substantiality in post-Coronavirus time should be prioritized. In China's consumer market, the demand for farm products increases due to changes in the diet structure caused by improving living standards. At present, food and clothing are no longer a problem for most Chinese, but eating better and healthy is a crucial consideration. Accordingly, the demand for green agricultural products will keep increasing in the post-Coronavirus time, which will, in turn, push the protection of the environment and maintain substantial agrarian development. The increase in demand for meat will inevitably promote livestock farming, and the consumption of grain by livestock is far higher than that of human beings.

2. Increasing the consumption of household electrical appliances is very important in keeping substantiality in the post-Coronavirus time.

Under the background of the reform of consumption channels, consumption upgrading, and consumer demand diversification, the household appliance industry should speed up its transformation and upgrade to high-end, intelligent, and quality development.

3. To increase tourism consumption is also very important in keeping substantiality in the post-Coronavirus time. With the increasing diversity of tourism products and the substantial tourism market environment, the tourism market grows; Tourism consumption continues to rise. Residents travel in a variety of ways. Actual tourism consumption needs to have innovative content and broaden cultural and creative product display and sales channels. China has the most extensive stock of tourism and shopping markets globally. Tourism should also seize the critical period when China expands consumption upgrading. It promotes economic quality and efficiency, and plays promote economic quality and efficiency and plays promote economic quality and efficiency and play, promotes economic quality and efficiency and plays a more vital role. There is an increase in cost pressure caused by rising food prices in the indispensable supporting industries of tourism and the hotel industry. However, the pressure can be effectively relieved through price increases, so the impact of inflation is relatively small.

4. Consumption of new services, especially old-age care and medical care, as a means of substantiality in the post-Coronavirus time will undoubtedly have a considerable increase. The demand for health care will rise further with the arrival of China's aging and improve people's living standards. This consumer demand to meet the spiritual level is still relatively low in China and has a substantial development space. Also, the growth potential of the financial service industry is enormous. The scale of China's stock and bond markets is growing day by day. The high-income and middle-income groups' investment and financial management needs have not been fully met. In the past, most people chose to buy houses.

5. Increase the intensity of international consumption growth in China. Actively increase domestic and international consumption. First of all,

with the in-depth development of the world, actively develop cross-border e-commerce to meet the diversified needs of consumers, thus promoting the upgrading of Chinese consumption. China needs to support multilateral trade firmly, establish free trade, build an open world economy, and expand the scale of international trade. Consumption has become the main engine and driving force of China's economy, and China should continuously expand consumer demand. The construction of a global consumption center city and the rational allocation of resources are conducive to further increasing economic development's essential role. China needs to continue improving the domestic transportation infrastructure and comprehensive service facilities, build a new pattern of accessible tourism, and continuously enhance tourism's international influence.

Fourth, increase the actual income of urban and rural residents and issue consumer loans to farmers. Although the contribution rate of consumption to China's national economy is expanding, Chinese government officials must also pay attention to such a macro-economic phenomenon. In recent years, some consumer goods have been selling well at the micro-level, and the "Double Eleven" sales have hit new highs over and over again. However, the total consumption of urban and rural residents has begun to weaken. According to data from the CNBS, the real growth rate in the disposable income of urban households slowed to 5.4% in the first three quarters of 2019, the second-lowest since the first quarter of 2008 and the lowest level in nearly a decade. The total household income of urban residents is growing slowly. The overall growth rate of wage income, operating income, property income, and transfer income of urban residents is slowing down. According to the CNBS, in October 2019, the social zero was 7.2% year-on-year, the lowest since 2003 (see Figure 6-4).

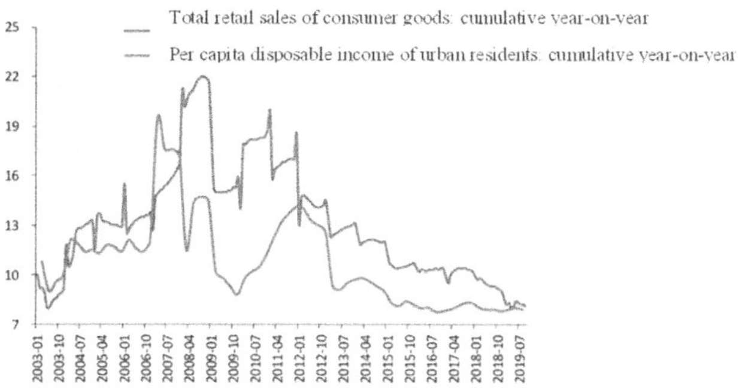

Figure 6-4 Trends of per capita disposable income of urban residents and total retail consumption

Source: Based on relevant information from China National Bureau of Statistics.

It is not conducive to the growth of domestic consumption. The slow growth of the disposable income of urban households and the rapid growth of residents' debt ratio will inevitably lead to the decline of domestic consumption in the future. It is very unfavorable to long-term economic development. On the one hand, the economic growth rate declines year by year. The income growth rate of urban and rural residents is slowing down, and consumer spending is much cautious.

On the other hand, enterprises have experienced several rounds of leverage. With a high leverage ratio, increased pressure on debt burden and interest expenditure, it has squeezed out consumption to a certain extent. Simultaneously, the growth rate of consumer loans has slowed down, and advanced consumption has been suppressed.

Effectively improving urban and rural residents' income levels is an integral part of a country's macroeconomic management (Cohen and Soto 2007). First of all, China should start by promoting employment to increase income and thus improve consumption ability. Chinese government officials should emancipate their minds to open up channels to expand employment. Especially in the third and fourth line areas, the government should do everything possible to boost employment. Include self-employment and informal small business hawkers so that all citizens who have the ability and desire to work can obtain employment and earn the labor income. In 2018, China's working-age population aged 16-59 will continue to decrease. The total working-age population is still nearly 900 million, but the total employed population is still 780 million. The total number of employed people declined for the first time (see Figure 6-5).

Through the analysis of employed population statistics, China is still rich in labor resources. Therefore, under the background of China's overall stable economic operation and the sustained efforts of various policies to stabilize and promote employment, it should be achieved through increased labor force participation. The government should expand and ensure jobs, by all means, strive to solve structural employment conflicts. Use the "Internet" to develop new forms of employment, promote multi-channel employment, further support entrepreneurship to encourage employment, realize the benign interaction between economic development and employment expansion, ensure a stable and good employment situation, and promote the improvement of the labor income level of urban and rural residents.

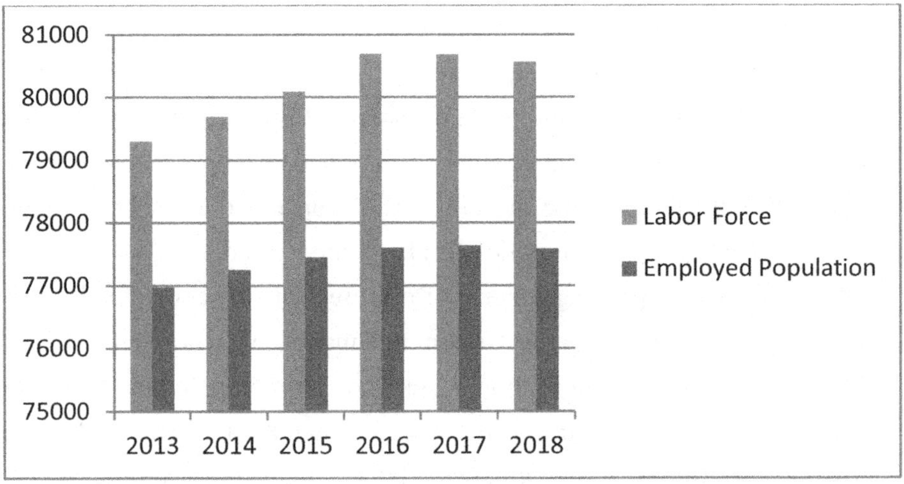

Figure 6-5 Changes in the National Labor Force and Employed Population from 2013 to 2018

Source: Official Website of China National Bureau of Statistics

China should increase residents' property income through multiple channels. Property income is mainly the return residents get by providing funds or assets to other economic activities. One of the most important channels is to invest in the stock market (Diamond 1967). Stock assets can avoid inflation risks, and stock investment is an effective way for residents to share enterprises' growth benefits (Lettau and Ludvigson 2001). Consumption level is mainly determined by residents' wealth income and wage income level s. With the continuous increase of residents' income and the stock market participation rate, stock investment should become one of the primary forms of residents' wealth income. Simultaneously, the stock market's wealth effect will affect residents' consumption levels to a certain extent (Acemoglu and Guerrieri 2008). As of 2019, the number of listed companies in the Shanghai and Shenzhen stock markets has reached 3,733, with a total market value of 54 trillion, 60% of the total GDP in 2018. At present, the total market value of the U.S. Stock market is about 35 trillion U.S. Dollars, equivalent to 225 trillion yuan, 171% of 2018 GDP. Therefore, China's stock market has great potential for development.

However, the domestic stock market has been depressed for a long time. The vast numbers of investors have suffered severe losses. From the national economic perspective, it is crucial to effectively increase residents' income in the future. It requires the domestic securities market to effectively restore the wealth mechanism and improve residents' income from property income. Otherwise, the future will seriously affect domestic economic development. As China's stock market scale continues to expand, it is necessary to ensure the long-term and healthy development of the stock market. Create better investment opportunities and allow investors to benefit from them, thus increasing income and new consumption growth points. Respecting the market laws and maintaining the steady rise of the stock market index is conducive to the reasonable matching of resources and can improve investors' consumer confidence. As such, it drives the rapid and high-quality development of the economy.

Nonetheless, the domestic capital market's management has neglected the stock market's investment and financial management functions over the past few years. It has blindly strengthened its financing features and continuously expanded them endlessly. The state is trying to open the door for more enterprises from direct financing and relax the securities market's financing channels and the bond market, so the expansion is understandable.

China should vigorously improve the income level of farmers, especially the monetization level of farmers' income. At present, the income of urban and rural residents in China is still relatively low compared to developed countries. The farmers' income is still meager, and further efforts are needed to increase their actual income. Since New China's founding 70 years ago, it has experienced the most significant and fastest urbanization process in world history. The continuous expansion of the city scale and the constant enhancement of its economic strength will further promote economic development. We estimate that every one percentage point increase in the urbanization rate will drive consumption growth by nearly two percentage points. According to the data of CNBS, by 2018, the overall level of urbanization in China has reached 59.58%. Nevertheless, there is still a big gap compared with more than 80% urbanization in developed countries like the United States.

Urbanization is a long-term process, and it is difficult to achieve the phased goal of promoting social and economic development by increasing consumption as soon as possible. To this end, we propose government-sponsored 20-year interest-free bank loans for rural residents' consumption. Regional and income differences are based on the existing rural population and will issue interest-free loans of 3,000-5,000 yuan RMB per person per year. Let us briefly explain the economic and sociological significance of issuing such loans as follows:

First, it can increase the domestic market as soon as possible. The Chinese government often says that domestic demand is insufficient, and sufficient domestic demand is inadequate. With the current living standard of Chinese farmers, the demand is apparent. There is a desire to demand but no ability to demand. This method is more effective than the salary increase for civil servants because most civil servants may deposit their increased salary in the bank.

Second, doing so can stimulate the production of daily commodities to expand urban employment. It can also solve the reemployment pressure brought by laid-off workers in cities to the country and is also conducive to absorbing migrant workers' jobs from rural areas to cities.

Third, this practice can cultivate the farmers' awareness of the commodity economy. Through publicity and education, farmers, especially those with potential, can be guided to convert part of the loans into production investment. It can improve agricultural products' commodity rate and added value, thus achieving higher financial results.

Fourth, doing so can strengthen the government's image among farmers, ease the tension between farmers and the government over the years, and is conducive to the actual implementation of the spirit of developing the economy and improving and improving people's living standards since the Third Plenary Session of the 18th CPC Central Committee. Of course, avoiding adverse problems in this process should be studied in advance.

In 2018, there are about 564 million farmers in the country. If the government gives each of these 564 million people a discount loan of 3,000 yuan per year, the state will increase its annual consumption by 152.8 billion yuan (3,000 × 700 million × 90%). In other words, it will directly increase its GDP output by 152.8 billion yuan. If the multiplier effect is taken into account (we estimate that in China, the multiplier effect of consumption on GDP growth is four times), the consumption growth can bring about 609.12 billion yuan of new GDP opportunities per year. Thus, it increases GDP growth by nearly seven percentage points (Tian 2013).

If the country's tax revenue is 23% of GDP and the discount rate is 7%, then the state will increase its tax revenue by 1.95 trillion yuan per year. The government's discount interest for farmers is 0.12 trillion yuan, which means that the country will increase its fiscal revenue by 1.83trillion yuan per year because of this policy. The state can use this income to improve the agricultural production environment, increase agricultural commodities' rate, increase agricultural productivity, and increase farm products' added value. In such a virtuous circle for several years, farmers' economic status will significantly improve, and their income will continue to increase. At that time, farmers will not be afraid of not repaying their loans.

At the same time, China should also consider other economic and social benefits of this monetary policy. The expansion of domestic demand under the multiplier effect will enable the previously unemployed urban workers to get employment opportunities. It will provide about 33.75 million employment opportunities every year due to the implementation of this economic policy. We estimated this employment increase based on the assumption that the wage accounts for 40% of the national income, the annual wage income, and each worker's social benefits are 60,000 yuan. As these newly-added employees have income, they will drive another wave of market demand. China's economy will naturally develop comprehensively and excellently if they repeat this.

Conclusion

Internal consumption-driven and market-promoted choices are likely to be the best choice for substantiality in China's post-Coronavirus economic development model. Developing the economy, deepening reforms, and doubling Chinese people's income are the leading spirits always stressed by state leaders. Therefore, accelerating income growth will be a trend. In recent years, the economies of the United States and most Western countries have begun to reduce their demand for Chinese products due to the impact of the economic crisis. The Chinese government is taking note and has already started to shift the focus of economic development to expanding domestic demand to mitigate sluggish foreign markets' impact.

China's economy was stable; the consumption operation was relatively stable on the whole. The consumption structure was continuously optimized, and the contribution rate of consumption to economic growth has further increased. Giving full play to its potential will make more enormous contributions to economic growth. China should continue to adjust its economic growth structure to promote the continuous improvement of endogenous consumption. This chapter assumes that the income of urban and rural residents will grow at an average annual rate of 12%, and China's average yearly social consumption will also grow at 12% in the next ten years. This growth will undoubtedly reduce China's GDP growth dependence on investment and exports, which is in line with the long-term development trend of China's economy.

In the future, the main driving force of China's substantial economic growth will be consumption, focusing on cultivating the consumer market and improving the people's consumption ability. China's macro-economic management department must cultivate an endogenous consumption-driven economic growth model. China will promote the new format mode of the Internet, big data, artificial intelligence, and the deep integration of technologies in the real economy. Stimulate people's consumption; stimulate the potential of cultural and tourism consumption and other measures, give full play to the active internal consumption market with a population of 1.4 billion, and make endogenous consumption the continuous endogenous driving force for China's sustained economic development.

Chapter 7
Independent Planning System and Metropolitan Development

The optimal allocation of public management and administrative resources has played a key role in the fundamental economic development in China in recent years. The new administrative system of large cities (metropolises) with independent planning has become an innovative format to utilize the soft renewable resources of administration, a new attempt to reform the economic system by the Chinese government. The greater Chaoshan area needs to be agglomerated and unified to develop the regional economy by implementing an independent planning system. Agglomerating and integrating Shantou, Jieyang and Chaozhou into the greater Chaoshan Special Economic Zone with an independent planning system is practically feasible and has a decisive strategic significance in promoting the overall economic and social development of the whole eastern Guangdong area. Discussing and researching public management and administrative resources as soft and renewable resources in economic development will certainly be an important focal point for future regional economy study.

Introduction

The issues of public management effectiveness have increasingly gained prominence in the macro-economic situation in most developed countries (Buleca and Murab, 2014). At the same time, regional development strategy and public management have been among the hottest topics among Chinese scholars in recent years. Public management and administration involve institutional changes regarding governance. Institutional change is a process that reshapes an administrative district's original institutional arrangements and restructures interest distribution patterns. Different stakeholders play the game to maximize their interests, leading to new institutions-agreements formation due to various related factors. The games involve relationships between different ideas of governance and between the central and local governments and local governments (Jin, 2007). Public management and administration is part of a wider sustainability culture change movement and is widely recognized as an environmental leader, advocating other levels of government. Public management and administration play a central role in adopting sustainable initiatives (Strengers, 2004; Williams et al., 2011).

Recently, the Chinese central government announced that to enhance the further growth of the national economy, it would let market power play a decisive role in production resources allocations. The government also called people to accept and understand the new normal in Chinese social and economic development. The core characterizations of the new normal have put forward challenges to public management and administration, given that the Chinese central government's new policies prefer market power to administrative power in production resources allocations. However, letting the market play a decisive role in determining resource allocation does not mean removing public management and administration but rather enhancing its role in policy decision-making at the up-level. Public management and administration have played a pivotal role in deepening economic reform, which, in turn, is conducive to improving the economic and social environment (Kerlinová and Tomášková, 2014; Zhang and Bai, 2015).

In recent years, public management and administration, comprising evidence-based policy and the results agenda, has become ubiquitous among policymakers (Taylor, 2014). It is significant to explore the methods of administration in the background of the new normal to form strategies to enhance governance capacity in terms of public management and administration, and to innovate modern technology for public management, and to build the implementation mechanism at the top-level design activities and to restore the system of the core ethical values in public management and administration (Zhang and Bai, 2015). In the context of regional economic integrative development, local governments should adjust policy and institutional arrangements; transform government functions, and carry out the evolution of governing notions and methods, transferring from administrative-region management to regional public management and administration (Liu, 2010).

On the other hand, "resource" as an important concept in economics can be defined as the aggregate input effectively creating output in any economy. In traditional economics textbooks, land, capital, labor, and entrepreneurship are listed as the most fundamental resources for production (Hausman, 1996). However, in broad terms, any material, energy, and information used to produce benefits in a foreseeable period can be categorized as a resource. As such, administration functions as resources in economic development, which is supported by the fact that the Greater Pearl River Delta has gained substantial benefits because of the effective regional administration behind the economic development. It was termed the foreign coordination model of regional economic development (Zheng, 2007).

Resources are characterized by effectiveness and scarcity. Starting from the meaning and basic characteristics of resources, the forces and operations of administration are essentially effective economic development resources. The management and administrative subject maintain or change the specific social, administrative public management system and order (Jin, 2007; Zhou, 2004). Public management and administrative resources refer to the aggregation of the material and spiritual factors supporting the existence, operation and development of the administrative public management system. Public management and administrative resources come from two elements of the administrative system: the structural element, the static framework of the existing system, and the process element, which is termed the administrative operation track of the system (Easton, 1989).

Public management and administrative resources mainly include the government agencies of a country or a region concerning the administrative environment, administrative organization, leadership, legislation, enforcement, finance, supervision, culture, and economic functions and activities. As the principle of the political economy implies, administrative resources mainly act to develop social productivity. It helps to mobilize and reasonably distribute all the other resources to develop a social economy, cultivate and maintain a stable, fair, democratic and harmonious social environment, promoting the constant improvement of people's material and cultural life. Moreover, adaptation to continuous change also brings the view of administrative development more closely in line with economic analyses of the impact of changes in the economy. Economic changes in global-local balances do not leave administrative resources intact (Bennett, 1997).

Public management and administrative resource is comprehensive concept that may not be directly measurable. In contrast, administrative management is measurable and single, making it one of the important parameters measuring the abundance of public management and administrative resources in a country or a region (Tian and Dai, 2012). Administrative management is a scarce administrative resource for developing countries, and how to realize its optimal allocation is an issue confronted by both western economics and socialist resource economics (Yang and Pu, 1998). The government should focus on providing public goods and services, playing the market's core and fundamental role in systematically and institutionally allocating resources. Leave what can be done by the market or the intermediary organization to that organization, with the remaining done by the government (Yu, 2005). The advantages of China's public management and administrative resources are mainly reflected in the formulation and perfection of laws and regulations and effective intervention of the market economy by the government (Tian and Dai, 2012). Moreover, it is crucial to distinguish between the "administrative institutions environment" and "administrative institutions arrangements." Still, the institutional factors that represent barriers to other factors' efficacy influence economic development (Rodriguez-Pose, 2013).

The logic behind China's rapid economic development within the last 30 years is a common topic of interest for economists. China's economic reform started from the late 1970s and early 1980s when the reallocation of public management and administrative resources changed the incentive structure in the economic system to improve efficiency and promote economic growth (Shi and Zhou, 2007). Theoretically, as a central administrative resource allocated to local government, independent planning has positively affected cities' economic efficiency in many aspects. The local government can use the public management and administrative resources allocated to formulate strategies more appropriate to the local conditions, thus improving economic efficiency and social welfare. After the power is delegated, the cities may make decisions at their discretion without referring to the provincial government, significantly enhancing administrative efficiency.

Reducing management levels can facilitate information transfer and quick and accurate economic decisions. The municipal government may allocate resources efficiently to improve overall economic efficiency with independent planning. In addition, fiscal decentralization motivates local governments to create wealth. Meanwhile, with the incentive of local official promotion, the delegation of economic power may be better used to promote the development of the local economy (Zhou, 2004). Finally, from the rent-seeking perspective, the delegation of economic, administrative power such as investment approval and foreign trade lowers the regulatory levels. It reduces the regulatory agencies, decreasing the cost of rent-seeking by the cities from superior governments, ultimately increasing social welfare (Shi and Zhou, 2007).

In modern China, independently-planned cities are most distinctly characterized by a budget directly linked to the central government, divided between the central and local finances without payment to the provincial finance. Such an independent planning system undoubtedly adds renewable public management and administrative resources to cities' economic and social development with independent planning, enjoying more rapid development than their prior performances under increased public management and administrative resources (Chen and Zhao, 2011).

The greater Chaoshan area consists of three cities, namely Shantou, Jieyang, and Chaozhou. Shantou leads the economic development of the east Guangdong region. It is the economic hub of the greater Chaoshan area; Jieyang is well known as the "jade capital of Asia" and "China hardware base"; Chaozhou is a famous hometown of overseas Chinese, the main export base of China ceramics as well as a historical-cultural ancient city. Moreover, Shantou is among the earliest coastal cities established as special economic zones since China's reform and opening up. Unfortunately, compared with other cities that have established special economic zones simultaneously, such as Shenzhen, Zhuhai and Xiamen, Shantou has not achieved the same level of development. Currently, Shantou lags behind these cities in terms of its hard power and lacks a matching soft power, thus suffering from the resulting troubles and losses during development (Tian, 2011).

Looking at the greater Chaoshan area, to revive its economy, the agglomeration of the three cities is a necessary choice second to none to make the best use of public management and administrative resources and maximize the effects of optimal resource allocation on economic development. Agglomeration economies are a broadly relevant phenomenon affecting many industries. There is heterogeneity between industries (Strange, Hejazi and Tang, 2006). José Lobo and Deborah Strumsky (2008) found that agglomerative features of metropolitan areas are more important determinants of metropolitan patenting productivity. Marius and Federica (2009) discovered that the consistent evidence supporting agglomeration boosts GDP growth to a certain level of economic development. In addition to the agglomeration, for the greater Chaoshan area, implementing independent planning is especially important in accelerating the building of its soft power. It will effectively mobilize and integrate its administrative resource advantages to develop a new unified administrative public management system.

Dynamics of Independent Planning System in Economic Development

Resource allocation is one of the most fundamental issues studied in economics and public management. Under China's existing public management and administration system, establishing cities with independent planning is a natural economic outcome according to the objective law that the production relation must conform to productivity. The administrative system of independent planning can raise the greater area central city and important coastal cities in the national macroeconomic management and economic system. Also, it will strengthen the functions of key cities that participate in macroeconomic management so that they are free from the traditional economic management system based on administrative blocks and levels. The evidence supports the view that decentralization improves economic efficiency. The agglomeration of connected administrative regions can also enhance economic development (Shi and Zhou, 2007).

During its reform and opening-up process in the recent period of nearly 40 years, China has rapidly entered into the global market system by integrating the independent planning mode into the opening-up strategy, institutional reform and innovation, importing and exporting resources in large quantities (Fu, 2013). Remarkably, the mean GDP growth rate of those cities with an independent planning system is about 5% higher than that of the national GDP growth rate (Zhang, 2014). As a method of effective administration, an independent planning system is an original form of exploiting public management and administration resources. It plays an irreplaceable role in developing China's socialist market economy. It is characterized by streamlining administration, instituting decentralization, and rectifying economic relations. Below, the current authors will further probe the dynamics of an independent planning system as a means of public management and administration in regional economic development.

Radiation Function as the Regional Economic Center

Urbanization has been a key element in the process of development. (Bairoch, 1988) Urban areas generate 85% of GDP in high-income countries (World Development Report, 2000), and the degree of urban concentration has a positive impact on economic growth (2003). The formation and development of the economic circle of urban agglomeration pursue the following law: an economic circle with one central city develops into a large economic circle with several central cities and further into a large economic belt of cities. Evidence shows dynamic gains from statically oversized cities. Agglomeration and urbanization are the engines of growth (Bertinelli Black, 2004).

Along this line, scholars put forward a new perspective of a comprehensive observation of regional and urban economic resource endowments to make a reasonable strategic choice for regional and urban development (Li, 2011). Urban and regional development studies focus on urban areas driving innovation and growth, with surrounding areas cast in a passive, residual role (Ward and Brown, 2009). Indeed, in China, independent planning significantly impacts the economic efficiencies within and outside the province. Cities with independent planning absorb a domestic investment per capita of 940 RMB more than their counterparts outside the province and nearly double their counterparts in the province. Similarly, the difference in FDI per capita is around 1.5 times greater (Shi and Zhou, 2007).

In China, the Yangtze Delta economic circle, with Ningbo as the economic center of the south wing of the Yangtze Delta, has become the sixth-largest metropolitan economic circle in the world. The northeast economic zone centering on Dalian has also developed through economic model transformation and plays a positive role. The Western Straits Economic Zone centering on Xiamen is starting to take shape. The Pearl River Delta economic circle surrounding Shenzhen is growing increasingly, and Qingdao has also developed into the core of the Bohai Bay economic circle. The Pearl River Delta and the Yangtze Delta cities are ranked among the top ten in the comprehensive evaluation of urban economic benefits. In contrast, for Bohai Bay, only Beijing and Dalian are ranked among the top ten (Wen, 2011). The economic development of Bohai Bay is currently at a stage of strong polarization, with each central city enjoying a higher degree of economic aggregation.

Connecting Link at the Mesoeconomic Level

The macro-economy covers the whole national economy. Based on the essential unit of economic operation (consumer and producer), the micro-economy is at the fundamental level of the large national economic system. However, regional economic agglomeration plays an increasingly important role in the regional and international economy at the macroeconomic level. The "intermediary" nature of the meso-economy determines its functions of coordinating the operation of the macro-and the micro-economy, not only in executing and extending macro-control but also centralizing and guiding micro-management (Yuan, 2003).

It is suggested that the metropolises with independent planning have dominated the links of industrial economic development in China since the 1990s (Deng, 2004) because the spatial proximity is a positive force for economic growth (Martin and Ottaviano, 1999). Baldwin and Martin (2004) stress that spatial agglomeration favors regional growth due to localized spillovers. Krugmand Elizondo (1996) suggests that given the fact that domestic transactions become more important and shorter distances can lower the cost, agglomeration matters more to closed economies than to open ones. On the other hand, Markus Brückner (2012) suggests plausibly that exogenous shocks that differentially affect the return in the agricultural sector have a significant effect on the rural-urban migration decisions in Africa.

Meanwhile, mutual restricting and promoting market mechanisms and the allocation of public management and administrative resources in the economic circles of urban agglomeration are very significant. During different stages of its development, the agglomeration of economic and public management and administrative resources is dynamic. When public management and administrative resources match the market mechanism, the administrative mechanism will organize and promote economic resources and promote the development of the regional economy. Otherwise, the administrative mechanism will impede the development of the regional economy.

Accordingly, the authors argue that a corresponding allocating mechanism of public management and administrative resources in the specific regional economic space is necessary to eliminate administrative barriers and unify the regional economy. Otherwise, the smooth flow of economic resources is impossible, and advantages between cities may not be complementary (Liu and Meng, 1999). The optimal allocation of public management and administrative resources realized through independent planning enforces the state's central leadership in the economy and vitalizes local economic development, helping to organically combine planning uniformity and market flexibility, both macro-and micro-control.

Rational Productivity Distribution and Coordinative Development

As the regional center and the joint point of the industrial and geographical division of labor, cities with independent planning are safe economic activities. They are also an economic organization to organizes and manage the economy objectively. Such cities play a special role in realizing rational productivity distribution and the coordinated development of urban-rural areas. In the urban industry competitiveness ranking, telecommunication equipment manufacturing is a significantly advantaged industry in Shenzhen which has developed an industry aggregate with national competitiveness and higher gross value added.

In Qingdao, transportation equipment manufacturing has higher industrial competitiveness and obvious market advantage, occupying a national market share of 2.2%. Petroleum processing, coking products and nuclear fuel processing is the most competitive industry in Dalian, Qingdao and Ningbo, with Dalian superior to Ningbo and Ningbo superior to Qingdao. The financial sector is ranked first in Ningbo, Xiamen and Shenzhen with the market and fundamental advantage, playing an important factor supporting and serving the rapid development of key sectors such as service and manufacturing industries. As to the service industry, Shenzhen is the most competitive, followed by Qingdao, Dalian, Ningbo, and Xiamen (Lei, 2012; Lei and Fu, 2015).

In short, the independent planning system is an effective measure to comprehensively develop and utilize administrative resources and an agent that promotes the rapid development of regional economies. The system has a series of advantages, including connecting links, central radiation, rational productivity distribution, and coordinated development of the urban-rural area. Consequently, implementing independent planning is an effective way to promote a city's macroeconomic development significantly.

The Effect of Independent Planning on Economic Development

Independent planning has enabled the economic development of certain cities in modern China to benefit from the combined effects of increased public management and increased administrative resources. Since the independent planning of Chongqing in 1984, there once were 14 cities with independent planning power. However, these cities have decreased since 1994, leaving only five (Dalian, Qingdao, Ningbo,

Xiamen, Shenzhen) remaining. These five cities have developed rapidly after implementing independent planning. They have increased the GDP per capita by around 9.13% alone, clearly exceeding the annual national GDP growth rate, implying that the effect of independent planning on GDP per capita is larger than other conventional factors. The capability of absorbing domestic and foreign investment, urban infrastructure, regional radiation and regional influence are greatly improved after implementing an independent planning system (Shi and Zhou, 2007).

Moreover, the competitiveness of a city is also substantially enhanced, as shown by a comprehensive factor analysis of the economic benefits for 36 provincial capitals and cities in China with independent planning. Shenzhen is ranked first, Dalian second, Ningbo third, Xiamen eighth, and Qingdao eleventh. Meanwhile, Shenzhen enjoys obvious economic benefits due to its leading role and scored highest for its resident living and industrial factors, followed by Xiamen (Lei and Fu, 2015; Sun, 2001; Wen, 2011). Based on previous studies (Shi and Zhou, 2007), we further examine the effect of independent planning by using GDP per capita as the dependent variable and using the fixed assets investment per capita and the city's population at the end of the year as control variables. The cities selected include five currently with independent planning, i.e., Xiamen, Shenzhen, Dalian, Qingdao and Ningbo. Three cities were removed from independent planning in 1994, namely, Xi'an, Wuhan, Nanjing, and Chongqing, which were removed in 1997. There are nine cities in total. Table 7-1 presents the descriptive statistics of key variables for these cities.

Table 7-1 Description of main economic variables for cities with independent planning

Variable	Sample size	Mean	Variance	Min.	Max.
GDP per capita	223	2676584	23562.35	357	115356
Fixed assets investment per capita	223	165.46	195.23	0.38	812.56
The population at the end of the year	223	927.18	935.56	68.65	3452.36

Note: data collected from RoyalFlush software

The data in this research is updated until 2015 with Assumption A: independent planning has a significant effect on GDP per capita. In particular, based on previous studies, this chapter suggests: with the perfection of market economization, the marketability to allocate resources tends to be stable, and economic development is slowing down; relatively speaking, and the government's ability to regulate and control the market is increasing, which means the effect of public management and administrative resources allocation on economic efficiency increases. As a result, Assumption B is developed: the effect of independent planning on GDP per capita derived from this chapter is larger than previous studies. Table 7-2 shows the specific results.

Table 7-2 Regression results

GDP per capita	Coefficient	Standard deviation	P-value
Log of fixed assets investment per capita	0.6568	0.0150	0.000
Log of Population at the end of the year	0.0048	0.03.25	0.856
Existence of independent planning	0.1538	0.0635	0.011
Constant	5.1854	0.2835	0.000

The final results show that independent planning has a significant effect on GDP per capita (p=0.011), implying that the reallocation of public management and administrative resources caused by independent planning has greatly improved overall economic efficiency. At the same time, according to the estimation of updated data, the public management and administrative resources increased by independent planning system contribute about 16.07% to the GDP growth of each city, larger than the contribution rate (9.3%) of previous data, which is in line with Assumption B.

Advantages of Implementing Independent Planning in Greater Chaoshan

The Guangdong provincial party committee and provincial government attach great importance to the development of the greater Chaoshan area. It was pointed out that the goal was "to accelerate the development of the urban cluster in eastern Guangdong centering on Shantou" in the tenth party congress of Guangdong province, thus establishing the regional strategy of developing the greater Chaoshan area with a focus on Shantou. Chaoshan in eastern Guangdong has historically enjoyed important strategic development.

Agglomeration of the Greater Chaoshan and the Necessity of Independent Planning

Guangdong provincial new development strategy has further identified the strategic position of eastern Guangdong. It is the important provincial economic growth pole, a key portal to the outside world, a demonstration area for marine economy development and a characteristic city agglomeration suitable for living and working. In the Economic Development Program of Eastern Guangdong (EDPEG), it is suggested that as of 2015, the GDP of eastern Guangdong should reach to 598 billion RMB with an annual increase rate above 13%; the GDP per capita would be 34150 RMB. Meanwhile, the infrastructure and people's living and the ecological environment will be further improved. At the same time, the EDPEG determined downtown Shantou as the center and Chaozhou, Jieyang and Shanwei as sub-centers. The level of town development would be raised to construct a characteristic brand famous city. The agglomeration of "Shantou-Chaozhou-Jieyang" would be promoted to form an urban circle, realizing coordinated development of the urban cluster in eastern Guangdong.

The three cities in the greater Chaoshan area have distinctive characters and respective advantages and disadvantages. Shantou, for example, is an important bridgehead of cross-strait cooperation and a hub connecting the Western Straits with the Pearl River Delta, possessing comparative advantages in cross-strait cooperation and cooperation between the Western Straits with the Pearl River Delta. Furthermore, Shantou is one of the central cities in the Fujian-Guangdong-Jiangxi economic cooperation zone with a unique "double platform" advantage, creating a favorable environment for Shantou's modern service industry development. High expectations have been placed on Shantou with more responsibility for driving regional development.

However, the economic and social development of Shantou also faces serious challenges. These challenges include mismatching public management and public management and administrative resources, unfavorable economic location, and unbalanced public management and administrative resources and social, economic development, which are negative constraints to the long-term development of Shantou. The current authors argue that independent planning as the means of effective public management and administration is an operational solution that can bring the potential of Shantou Special Economic Zone (SEZ), a city with convenient information and active commercial trade, to full play. Moreover, given that Shantou is similar to certain cities with an independent planning system, such as Xiamen, it is practical to implement independent planning in Shantou. Later extend that system to the whole Chaoshan area, which will strongly contribute to the overall development of the agglomerated greater Chaoshan area.

Starting from the new strategic thinking of independent planning, the current economic aggregate of the greater Chaoshan area is much higher than Xiamen, equal to 1.24 times that of Xiamen, and the permanent resident population is 3.8 times larger than that of Xiamen. As shown in Table 7-3, the economic development strategic position is as favorable as Xiamen; moreover, the strategic position of the regional economy will exceed that of Xiamen to a considerable degree after integrating the greater Chaoshan area. As a result, upgrading the integrated Shantou new special economic zone to a city with independent planning is practically feasible. It has decisive strategic significance in the economic and social development of the whole eastern Guangdong area.

Table 7-3 Economic data comparison of selected cities in 2015

City	GDP (RMB 100 million)	GDP growth rate	GDP per capita (Yuan)	GDP per capita growth rate	Permanent resident population (10 thousand)
Shantou	1850.01	8.71%	33494	7.84%	552.37
Jieyang	1890.01	6.15%	31315	5.44%	603.54
Chaozhou	910.10	7.05%	33455	6.72%	272.04
Greater Chaoshan	4650.12	7.12%	33083	6.67%	1427.95
Xiamen	3565.00	7.00%	99455	8.22%	367.00

Note: data collected from the statistical information websites of each city

Eastern Guangdong is an important development pole of the province. The greater Chaoshan area is the traditional political, economic and cultural center of eastern Guangdong, leading the development of eastern Guangdong in terms of the urban construction scale, economic aggregate, urban living environment, supporting infrastructure, education, health, and culture. However, there is still much room for improvement. Tables 7-3 and 7-5 show annual economic growth in the greater Chaoshan area is 10% to 16%. With the addition of the additional 3% to 6% brought by independent planning, it can be expected that the economic society of Shantou will experience radical changes in the following 20 years.

Economic Advantages of the Greater Chaoshan Area

As aforementioned, the greater Chaoshan area includes Shantou, Jieyang and Chaozhou. As one of China's five special economic zones, Shantou has been developing at high speed in recent years. Jieyang is located at the Chaoshan plain in southeast Guangdong and borders Shantou to the east. Chaozhou, renowned as the "jade capital of Asia" and "China hardware base," is a famous hometown of overseas Chinese and an important tourism city and the main export base of China ceramics. Further, its wood carving technique is one of China's two woodcarving systems. Table 7-4 shows these three cities' GDP and GDP growth rates from 2002 to 2015.

Take Shantou as an example: Shantou's GDP has increased 47 fold. Its urban area has expanded over 20 times its original area during the past 30 years; the general budget revenue of local finance has been raised more than 50 times with an annual rate of 15.7%. Shantou's urban per capita disposable income has increased at an annual rate of 8.1%. It is gradually forming an economic pattern that features the coexistence and competing development of different types of ownership and has preliminarily established an economic system suitable for the export-oriented development of the special zone.

Table 7-4 GDP and GDP growth rates of Chaozhou-Shantou-Jieyang

Year	Shantou		Jieyang		Chaozhou	
	GDP (RMB 100 million)	GDP growth rate	GDP (RMB 100 million)	GDP growth rate	GDP (RMB 100 million)	GDP growth rate
2015	1850.10	8.71%	1890.01	6.15%	910.10	7.05%
2014	1701.81	8.68%	1780.44	10.91%	850.20	8.95%
2013	1565.90	10.67%	1605.35	16.32%	780.34	10.46%
2012	1415.01	0.82%	1380.15	12.57%	706.47	9.53%
2011	1403.44	16.09%	1225.86	21.43%	645.00	16.46%
2010	1208.97	16.71%	1009.51	23.70%	559.24	9.61%
2009	1035.87	6.27%	8160.92	12.68%	480.18	17.51%
2008	974.78	14.67%	7242.33	23.59%	438.08	16.24%
2007	850.10	15.29%	5859.93	22.03%	372.8	13.57%
2006	737.38	13.21%	4802.22	16.00%	320.72	12.06%
2005	651.36	7.88%	4139.96	7.31%	282.39	13.85%
2004	603.76	14.57%	3857.8	7.44%	252.01	10.40%
2003	526.97	9.07%	3590.69	7.31%	221.36	6.15%
2002	483.16		3346.08		200.51	
Mean		11.39%		15.48%		12.35%

Note: data collected from the statistical information websites of each city

In the light of the current economic growth rate, it is estimated that by 2016, the GDP of Shantou will be over 260 billion RMB annually, and per capita GDP will be 45200 RMB annually, slightly exceeding the economic levels of moderately developed countries. The "12th Five-year Plan" of Shantou sets an economic growth rate of 20% over the following five years as a goal, which is a very challenging one without special economic growth measures. The following discussion involves the efficient use of public management and administrative resources, the focal strategic direction studied by the current authors.

Table 7-5 Development orientation and industry positioning for the four cities in eastern Guangdong (Chaoshan)

	City orientation	Industry positioning	
Shantou	Develop into the central city of eastern Guangdong region, a modern port city and the ecological coastal city	Vigorously develop modern service industry, enhance the aggregation and radiation function of the central regional city, and build eastern Guangdong's commerce, finance, information, technology, education, and culture center.	Accelerate the development of port-centered industries such as equipment manufacturing, ship repair and manufacturing, petrochemical processing and modern logistics. Prioritize the development of emerging industries, including new material, biological medicine and culture creativity, transform and upgrade traditional advantage industries like textile and clothing, crafts and toys, electronic information and printing and packaging.
Jieyang	Develop Shanhai commercial city according to the requirements of "water city in eastern Guangdong."	Vigorously developed airport logistic industry by Jieyang Chaoshan Airport.	Accelerate the construction of large petrochemical, large equipment manufacturing and energy projects, focusing on the heavy chemical industrial base. Prioritize the development of traditional advantage industries as hardware and stainless steel, mechanical equipment manufacturing, pharmaceutical and jade processing.
Chaozhou	Develop into a famous historic and cultural city and modern riverside city with significant domestic and international influences.	Develop and grow the cultural and tourism industry.	Prioritize the development of biological environment protection, fine chemicals, warehouse logistics, optimize and improve traditional specialty industries as ceramics, food, hardware and aquatic equipment, develop an important and characteristic industrial base in Guangdong.

Shantou, Chaozhou and Jieyang, originally belonging to greater Shantou, have a natural basis for cooperation regarding humanity, geography, society and economy with close governmental and non-governmental contacts and economic cooperation. The Planning for National Major Functional Zones explicitly identifies Shantou as the central city in eastern Guangdong, promoting the agglomeration of Shantou-Chaozhou-Jieyang. The Development Planning for the Western Straits Economic Zone highlights a development led by Shantou and supported by Chaozhou and Jieyang, thus facilitating the urban agglomeration of Shantou, Chaozhou and Jieyang (Shantou Daily 5 edition special reports, 2012). The Reply of the State Council on Expanding the Shantou Special Economic Zone (The State Council Document, 2011) also explicitly requires Guangdong and Shantou to be prepared for the overall planning after expansion. According to the intensive and creative development principle, the "industrial distribution" planning should be implemented to "work hard to shift the model of economic development," thus "promoting the sound and fast development of the eastern Guangdong region."

Shantou, Jieyang and Chaozhou, considered individual economic entities, each owns specific positions in the greater Chaoshan area. As the leading city in the agglomeration of the greater Chaoshan area, the position of Shantou in the regional development pattern is further underlined. Jieyang and Chaozhou also find their future development directions and even their positions in the overall national economic development under the development idea of agglomerating the greater Chaoshan area, shown in table 7-5 (Lin and Peng, 2011).

Public Management Resources and Development in Greater Chaoshan

Above all, the current authors argue that Shantou should become agglomerated with Chaozhou and Jieyang. Seeking the approval to agglomerate three cities into a new administrative region will be covered by the favorable policies and legislative power currently possessed by Shantou SEZ. As such, it will expand the economic advantage of Shantou SEZ to make the whole greater Chaoshan an SEZ with independent planning and sub-provincial authority for economic development management. Based on the above strategic thinking, the current authors propose developing and adjusting the greater Chaoshan area's public management and administrative resources in the following aspects.

Enhance the Development of Soft Power

Kroenig et al. (2010) argue that the term soft power is entrenched in the theory and practice of American foreign policy. Scholars have not yet developed or empirically tested a theory about the conditions under which governments can use soft power to their advantage, making effective policy especially difficult to design and implement. Investment and a positive migration policy should be introduced with independent planning. The authors also suggest that educational development and personnel training should be prioritized. Shantou SEZ has only one university, Shantou University and Shantou Vocational Technical College. Including Hanshan Normal University, the entire greater Chaoshan area has only three institutions of higher learning, which is far from the development need. In particular, with the creation and implementation of the greater Chaoshan agglomeration, building new technology, industrial development and talent cultivation bases in the greater Chaoshan area represents the general trend.

The establishment of colleges and other educational institutions is a long-term investment, requiring accumulations over a long period. Only if we consider that education is the basis of progress and talent is the key can we grasp the opportunity and confront bigger challenges. Education will certainly benefit from the various conveniences brought by the above independent planning since the economy, technology, and education are interlinked and move ahead or step back altogether. We must consider the strategic significance of independent planning from an overall perspective. To enhance and develop soft strength and power should become a rational and feasible choice facing most decision-makers for urban development (Wang, 2009). Accordingly, the underdeveloped soft strength becomes a barrier that obstructs SEZ construction and needs to be removed (Zhu, 2007).

In addition, the tourism service industry should be vigorously developed. After implementing independent planning, Shantou will be able to make an overall arrangement of the urban tourism resources of the whole city and even surrounding cities, driving the successful development of other industries, thus improving the overall development level of the greater Chaoshan area. The Chaoshan area possesses rather comprehensive tourism resources, including the natural landscape, abundant cultural relics and certain tourism service infrastructure (Wang and Yang, 2012). Therefore, it would be advantageous to develop tourism (Ma, 2003). However, for various reasons, tourism in Shantou has been developing at a slower speed compared with surrounding cities. For example, compared with Xiamen, Shantou greatly lags in this industry. Consequently, the tourism development strategies of the Chaoshan area must be formulated from several aspects, with the input, publicity, planning and policy measures optimized and improved.

Strengthen Infrastructure Construction

Better infrastructure construction helps attract more direct investments, improving the efficiency of turning investment into output. Meanwhile, independent planning will attract even more investment with certain spillover and accumulation effects which require better infrastructure to increase investment return. Independent planning will enable Shantou to plan and integrate the surrounding infrastructure, raising the accessibility between cities. Additionally, the transportation system is undoubtedly a weakness of Shantou. As a result, an urban express ring road must be constructed to build a supporting system for urban-rural agglomeration. As for the most fundamental communication media – bus, the docking between the public transportation service and the central city of the greater Chaoshan should be accelerated; simultaneously, the rail lines should be increased, as the current handful of lines is abnormal for a city. Moreover, ports are also an important transportation condition. Governments at all levels of the greater Chaoshan area should strengthen infrastructure construction, improve and optimize the hardware and software environment supporting production and living.

Reinforce Population Scale to Adapt to New Development Needs

Roemer, Lucas and Scott put forward the new theory of economic growth. The new theory introduces knowledge and human capital factors into the economic growth model, arguing that the accumulation of specialized knowledge and human capital can generate incremental revenue, enlarge total revenue, and improve labor and physical capital productivity. The production theory points out that during social production, the mutual migration between migrants and local workers will promote the growth of marginal productivity. Schulz once estimated that after the Second World War, only 20% of American agriculture growth could be attributed to physical capital investment, with the remaining 80% resulting from education and technology. In particular, he emphasized that the common fault of developing countries is the indifference to human resource investment. They are willing to generously invest in the construction of tangible buildings and equipment procurement but stingy with human resource investment, making the restricted labor growth a bottleneck for economic development (Theodore, 1990).

Taking Shantou as an example, we assume that the GDP of Shantou will reach 360 billion RMB as proposed in the "12th Five-year Plan" of Shantou in the following five years. The estimation is conducted on the basis that the GDP per capita will then be 45200 RMB, and the population growth rate will be higher than 8.75%, meaning that the population will reach 8 million. The population of the greater Chaoshan area will be 21.19 million at the same speed. To maintain a population appropriate to economic growth, the population growth rate of the greater Chaoshan area must be higher. It is difficult to be realized through the natural growth rate alone, so we must seriously consider the migration factor in social and economic development.

To this end, the current authors suggest to 1) carry out a positive migrant policy, 2) carry out positive investment migrant policy, 3) carry out positive technical migrant policy, all of which will increase the productive labor force, elevate the education level with same population density, absorb talented people with advanced knowledge, absorb quality and sustainable investment, and which will maintain a population appropriate to the economic growth. Suppose the above three positive migrant policies can be implemented successfully. In that case, there will be tens of billions of construction funds and tens of thousands of young and skilled laborers each year in Shantou, driving the GDP growth of the greater Chaoshan SEZ at least one percentage point higher. Hence, we suggest the decision-makers of the newly established greater Chaoshan SEZ take this into serious consideration when developing the specific policies and schemes concerning the migrants in Shantou SEZ.

Optimize "Bringing in" and "Going global"

Centering on Shantou, the greater Chaoshan area will develop from an economic circle with one central city into a large economic circle with several central cities and further into a large economic belt of cities. The implementation of independent planning will use public management and administrative resources to strengthen mergers and cooperation between companies or expand enterprise scale by inviting investment. It will ultimately realize the objective of releasing economic development vitality. Take Shantou as an example: Shantou should give full play to its comprehensive advantages of being an SEZ, a port, having much commerce and a favorable location, and the city should improve its internal and external openness, promoting reform, development and innovation (Zheng, 2011). Shantou's larger industrial enterprises are insufficient. The scattered small enterprises cannot confront the fierce external competition. Therefore, as to the greater Chaoshan area, besides increasing internal funding and consolidating industries, external funding and technology introduction are also necessary. Independent planning has a significant effect in absorbing FDI, with the FDI per capita 1.5 times higher than if independent planning does not exist. Moreover, the authors have confirmed that domestic investment is indeed stimulated by inward investment (Deiffield and Hughes, 2003).

Conclusions

Public management and administration should maintain their role in directing regional economic development even though market power reserves its decisive role in allocating resources. The advantages of public management and administrative resources, and independent planning are undoubtedly crucial to the greater Chaoshan area's long-term economic and social development, especially its agglomeration strategy. Furthermore, research conducted from a practical and political point of view is of great value to the overall planning and strategic layout of the economic and social development of the whole eastern Guangdong region.

This research provides evidence that independent planning significantly affects GDP per capita. The results show that the reallocation of public management and administrative resources greatly promotes overall economic efficiency. More importantly, according to estimations with updated data, public management and administrative resources increased under an independent planning system. They contributed to the GDP of each city with independent planning in an increasing marginal trend.

Based on previous studies (Tian and Dai, 2013), this chapter demonstrates the necessity and feasibility of independent planning for the greater Chaoshan area. It proposes suggestions from multiple perspectives, including the economic development practices of cities in China, with independent planning and the strategic layout of eastern Guangdong's economic and social development and eastern Guangdong's economic and social development status quo. Discussing public management and administrative resources as soft and renewable in economic development will certainly be an important focal point for future regional economy study. The authors also hope to conduct further, more comprehensive and systematic discussions and research in this area, offering advice on the agglomeration and development of the greater Chaoshan area, thus realizing a blueprint for the superior development of the economy and society in eastern Guangdong.

Chapter 8
Impacts of Western Films on Contemporary China

As globalization moves ever so faster, cross-cultural communication activities of films are becoming increasingly frequent. In an environment full of complex and unfamiliar communication techniques, only by truly exploring the internal and external influencing factors and mechanism of its communication process can we improve the cross-cultural communication effects of films. Therefore, this research collects discourse data of Chinese audiences and scholars in Douban and CNKI on ten outstanding Western masculinist films that flowed into China over several years. It uses the grounded theory to explore the common relationship and construct a corresponding model to capture the mechanism. It is found that five main categories, which consist of situational content of films, the relationship between the film and the West, the interaction between the film and Chinese audience, negative identification factors, and cognitive, motivational approaches. Dynamics adjust Western films' cross-cultural communication effect in China. According to the above, this chapter constructs a model of factors affecting the communication effects of western masculinist films in China. Combined with the above-stated relationship to build up mechanism named OTHER- OTHER IN MY VIEW- WE, to seek a more effective way to enrich the academic fields cross-cultural communication in films, promote the modernization of cultural integration between China and the West.

Introduction

Films effectively exchange thoughts between the East and the West as a medium for carrying cultural and social ideas. But the importance of films has not been settled as it should be in China, which has degraded the effectiveness of cross-cultural communication. Until recent years, Chinese filmmaking has evolved around the idea of "telling Chinese stories and letting the world hear Chinese voice," and finally receiving attention for strengthening cultural expression. In existing research on how 'Chinese story going into the world' and how "Western films going into China," few scholars stand in as the middleman to provide perspective to discuss the real feedback from the film to improve communication. Therefore, it is evident that the corresponding model and mechanism in analyzing the relationship between the modern Chinese process and worldwide film cross-cultural communication have been lacking.

A major concern in this article hopes to find out why Western films can be widely disseminated in China regardless of culture and ideology. Analyze the comments of academia and the public through films, and find useful suggestions for promoting the interactive effects of world culture.

With the global village envisioned McLuhan becoming a reality, the internet has breached the limitations of time, space, and national boundaries. Different cultures are blended into the world in a fast, low-cost, and efficient way. According to a 2020 survey reported by the American Film Association (MPA), China has occupied the world's largest film market due to its huge population and consumer base, thus becoming one of the most important markets. As films are a significant part of cultural exchange, attracting many international films into the Chinese film market to tell their stories and share their thoughts, values, and even culture with the Chinese audiences. Therefore, analyzing the cross-cultural communication effects of Western films in China while broadening the academic fields of film communication, cross-cultural communication can benefit contemporary cultural communication between China and the West.

In the past, academia used different visions to explore the communication effect of films, with systematization divergence, to describe the different objects such as media (Baek, Yang and Ahn 2017; Nakatsu, Tosa and Ochi 2001), systems (Yoon, Polpanumas and Park 2017; Hennig-Thurau, Wiertz and Feldhaus 2015), groups (Strasburger and

Donnerstein 2014), academic discipline (Babaii and Asadnia 2021), and more, investigating their functions in cross-cultural communication. Some scholars discuss film's communication impact from specific content production (Chung and Eoh 2019; Marquez 2020), with a grand narrative to analyze policy and industrial development's influence on cross-cultural communication via films (Kirby 2018; Chen, Chen, Chao and Wang 2021). A summary of some relevant concepts to different disciplines, such as sales and distribution of films. Evaluate film communication effects according to their box office and popularity (Song, Kim, Lee and Kim 2017). Discuss different kinds of films' watching impact on audience' s psychology, emotion, and behavior (Erk, Toet and Van 2015). And explore structural changes with the economy, law, ideologies imposed by films development. Among these reviews, considering films of feminism consist not only of female creators, topics, and consciousness, but also concentrate on stereotypes and discrimination of gender, expands to the analyzing about culture, rights, and society, trying to break the patriarchal mechanism and change the status of development for the female group. So that feminist films often consist of strong awareness of equal rights, the description of female roles in films is more positive. This chapter divides films storytelling mainly based on male perspectives and male characters, which contains dominant male perspectives or strong masculine ideologies. In addition, female characters in these films have not played an important and positive role in the development of the film, and even occurrence that films stereotype and discriminate against women. Apart from feminism, film, for easy to explain, will be referred to as masculinist film in the following paragraph. After analyzing, we found, compared with enthusiasm focus on female-dominated perspective, investigation of masculinist films' communication was mostly neglected and even pushed away from the center of academia.

Considering male consciousness is a fundamental part of any film since masculinist films are still an important part of modern films, their production and dissemination have their reasonable meaning of existence

(Jonathan 1998). Therefore, it is important to discuss their role and function in film's cross-cultural communication. Based on this, we argue that studying masculinist films, whether historical or contemporary, has profound academic value. Moreover, it makes research of film cross-cultural communication effect more universal. However, discussions around the effects according to audience-specific feedback have been limited (Chiu, Chen, Wang, and Hsu 2019). Even less attention is paid to the content of masculinist films. Thus, a mature theoretical framework has not been established for this issue. Analyzing Chinese audience reaction obtained in cross-cultural film communication can assist scholars in studying how to promote cross-cultural communication among China and the West, provide a significant theoretical and practical view in effectively reducing deviations in cultural expression.

To maximize sample contents, this article takes two perspectives from the Chinese audience, concentrates on Western films that have been widely transmitted in China, seeking out common characteristics between different viewpoints to construct mechanism and theoretical model. Given this, based on the grounded theory, we select ten representative masculinist films in China as samples to probe the influencing factors and mechanisms affecting the communication of Western films in China. The following paragraph in sections 3 and 4 carry out coding and category definition to build up the model based on theoretical saturation, which explains films situational content combines the relationship between the film and the West and jointly influences the generation of OTHER IN MY VIEW- WE mechanism. Then, based on the influencing element of the interaction between the film and Chinese audience, this essay carries out the construction of the "OTHER IN MY VIEW- WE" mechanism dynamically affected by negative identification factors and cognitive, motivational approaches. Together, the above five elements constitute the model of "affecting factors of disseminating Western masculinist films in China." We then construct the OTHER- OTHER IN MY VIEW- WE mechanism (see for details in 4.3.) to explain the cross-cultural communication effect.

On this basis, this article advocates that cross-cultural film communication should be aware of the unsuitable expression, which could lead to conflict with local culture and values. Then, to expand the range of identification space, cross-cultural film communication ought to use the attraction of creators and actors to enlarge the scope of transmission and increase the audience's interests. This article utilizes existing communication approaches to help Western films enlarge their communication in China and seek a more effective way to get along well with China via cultural communication.

The structure of the paper is as follows five parts: literature reviews, research design, category extraction and model construction, discussion of model interpretation, and case study. Suggestions and analyses on limitations and prospects of this topic are provided as concluding thoughts. The following chapters will start with an existing academic review to summarize and sort out the academic explorations on masculinist film cross-cultural communication, to outline this article's research value and rationality.

Literature Review

Presently, academia adopts two perspectives around cross-cultural communication of masculinist films: explicit and implicit, inward and outward. These are made to analyze and explain influencing elements in film production, expression, communication process, etc., due to the difference in focus and tendency between the two perspectives.

Visibility and Invisibility of Masculinist Films

According to the explicit and implicit male-dominated consciousness in films, academia presents a relatively well-balanced tendency to discuss problems brought by masculinist films to cross-cultural communication study.

On the one hand, based on the audio-visual language of films, existing study on visible male-consciousness films, on the ground of comparative framework, concluded that fixed elements selection (O'Brien and Liddy 2021; Eaklor 2012), role matching (Hennessy 2016), plot setting (Sharma and Wherry 2009) often appears in masculinist films. At the same time, they affirm that good masculinist films have enriched the expression of the film in communication, depth, and thoughts about the relationship between genders and rights. Scholars conducted a reverse analysis of invisible male consciousness films, refining their characteristics such as flat characters (Boyle, Millington and Vertinsky 2006), extreme plot (Wrigth 2012), misrepresentation of disadvantaged groups in the name of feminism (Abdi and Calafell 2017), and extending review from male-consciousness in film in a historical and societal context, pointing out the structural contradiction of discrimination in film development (Williams 2003), discuss the negative problems appear in masculinist films such as patriarchy, gender discrimination, homosexual hatred, and racial problem (Gopinath 2000), to describe social reality contradictions triggered by patriarchal consciousness, such as imbalanced employment (Liinamaa and Rogers 2020), cultural differences (BIELBY and BIELBY 1996), industrial imbalance (Minoo 2010), regional and religious violence, crime problems (Liddy 2016), and the expression of the dilemma of feminism (Duong 2015; Liu and Dahling 2016).

Academia praise masculinist films' contribution in correcting social problems and consciousness in civilization, history, and social concepts while protesting mainstream stereotypes, ideological oppression, rights exploitation, and social problems caused by patriarchal consciousness in film communication. Most studies relate films to industries and groups and discuss the imbalance of modern industry, culture, and society brought by male-dominant film consciousness. However, scholars rarely use academic insights, stand in the audience's perspective to analyze the relationship between communication and interaction of the audience feedback with film, which urgently needs to be noticed and discussed from academic fields.

Internal and External Exploration of Film-based Cross-cultural Communication and its Effects

From the inward and outward perspective, a brief review of the Western masculinist film's communication and its effects in China is given in this section to illustrate the similarities and disparities of The West and China's academic attention.

To explore cross-cultural communication and its effect in China, as "telling Chinese stories well" has been the Chinese government's practice put forward and practiced, Chinese scholars have focused on "letting Chinese films go into the world." By historical processes (Hu and Yang 2018), combined with practical solutions to problems encountered (Yn and Fu 2020), the Chinese academia is eager to advocate their films and culture towards the Western world. Some suggest via humanity, integrity, and openness (Long 2021) to enlarge the communication effect. Some scholars argue that the scope of communication must be considered, valuing the meaning of recognition attitude (Ming and Bao 2021). And several scholars put forward different academic spots on producers such as traditional media, individual filmmakers (Xiang and Wang 2020), filming companies (Xie and Sun 2013), and communication mediums such as a laptop (Liu 2019), cinema (Huang 2015), presentation and production choices such as color (Nie 2019), plot (Li and Zhao 2015), symbol (Long 2016) and so on, to tackle the dilemma of current cross-cultural communication with Chinese film. Those reviews above proposed demonstrating and exploring how Chinese films can achieve the maximum communication effect.

For cross-cultural communication and its effect in the West, scholars mostly focus their attention on audio-visual language, discussing the role and defects of film in cross-cultural communication with music, visualization, sound effect, translation, subtitles, and other elements

(Tavassoli and Lee 2003; DKJ 2019; Tia 2015). Scholars extend their concentrate on other disciplines such as society and psychology to emphasize the meaning and function of films (Berger 1996; Paolo 2007). The purpose of their research is to reflect on cultural communication, conduct effective communication results, and rarely pay attention to the practical problems on the communication of films after they spread into other countries and other cultures.

In contemporary society, films are the main force in conveying values and cultures. Many scholars put this issue on media, platforms, groups, or disciplines to investigate better communication effects, analyzing structural changes caused by policies, industries, and society. Studies on these two perspectives can dynamically enlarge film's cross-cultural communication outreach and further study space.

However, observing local academia and audiences, centralizing on constructing mechanisms and models is still in a relatively blind stage. Distinguishing the similarities and differences between imaginary and 'reality 'other' are the initial and highlight step of maximizing cultural communication. Hence, after comprehensively collecting and analyzing local Chinese discussion, observing Western film communication effect status in China. Takes masculinist films' communication effect as a topic, with the help of the grounded theory to develop a theoretical model and mechanism to conduct modern cross-cultural communication from the West to modernization China. Meanwhile, we aim to organize comments from the Chinese audience into diverse groups, refine the key points and difficulties of western film transmission to seek accurate and useful advice for cross-cultural communication.

Research Design

This chapter chooses grounded theory as the research method for two reasons: Firstly, investigation of local audience is still in an emerging stage, the academia has yet to establish a mature theoretical framework to accurately solve the problem of processing film cross-cultural communication, whereas using the grounded theory is a reasonable strategy at present. Secondly, taking the audience's comments as an object in the study of film cross-cultural communication effect is still exploratory. Given this, qualitative research is more prospective than quantitative research with the given context (Jia, Wang, and Xu 2021; Sun 2010).

We are given many sample films, which overage capacity constraints. This article selects multiple masculist characters among the types of films included for discussion. Combining the top 250 films listed on Douban, which is the biggest film review website in China, search with "patriarchy," "masculist," and "multiple characters," our study can obtain 39 films with details. Considering the subject of this essay is Western films, Chinese and Asian films are excluded, and a total of 23 films were obtained. We then follow multiple case studies and discard films with the same country, genre, director, and period. Ten films are ultimately selected for the following research. The list includes *Scent of a Woman, The Godfather, Once Upon a Time in America, The Green Book, 12 Angry Men, Call Me by Your Name, Malèna, The Lord of the Rings, Trainspotting, Pulp Fiction.* Within this sample of 10 films, the earliest one was released in 1957, and the latest 2018, which covers a long period enough to provide a sufficient timing perspective reducing bias from historical sequence. The sample also contains multiple variations such as plot, crime, settings, adventure, and so on to ensure diversity of comments for the following discussion.

Getting close to the audience for observation and direct feedback collection can help academia understand the real effect of film in cross-cultural communication. With this in mind, we conduct searches on Cnki and Douban, two online platforms that aggregate opinions about films from the Chinese academia and the public. Literature and comments in these two platforms contain abundant texts about the films in question, thus making them an important indicator for learning the relationship between films and the Chinese audience (Koh, Hu, and Clemons 2010). Then, this chapter classifies and categorizes sample film comments into initial data, extracting data characteristics into different sorts to support the database of open coding.

In the stage of classification and categorization, this section use Douban comments and Cnki as resources of initial data, the detail of which can be seen in Table 8-1, following communication and China as the keywords for search and filter. Screening criteria in detail abide by three points: 1. Logically texts should have a certain length. 2. Discussion should be from the perspective of the Chinese audience. 3. Contains comments on film's contents and production to reach cross-cultural communication.

Table 8-1 Initial data resources

Movie Title	Access Address of Douban	Access Address of CNKI
Scent of a Woman	https://movie.douban.com/subject/1298624/	https://kns.cnki.net/KNS8/AdvSearch?dbcode=CJFQ
The Godfather	https://movie.douban.com/subject/1291841/	https://kns.cnki.net/KNS8/AdvSearch?dbcode=CJFQ
Once Upon a Time in America	https://movie.douban.com/subject/1292262/	https://kns.cnki.net/KNS8/AdvSearch?dbcode=CJFQ
Green Book	https://movie.douban.com/subject/27060077/	https://kns.cnki.net/KNS8/AdvSearch?dbcode=CJFQ
12 Angry Men	https://movie.douban.com/subject/1293182/	https://kns.cnki.net/KNS8/AdvSearch?dbcode=CJFQ
Call Me by Your Name	https://movie.douban.com/subject/26799731/	https://kns.cnki.net/KNS8/AdvSearch?dbcode=CJFQ
Malèna	https://movie.douban.com/subject/1292402/	https://kns.cnki.net/KNS8/AdvSearch?dbcode=CJFQ
The Lord of the Rings	https://movie.douban.com/subject/1291571/	https://kns.cnki.net/KNS8/AdvSearch?dbcode=CJFQ
Trainspotting	https://movie.douban.com/subject/1292528/	https://kns.cnki.net/KNS8/AdvSearch?dbcode=CJFQ
Pulp Fiction	https://movie.douban.com/subject/1291832/	https://kns.cnki.net/KNS8/AdvSearch?dbcode=CJFQ

This data comes from Douban and Cnki Sources.

Table 8-2. Open Coding Database

Movie Title	Amount of Comments Data	Amount of Literature Data
Scent of a Woman	63	16
The Godfather	86	31
Once Upon a Time in America	65	23
Green Book	105	30
12 Angry Men	65	21
Call Me by Your Name	71	15
Malèna	58	24
The Lord of the Rings	70	35
Trainspotting	75	13
Pulp Fiction	92	25

This data comes from Douban and Cnki Sources.

The above screening criteria set restrictions on sample length, logic, speaker identity, topic relevance, etc. We finally obtained 233 valid documents and 750 valid text comments to compose an open coding database (Table 8-2). This database includes a discussion of cultural, historical, legal, policy, and other aspects. And in the following chapters, we categorize them from this database first and divide the data by their properties while following the principle of theoretical saturation to accomplish the coding process.

Category Extraction and Model Construction

This section decomposes, categorizes, and conceptualizes the collected data to compose open coding in two steps. The result of this process can be seen below.

Table 8-3. Partial of Initial Coding and Category

Partial Open Coding and Initial Category Refinement		
It might be the fifth time to watch the film, but I will still be shocked by it. Is Coppola (the director) the best filmmaker on the planet?	A1 Reputation of Director	B3 Creators Attraction
What the director has done is fantastic. He draws a story with almost no drama but shows a beautiful world as a dream.	A2 Ability of Director	
This film exposed the fragility and helplessness of women in the era of patriarchy in Italy.	A10 Problem of Rights	B1Abstract content

A story about a gay lie to fool adolescence: I have never opposed gay love, but I hate the film that treats all female characters perfunctorily to celebrate the so-called same-gender love.	A12 Problem of Sexual Distinction	
Lumet's scheduling and mirroring are terrific, with the support of superb shooting and performances and perfect coordination of choreographer and director, giving this wonderful artwork tension from start to finish.	A20 Shooting Technique	
It may have been more than a year since the last time I watched 'The Hobbit.' I didn't watch half of the film because the film's length is too long.	A23 Movie Duration	
I watched it again and again. Although the film content is very good, more important is it represents the memory of past years, the years about the university of chatting with roommates in the dormitory about this film. When I re-watch it, everything was like yesterday once more.	A27 Viewing Frequency	B11Watching Experience
Some people see it affectionately as a political metaphor film, others watch it as a youth memory, and some frankly see it as a sensual erotic film.	A30 Viewing Purpose	
I first watched the domestic remake and then watched the original version even though there is only one scene but truly exciting.	A32 From Remake to See the Original	B10 Watching Purpose
I watched the "Green Book" because Chen Xiaoqing recommended it in "Yuan Zhuo Pai." As he said: After watching this film, he especially wanted to eat KFC. Lip's passion for food in the film infected him.	A33 Recommendations from Others	
There are more adaptations than I thought. The shortening of the time length and several changes to the storyline add an entirely new story.	A36 Interests from Original Fiction	B6 Longitudinal Comparison
With the eloquent laid out step by step, the two outstanding boys tentatively explore and close to each other, and finally get in touch. It's rare to see such enlightened and indulgent parents in China; after all, the movie shows a better, idealized reality to me.	A37 a Gap between Film and Reality.	
This movie by Francis Ford Coppola is different from Martin Scorsese's 'Good Fella,' but all have their charms. Maybe the latter is not as well-known as the former, but both can be described as momentous of gangster movies. The Godfather is more narrative and romantic based on the original novel, while "GoodFella" is more realistic and is based on a true story.	A39 Comparison of Movies of the Same Genre	B5 Horizontal Comparison
I know that director is trying to enhance the warm tones of the northern Italian countryside, but I suggest he watch L'effrontée and other French films in the 80s to learn how Europe can be present. The film is too busy to illustrate the life and lack of passion; come on, I feel that the director is asleep in directing.	A40 Comparison of directors of the Same Type	

The data comes from Douban's comments.

After importing data searched from CNKI and Douban. We put them into the NVIVO software for sentence-by-sentence reading. First, incomplete and weakly relevant comments and text are deleted. Next, in the reading process, numbering and naming texts, for example, if some elements appear in data several times such as "color of the image is attractive," "unforgettable sounds," are summarized into abstraction elements as "color" "sound" in the open coding stage. Subsequently, similar comments and titles are summarized, and initial conceptual coding is made. For example, suppose the appearance of actors increases the audience's interest in watching films, which is mentioned in the open coding stage. In that case, this study classifies similar comments as the initial coding as "good-looking appearance" as an attraction factor. Accordingly, we summed up 84 initial coding in this stage, shown in Table 8-3.

After extracting, this chapter sort out initial coding into the initial category: such as "viewing frequency, viewing age, viewing time, viewing purpose, sequence of viewing, and imagination," are all belonging to the initial coding that affects the audience watching experience. So we summarized this coding as an initial category named "watching experience." Fourteen initial categories are summarized in the way of arrangement, as shown in table 8-4.

It should be noticed that the comments and text collected in this article are based on Chinese audiences and Chinese scholars regarding masculinist films. Meanwhile, its concentrated topic is influencing factors and practical results of Western masculinist films communication in China. Thus, this chapter's coding, categories, model, and mechanism can only apply to Western masculinist film communication in China. Still need repetition test for films from Asia and other districts, to acquire universal consequent.

Table 8-4. Diagram of initial categories and main categories

Explanation of Initial Category	Initial Category	Main Category
Based on the film, it extends to critics' thinking on abstract and grand content such as society, culture, and ideas.	B1Abstract Content	C1 Situational Content of Films
Discussions on audiovisual elements such as the specific plots, contexts, and content of the film.	B2 Concrete Content	
Based on the strength and achievements of the creators, such as directors and screenwriters, the audiences have additional favors and trust in the film, so they are more willing to make positive comments on the film.	B3 Creators Attraction	C2 Relationship Between the Film and Other Elemnts in the West
Because the audience loves the actors and stars, they have empathy leads to positive comments for their film.	B4 Actors Attraction	
Extending in the film industry, audiences compare similar types of films and creators.	B5 Horizontal Comparison	
Extending to the outside of the film industry, a comparative discussion of the literature, works, historical events, and real events involved in the film.	B6 Vertical Comparison	
Discuss the similarities and differences between the film and the audience's consciousness, thinking, philosophy, values, etc. from the perspective of the Chinese audience's cognitive concepts.	B7 Cognitive Space	C3 Interaction Between the Film and the Audience in China
Based on personal living space, talk about the relationship between the film and the audience's own experience (strong individuality).	B8 Living Space	
From the perspective of Chinese audiences, talk about the group preference feelings of Chinese audiences.	B9 Chinese Audience	
Recommendations by others, search for clips, promotion, remakes to see the original version, etc. to promote the different feelings of the audience watching the film.	B10 Watching Purpose	C4 Cognitive Motivational Approaches
Discuss the similarities and differences of the movie's feelings from the audience's viewing age, age, frequency, purpose, and viewing order.	B11Watching Experience	
Due to changes in times and customs, the intensity of the audience's cultural understanding of the film also changes.	B12 Intensity of Cultural Understanding	C5 Negative Identification Factors
Content in the film contradicts to local culture, resulting in differences in understanding conflicts.	B13 Intensity of Cultural Conflict	
The difference in core social values has led to disputes on the portrayal of certain issues, which in turn led to disapproval.	B14 Value conflict	
This data comes from Douban and Cnki Sources.		

Spindle Coding

This study decomposes the original comments and textual data into the 14 initial categories in the previous section. And after further refinement, we assemble five main categories shown in Table 8-4. Among the main categories, the intensity of cultural understanding (B12), the intensity of cultural conflict (B13), and value conflict(B14) are all belong to the negative influencing elements of identification, which can be defined as negative identification factors (C5). Creators attraction (B3), actors attraction (B4), comparison of horizontal and vertical aspects(B5 and B6) all belong to the relationship between film and the West, so that can be defined as the relationship between the film and other elements in the West (C2). Living space (B8), cognitive space(B7), and Chinese audience (B9) are all the discussions between Chinese audiences and Western film, to become one of the main categories (C3). Specific and abstract contents (B1 and B2) can be put in the situational content of films category (C1). Lastly, watching experience (B11) and watching purpose (B10) are the effective factors to impact on Chinese audience attitude, which selected into the cognitive, motivational approaches category (C4). In combination, the study concluded the *situational content of films, the relationship between the film and the West, the interaction between the film and Chinese audience, negative identification factors, cognitive, motivational approaches* as the five main categories to present spindle coding.

Construction of Model and Mechanism

From organizing initial categorizes into main categories, this essay extends the meaning of the categories above and links the five subjects to enter into modeling in the next step.

In this section, we carry out coding and category definition for the construction of the model to capture the previously hypothesized cross-cultural communication mechanism and model of influencing factors of western masculinist films transmitted in China. The model explains the situational content of films as a fundamental factor to push films' cross-cultural communication. After the Chinese audiences look over the film in the background of the West, link the relationship between films and Chinese culture and society, with the impulse on negative identification factors and cognitive, motivational approaches on Chinese; jointly propel the identification of Western vale and culture. Thus these five main categories dynamically make up the mode of affecting factors of disseminating Western masculinist films in China, as shown in Figure 8-1. From the function of these five main categories, this chapter analyzes the internal connections between them, and connects the relationships between the initial categories through the coding, combines the process of film transmission to set up a storyline for its cross-cultural communication:

First, after Western masculinist films entered the Chinese market, the situational content of films (B1 and B2) was defined by the Chinese audience as specific symbols of Western civilization, thus forming the identity of OTHER for distinguishing in this stage.

Secondly, step into the stage of understanding, the audience will start from two aspects to deepen understanding of films: (1) Compare films with the history, culture, and reality development (B3, B4, B5, and B6) in the background of the West. (2) Based on the contexts of China, the Chinese audience explores the differences in cognitive and living space between Western films and China (B7, B8, and B9). With the accomplishment of two aspects above, complete the stage of OTHE IN MY VIEW.

Thirdly, after having a deep understanding of the film, Chinese audiences generally combine with their watching motivations to conclude different feelings about films(B10 and B11). With the impact on negative identification factors (B12, B13, and B14) through values and cultural conflicts, the Chinese audiences strengthen their identification or rejection of films. In the way of identification, converged values and culture in the film become a part of the audience's thinking, stepping into the construction of WE.

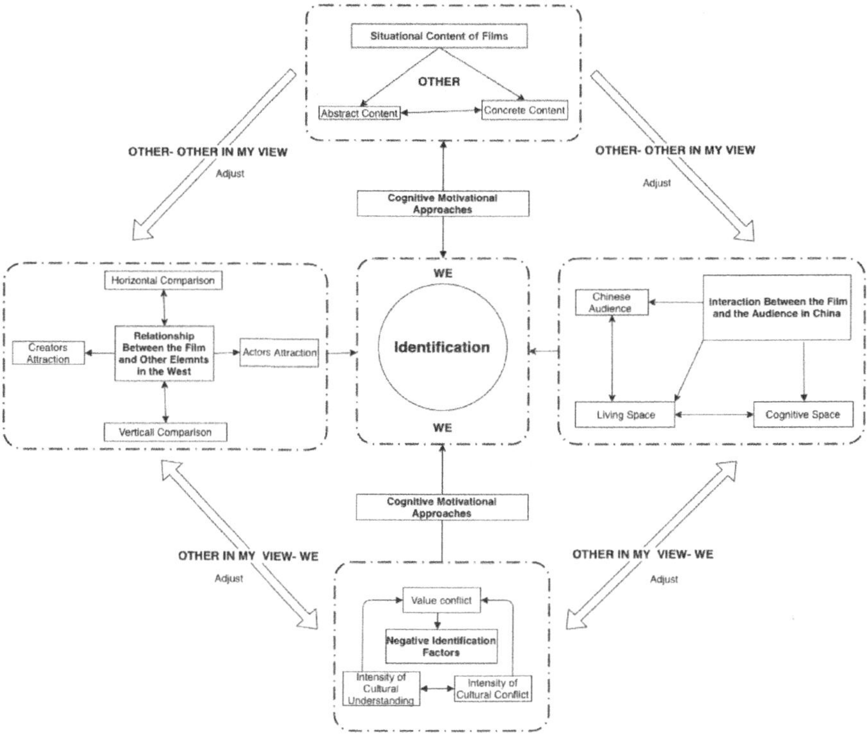

Figure 8-1. Model of Factors Affecting the Communication Effect of Masculinist Films in China

Three stages are composed of the five main categories; draw the storyline that illustrates Western masculinist film cross-cultural communication mechanism named OTHER- OTHER IN MY VIEW- WE. Then, with the help of deep understanding to gain the audience's empathy towards the film and culture, complete the transformation from the West to China.

Theoretical Saturation Test

In this stage, we randomly select five comments and textual data from *Django Unchained*, another masculinist film found in Douban's top 250 lists of films, to prove whether if the model and mechanism proposed to pass theoretical saturation or not. Then, carry out the coding listed in the previous sections again. This chapter does not identify new main categories or find new connections between them in coding and categorizing. Therefore, this essay argues that the model and mechanism in 4.3 are successfully passed the theoretical saturation.

Affecting Factors of Masculinist Films Conclusion and Suggestion

Based on the above-stated method, this article establishes a model to capture and explain the cross-cultural communication effect of Western masculinist films in China. The five categories play different roles in masculinist film cross-cultural communication. And in this chapter, our study will combine specific practical case studies to explain the logical relationship between each category.

The situational content of films determined by abstract and specific contents poses the necessary external condition for their cross-cultural communication effect. It is also the mediating factor for the OTHER-OTHER IN MY VIEW mechanism.

Analysis shows that specific content around the film is the discussion's primary topic through the database. From the appreciation of specific film contents, the audience is stimulated to talk about the abstract contents, thus affecting the film's purpose in cross-cultural communication identification, which can directly influence the setting of the OTHER-OTHER IN MY VIEW mechanism.

The specific contents of a film contain a story plot, photography, scene-setting, color, music, costumes, time length, translation, etc. These properties have a high frequency of occurrence in the initial coding of this study, amounting to 197 times. Among this coding, we observe similarities in terms of time length, photography, scene-setting, and music, to influence Chinese audiences' feelings. For example, "I watched half of it but didn't finish it.' indicates that the length of a movie is too long. (A23)," and 'The scene-setting of this movie is so beautiful that it greatly portrays the heartbeat of adolescence. (A20)," appear tendency to show that good specific content can bring positive comments and evaluation from the audience. When the presentation of the specific content is more fitting for a modern aesthetic, it can increase the audience's discussion passion and enhance the construction of identity.

This finding can also explain criticism directed towards a movie when inappropriate content is presented, even when the film contains good specific content. An example of such can be: "Perhaps because of the development of film technology, or too much expectation, I felt that Lord of the Ring is not good as Hobbit. (A25)," "Bad title translation constitutes as clickbait. (A53)," "The Consciousness of Idiom Translation in the Film Subtitle Translation Taking Scent of Women as an Example. (A69)." Among these examples, it can be noted that attention and comments from the public perspective can promote interactive discussion in the academic fields. The initial coding appears in half of the samples referring to the translation problem of Scent of Women both from public and academic perspectives. However, no discussion of obvious translation problems can be found in samples from the other seven films, nor was it noted in another capacity. In addition, for films with excellent specific content, the audience shifts their focus to abstract content, which drives academic attention. For instance, this chapter finds out the public takes race as the main topic in The Green Book, driving academia' attention to racial issues, such as "a very old-school but well-organized film, a little bit of self-consolation about the history of the 1960s in the West. (A14)," "A key words analysis of ethnic discourse in the film Green Book of race, power, and ideology. (A74)." It also proves that under the good expression and production of specific contents, if Western films can adjust their abstract contents in advance, it could be beneficial to be accepted by Chinese audiences and scholars.

Therefore, it can be argued that specific and abstract contents together constitute situational content of films. Firstly, films should stimulate the audience's curiosity and interest with high-quality film content to take the first step in receiving attention from the Chinese audience and scholars. Therefore, promoting the western masculinist films' cross-cultural communication effect in China is important to assure the high quality of films' situational content and attract Chinese audiences to watch the film without suspicion of the film itself.

The relationship between the film and other elements in the West includes the attraction of creators and actors, horizontal and vertical comparison. These are the external conditions that affect identification. After the audience knew film via situational film content, combined with the horizontal and vertical comparison of Western historical and literal context, to accelerate the construction of the OTHER IN MY VIEW mechanism.

The Additional Function of Creators and Actors

A good director is not only the guarantee of a good ticket office, but they can also ensure the quality of a movie. Employing reliable directors for film production can be the first and crucial step in promoting cross-cultural communication. Coding shows that all directors enjoy international popularity within the sample of 8 films. According to the analysis of initial coding, 18.19% of the public audience clearly stated that directors and actors are considered to be the main factors for their desire to watch the film, and expressed a strongly positive view towards these subjects, words such as "series work, strong aura, good acting skills, high popularity, handsome, beautiful" occupies a relatively large part of the database. Their emotional tendency is shown as positive in 4.2 out of 5 points. Therefore, analysis indicates that the quality of directors and actors contributes aggressively to the communication of masculinist film in China, which has produced a positive impetus to public acceptance of the film.

The Comparison of Horizontal and Vertical Category

Emotional tendencies observed in vertical and horizontal comparison in the database are similar to those in the above sections. This article summarizes it as the same contents to avoid repetition due to length constrain.

We find an inverse relationship between emotional tendency and time sequence among coding in the horizontal and vertical comparison categories. The finding is presented as follows: the further away from the film's release, the lower the audience's tolerance towards the film, and the coding shows more objectivity and prudent tendency. The closer the release window, the more tolerant the audience will become. It is evident in comments such as "The shortage of the film is Cliché, but it enlightens us a lot. (A39)," "It is a classic American movie with a funny plot and comfortable storyline. It is easy to have fun watching. (A47)." On the contrary, as years recede, the audience's comments gradually become sharper, and the emotional tendency towards film identity declines.

At the same time, our study detects a trend of an active analogical tendency that exists between public and scholars' perspectives, comparing similar kinds of films, directorial works, and literary works into one space. For example, The Godfather and Once Upon a Time in America are gangster films. Hence the title that appears in each others' database took the probabilities of 10.2% and 10.44%. Twelve Angry Men has been reproduced several times, such as remake and original version have become highly frequent vocabulary in their database. The original novel and fictional story can be observed from The Lord of the Rings database. Titles such as The Wedding Banquet and Brokeback Mountain, also actively mentioned in the database of Call Me By Your Name. Thence, as a regulated variable of the OTHER IN MY VIEW mechanism, time is inversely proportional to horizontal and vertical comparison. It also shares a proportional relationship with the additional function of creators and actors. It follows the analogical tendency to influence the completing progress of the OTHER jointly- OTHER IN MY VIEW mechanism.

The interaction between Western film and Chinese audience includes the aspects of living space, cognitive space between film and Chinese audience. It is the internal condition to build the mechanism of "WE." as the Chinese audiences illustrate the basic image of OTHER IN MY VIEW, through audience understanding of the differences among China and film presentation, to establish the WE mechanism.

The interaction between film and Chinese audiences is a moderating variable when adjusting the relationship between films and Chinese audiences' cognition within social reality. In the database of literary coding, this chapter finds that Chinese scholars mostly focus their research on the alertness and divergence with Western masculinist films and the Chinese society, deep into cognitive space such as cultural differences and social issues, to explore the gap between the West and China. For instance, "A Comparative Study of the family system in The Godfather and Chinese traditional family system (A77)," "The exotic journey of light and shadow youth, comparison of Sunny Days and Once Upon a Time in America(A79)." And lack of coding shows a link between the films and audience feedback in the database. It leads to establishing the OTHER IN MY VIEW- WE mechanism mostly through comparison, and its connection to modern China is relatively weak. This trend can also be detected in the database coding of the audience; when cognitive factors are stronger than literal factors, identification of audience to film would be not obvious in coding. When the overlap is reduced between OTHER-OTHER IN MY VIEW in the film, empathy and identification among coding presented by the public audience would be declined.

On the contrary, when the audience's own experience coincides with the film, their inclination of empathy and identification towards the film will be significantly strengthened, be it negative or positive. Thereby, this tendency promotes or inhibits the film's capability in cross-cultural communication. It is evident in comments such as "This love story that doesn't ask for a happy ending is meaningless in itself, but dad's words were great in the end. It's time for Chinese parents to learn how to treat puppy love. (A75)."

In this stage, these moderating variables are also influenced by negative identification factors and cognitive motivational approaches (to be discussed in detail in the following section). If the film does not contain conflicts in values or cultural concepts with the Chinese audience, the moderating effect of interactive elements such as the audience's experience, cognition, and social reality pose strong adjustment in the OTHER IN MY VIEW WE mechanism. Otherwise, the moderating effect of interaction changes when there are strong conflicts between the ideas presented by the films and the Chinese audience's values or cultural concepts. An example of this can be seen in the comments, "As the film portrays women as rough and rigid, and full of ridicule, I don't like it very much. But if the gender is changed and I was a man, I would like it very much. (A77)," "I began to learn to stand by a male perspective to appreciate and admire another male body. (A74)."

Negative identification factors, combined with cognitive, motivational approaches, separately are the external and internal regulated variable conditions of Western masculinist films' cross-cultural communication effect. By influencing the relationship between the Chinese audience and the films, the internal distance of the OTHER IN MY VIEW-WE mechanism can be adjusted.

As a regulated variable, cognitive, motivational approaches' functions are predominant. They can either greatly promote or suppress the identification effects of Chinese audiences. For example, "I watched this film several times, and each time inspires me different touching (A58)," "Perhaps because I watch Hobbits first, or the vision technology development is too fast, I watched it in high expectation, but it disappoints me. In my thought, The Lord Of The Ring is not good as Hobbits (A52)."

On the other side, the strength of the negative identification factors can affect the consistency of the OTHER IN MY VIEW- WE mechanism in an inverse relationship, which is not a simple linear pairing. Only by recognizing the importance of negative identification can it ensure a good cross-cultural communication effect. It is evident in comments such as "Of course, I am not talking about homosexuality, I am talking to those who knew they are homosexual and still tangled with girls. Even with the guise of literature and art in the film, it's still unacceptable for me. (A62)," "I am not a queer viewer, nor am I kind, like an angel, I am unable to appreciate gay love from girls' pain and tears. (A77)," "Research on the Localization of Western Films, Taking Film Twelve Angry Men as an example (A78).'"

In addition, negative identification factors can dynamically adjust the influence of cognitive, motivational approaches. It shows if the negative identification factors are too much, it would profoundly impact the function of cognitive, motivational approaches. Accordingly, it leads the Chinese audience's refusal to accept films and shut down the progress of the OTHER IN MY VIEW- WE mechanism. It also can be seen in comments such as "Except for attractive background music, there are only murders, arson, theft, violence in the film. (A57)," "Two rape scenes in the film, especially the latter, are painful to watch. I hate this not as a feminist, but the plot is purely in serving of male character's disgusting fantasy (A56)."

On the contrary, the adjustment of cognitive, motivational approaches would not significantly impact the negative identification factors, as evident by comments such as "I have watched the film twice, but I am still not into it. For me, the only admirable thing about the film is the actors' performance, and the rest are all trash. (A58)."

On this basis of interpretation and practical cases study, this chapter aims not only at Western masculinist films but also at a wider range of films. These paragraphs above, combined with academia and public discussions, argue Western films' possibility to develop identification with Chinese audiences. Advocate the essential to improving film content standards first, then use universality expression to enrich audiences' empathy space. During this process, preventing offensive expression conduct in film incur culture and values dispute. Using the creativity of the creators and actors to expand the scope of transmission can increase the audience's interest. It can help western filmmakers better engage with the Chinese audience and the Chinese market.

Conclusion and Suggestion

Based on the database, we use the grounded theory to construct a model and mechanism to reward Western masculinist film cross-cultural communication activities in China. This essay demonstrates five main categories, experimental each category's function for verifying the proposed model. Then, by combing the relational structure between these five categories, this study puts forward the OTHER- OTHER IN MY VIEW- WE mechanism for audience acceptance in China to propel cross-cultural communication effect.

The inevitable trend of globalization means that cultural communication is more frequent than ever. The local transformation it brings has a profound impact on the presentation of culture in local mobility (John 1999). Among the cultural communication process, film, as one of the major mediums of cross-cultural communication, is studied in this essay to explore the modern cultural fusion between China and the West.

Focusing on the quality of film content to present a good image of the West is the primary guarantee for promoting Western film cross-cultural communication effect in China.

When considering cross-cultural communication, plots and images of films are the first components to be presented to the audience, thus having a greater impact on their evaluation of the film. Therefore, as the main media of cross-cultural communication, films need to ensure their quality of content in terms of images, soundtrack, photography, color, story rationality, etc., to generate interest.

With the help of creators and actors' attraction to increase the Chinese audience's passion for watching Western films

The audience's interest is crucial in promoting empathy and recognition for films. As an important subject of filmmaking, directors, screenwriters, and actors are powerful promoters of films' cross-cultural communication abilities. On the one hand, creators and actors with a good reputation and strong influence can generate a good initial impression. On the other hand, well-known actors and creators would have more followers, bringing more audience exposure.

Stand by the Chinese audience's perspective to expression, further expand the empathy space between China and the West

The interaction between the film and the Chinese audience proposed in this chapter is important to strengthen public and academic recognition. The more universal the contents expressed in the film, the easier it is to stimulate discussion within these two groups, and the more likely positive feedback is heard.

Pay attention to the importance of modern communication channels, actively develop them to help the Western film show up in Chinese audience

The speed and mode of presentation with films can impact cross-cultural communication effect. Therefore, straightly reach to the target audience is the most economical and efficient way to broaden cross-cultural communication. Instead of increasing publicity and exposure randomly, filming companies should be aware of the importance of overseas distribution management. Strategic corporate with suitable companies and platforms in China to obtain useful data such as users portraits to conduct a more effective viewing rate for film. Or, even coordinating with theaters to replay relatively released films with modern technology to expand upcoming film communication coverage also becomes an economic exposure.

Be alert to the possibility of negative conflicts in stabilizing the establishment of the WE mechanism

Although different cultures have been converging as globalization progresses, each country still has a strong tendency to identify and maintain its basic values, which are rarely affected by economic and technological changes, showing a certain inherent attribute. Therefore, when a film contains elements that strongly conflict with local values and culture, it is prone to arouse the audience's antipathy to interrupt the possibility of identification and empathy. Given this, it is important to prevent conflicts in culture and value during filmmaking to utilize the "WE" mechanism effectively.

Limitations and Prospects of Research

As mentioned above, the model and mechanism developed in this chapter are typically appropriate to multi-character Western masculinist films. Although it has value for the construction of film cross-cultural communication effect theory, considering the amount of coding, which is made up with comments and literature, is limited, and the subjectivity of coding cannot be avoided. Accordingly, the reliability and validity between variables and the model and mechanism need to be further tested via quantitative research.

In addition, this chapter takes Western masculinist films as the main subject for investigation, which cannot be accurately applied in any other context. Furthermore, it lacks coding from film industry employments, ethnic Chinese, and English comments. Therefore, additional study is needed to examine the cross-cultural communication factors of other foreign films and their effects in China.

Combined with cross-border thinking, this essay devotes itself to examining modern film's cross-cultural communication effect. Furthermore, we hope the model and mechanisms constructed can provide a foundation for cross-cultural communication research between China and the west. We are using films to illustrate cross-cultural communication problems, seek effective and practical solutions for the obstacles between the two cultures and help gain recognition to cultural communication under greater context.

Chapter 9
Enterprise Reform and China's Modernization

In China's modernization, enterprises have experienced a complex process of change, which has promoted or restricted the process of China's modernization. From the perspective of government function adjustment, this chapter studies the enterprise transformation process in China's modernization from a historical perspective. It is found that although micro problems such as corporate governance and principal-agent are very important, they are only the second problem. The first problem should be the adjustment of government functions. The transformation practice of western countries has also proved the importance of flexible adjustment of government functions. In China, during the imperial period, enterprises in modern China did not develop due to the failure of government function adjustment. Thus, to catch up with and surpass the world powers, the new China after 1949 adopted a planned economic system, which is reasonable in the path. The Chinese government carried out the social transformation of market economy orientation after 1979. From then, the enterprises have become modern enterprises in the market economy. The findings of this chapter are of great significance to enhance the institutional innovation of enterprises and promote the process of China's modernization.

Introduction

As Madison (2007) pointed out, as early as the 10th century, China was already a prominent country in the world economy regarding per capita income, and it lasted until the 15th century. In terms of technology, the development and utilization of natural resources, and its vast territory's management ability, China has surpassed Europe. This kind of leadership in history is based on agricultural civilization. European countries gradually surpassed China in per capita income, technology, and scientific capacity with industrialization in the subsequent modernization process. The transcendence of China by western countries is closely related to the industrial revolution. In industrial society, the main organization undertaking the task of wealth creation is enterprise.

In the process of China's modernization, to make China strong again, the pursuit of strong industrial production capacity has always been the goal of Chinese people of insight. However, strong industrial production capacity is realized by the organization of enterprises. Therefore, to study China's modernization process, we must study China's enterprise reform.

Modern enterprises originated in western countries. Therefore, the research results of western economists on enterprises need to be analyzed. In western countries, economists' researches on enterprises are as follows:

First, the scope of enterprises. Coase (1937) argued that allocating resources through authority or command within the enterprise is remarkable. While in the market, resource allocation is carried out through the price mechanism. However, many long-term contractual relationships blur the boundary between the market and enterprises. It may be more useful to treat enterprises as special types of interrelated contracts (Klein et al. 1978). Enterprises adopt the multiproduct feature due to market failure and excess capacity (Teece 1982).

Second, employment relationships and internal organization. Alchian and Demsetz (1972) argued that the essential feature of the enterprise is not the relationship under the control of authority but a contract organization or team nature. As the enterprise owner, the capitalist enjoys the residual claim, is the central employer and central contractor, and is the final supervisor of team production activities. Cheung (1983) reinterpreted Coase's enterprise theory. He argued that it is not entirely accurate to say that enterprises can replace the market. It is exact to use one contract replaces another contract." The market has limitations in the qualification evaluation of employees within enterprises. Because the direct superior is familiar with the characteristics of employees, the hierarchical structure of enterprise employment relationships has advantages (Williamson et al., 2009).

Third, control of the enterprise. Grossman and Hart (1986) noted that an enterprise is composed of assets owned or controlled by it. Ownership is control. The enterprise explained by neoclassical economics is only a cartoon of modern enterprises. The various methods used by economists to solve enterprise problems - neoclassical, principal-agent, transaction costs, contractual relationships and property rights seem to be integrating (Hart 1989). The continuous evolution of ownership arrangement aims to meet enterprises' need for capital, risk-taking and decision-making services. It reflects the needs of agency problems. Production workers have less control, which may be due to the limited wealth of workers and the need to diversify investment to reduce costs (Putterman 1993).

Can the research results of western economists explain enterprise reform in the process of China's modernization? The practice of each stage of market economy development in western countries has proved that adjusting government functions is an important prerequisite for the development of modern enterprises in the market economy. In the period of free competition, the restriction of royal power by the constitutional system led to the British Industrial Revolution and the emergence of modern enterprises. In the period of acute class opposition, it is precise because of the government's legislation on the market and the establishment of the social welfare system that acute class opposition can be eased and modern enterprises can develop. During the monopoly period, the government's attack on monopoly made the market economy compete again, and modern enterprises developed further. After World War II, the government's comprehensive intervention brought the market economy back on track, western countries entered the rule of law stage, and modern enterprises grew. Therefore, adjusting government functions is the main reason for the smooth development of modern enterprises in western countries.

Looking back on the historical process of China's modernization, enterprises problems were not coming from themselves at the beginning but closely combined with the functions of the government. China's modern enterprises did not appear because of government function adjustment failure in China's Qing Dynasty. The gap between China and developed countries is becoming larger and larger. Therefore, the enterprise reform in China's modernization essentially adjusts government functions. Therefore, when studying the enterprise reform in China's modernization, we can and must choose to study it historically and dynamically from government function adjustment. Based on this logic, this chapter chooses to study the enterprise reform in China's modernization from government function adjustment.

Reasons for Hindering the Growth during the Imperial Rule

Traditionally, China is a country based on agriculture, ruled by emperors who exercise power on behalf of the government. During the Qing Dynasty, there were three types of enterprises in China. During the Westernization Movement, they were royal enterprises, small handicrafts, and government-run enterprises.

The government-controlled the production of royal enterprises during the Chinese imperial dynasty. Salt, porcelain, and silk products were directly related to the consumption of the royal family. Their craftsmen were from military artisans, not the commodity economy. The existence of these official Enterprises was tightly linked with power, which could not stimulate the development of a market economy, but was an obstacle.

From the perspective of the small handicraft industry, the huge population has created a stable small-scale peasant economic structure and stabilized at a low equilibrium level. Due to the limitations of small-scale peasant economy in capital accumulation, its operation law is completely contrary to the capitalist market economy in western countries. The result can only be decapitalization, which further solidifies the structure of a small-scale peasant economy. Thus, small handicrafts can't develop into modern enterprises.

During the Westernization Movement, a group of enlightened officials represented by Zeng Guofan, Li Hongzhang, Zuo Zongtang and Zhang Zhidong established many modern enterprises run by the government more than 30 years since 1861. The earliest was the military industry and then established new civil enterprises in the forms of "official run," "official supervised commercial run," and "official commercial run," of which "official supervised commercial run" is the main form. These enterprises used hired labor and introduced machinery, equipment and technology from developed countries. They are different from the official enterprises in feudal society. They are the earliest modern enterprises in China. However, these enterprises are subject to the supervision and control of the government and have no autonomy. They follow the habits of feudal yamen bureaucrats in the internal management system. The enterprises are full of overstaffing, corruption and so on, resulting in low production efficiency. In addition, in terms of firm governance structure, in the official supervised commercial enterprises, the decision-making power, supervision power and personnel appointment and removal power are concentrated in the hands of the government, and the commercial shareholders are in a weak position. In such enterprises, the contradiction between officials and business people is the major problem. Ordinary business people often have scruples when investing in such enterprises. The emerging enterprises in the Westernization Movement had the characteristics of the capitalist market economy. Therefore, these enterprises belong to the new enterprise form. However, bureaucratic vices have profoundly affected these new ventures in terms of business results. The economic effect of enterprises, therefore, is very poor. Many of them cannot last for a few years. So such enterprises are not modern enterprises in essence.

In sum, in the imperial period, the bureaucratic system under the emperor's rule constituted a solid system, which firmly bound the development of the modern market economy and hindered the growth of modern enterprises. Under the constraints of this system, due to the lack of government function adjustment, small handicrafts could not grow into modern enterprises. The official enterprises of the westernization movement could not evolve into modern enterprises.

Enterprises in the Period of the Republic of China

During the Republic of China (1912-1948), from the Beiyang government, which was the first Chinese government recognized internationally after the fall of the Qing Dynasty to the Kuomintang of China (KMT), which was founded in 1894 by Sun Yat-sen, it began a difficult exploration process under the chaos of internal and external difficulties. The transformation of enterprises is carried out in both government-run enterprises and private enterprises.

The Dilemma of Government-Run Enterprises

With the change of the Beiyang government and the Kuomintang, the ownership of some government-run enterprises established during the Westernization Movement also changed, such as China Merchants Shipping Group and Daqing Bank (reorganized into the Bank of China during the Kaiyuan Period). The owners changed several times, but they had a close relationship with the regimes in various periods. In terms of property rights, the property rights of these State-Owned enterprises are vague, and the responsibilities of shareholders, boards of directors and managers are not clear. The change of government has a significant impact on the enterprises. It also affects the sustainability of the development policies of state-owned enterprises.

In the Republic of China, the power of the warlord government was higher than the rules of the market economy. Therefore, political power is higher than private property rights in market transactions. When the government nationalizes private enterprises, it is often not based on negotiation. Still, it uses power to set prices unilaterally. The price is lower than the market price, resulting in damage to the interests of private shareholders and no protection of private property rights.

There is no effective supervision and restriction mechanism regarding enterprise governance structure, and rent-seeking activities and insider control are intertwined. It means that the enterprises lack an effective governance structure. In essence, these state-owned enterprises are not modern enterprises.

The Plight of Private Enterprises

During the period of the Republic of China, wars continued. As far as the government is concerned, the warlord government changes frequently, the situation is turbulent, and thus there is a lack of the most basic market economic order. In this context, the development of private enterprises is very difficult. However, many excellent private enterprises and entrepreneurs have arisen even in this dilemma. For example, Jian Zhang's Dasheng cotton mill, the Jane brothers' Nanyang Tobacco Company, the Rong family's flour processing, Xudong Fan's Jiuda and Yongli salt and alkali industry are all representatives of China's national capital class. However, in the environment of the Japanese invasion, bureaucratic plunder and banditry later, the market order was chaotic, and these private enterprises were very difficult.

As far as the consumer market is concerned, the social security system has not been established in extensive rural areas due to the absence of government functions. As the main means of production of agricultural society, possession of land is unequal. Coupled with the impact of disasters, war and inflation, the output value and income fluctuate violently. They can only barely make a living and have no surplus to deal with frequent accidents. Therefore, the consumer market is very limited. Under the dilemma of foreign invasion, people's livelihood declined due to the constant war. As such, neither government-run enterprises nor private enterprises could obtain sufficient development space.

"Decentralization" during the Planned Economy Period

Although the country achieved independence and sovereign integrity after the founding of New China in 1949, the international situation was still very severe. The key to the survival of New China is whether the military industry can be built quickly.

The rapid construction of the military industry is inseparable from advanced scientific and technological strength and financial strength, and a large number of talents. Under the long-term imperial rule and in successive years of wars, the People's Republic of China was very poor and lacked technical talents. Based on these objective realities, China chose the Soviet planning system. In 1953, the general line for the transitional period was proposed. It was planned to take 15 years. But in fact, it took less than three years to realize the socialist transformation of private capitalist industry and commerce and establish a planned economic system in an all-around way. At this time, enterprises have become appendages of government plans and have lost their independence.

After establishing a planned economic system based on state ownership, the Chinese government has not stopped exploring the construction of state-owned enterprises. From 1958 to 1976, the key content of the reform was to try to adjust power and interests among governments at all levels while maintaining the resources allocated by administrative orders. For example, the decentralization of power in the 1958 economic management system includes planning power, corporate jurisdiction, material distribution power, investment and credit management power, fiscal and tax power, labor-management power, etc. The Chinese government has appropriately taken some measures to delegate power to enterprises. However, various localities and units competed for resources and worked separately, the production order was in chaos, and economic efficiency fell sharply. At the end of 1958, many industrial and commercial enterprises fell into losses, and the economy encountered serious difficulties. As a result, in the early 1960s, the central government re-established a highly centralized system. Although the economy was stabilized and restored, the drawbacks of the centralized planned economic system reappeared, and it was compelled to carry out reforms again. In 1970, the system was "decentralized" again, and the economy repeated the situation in 1958. After 1971, the central government once again centralized power. The past 20 years have proved to be a mess when released and death when withdrawn. Under the planned economy system, China abolished the market economy, and enterprises became the executive units of government plans without autonomy. Because there is no market competition, there is no sufficient information index that can accurately reflect the enterprise's business performance. Judging from the practice results, under this kind of institutional arrangement without autonomy, the biggest shortcoming of state-owned enterprises is the lack of incentives for innovative activities. Although China has successfully developed the "two bombs and one satellite award," it is only limited to the strategic industries that the country focuses on during that time. Meanwhile, the patriotic passion of scientific researchers is also the reason for their selfless dedication. As for most civilian industries, such as color TVs, motorcycles, automobiles and other industries, during the planned economy period, the gap between China and developed countries is getting wider and wider.

The planned economy allocates resources through administrative orders and essentially requires centralized power. If power is decentralized, the enthusiasm of lower-level governments can be mobilized in the short term. However, decentralization soon exposed the drawbacks of not only harming the unification of government orders but also promoting local protectionism, forming a "princely economy." Therefore, the best way is to carry out market-oriented reform and establish a market economic system in which the market plays a fundamental role in allocating resources.

Changes in the Corporate System after Reform and Opening-up

After the reform and opening up, the reform of China's state-owned enterprises evaded ownership for a long period. It did not touch the original ownership system, called the "delegating power and transferring profits" stage.

Expand Enterprise Autonomy (1978-1992)

Following the reform direction proposed at the Third Plenary Session of the eleventh Central Committee, the Chinese government has promoted expanding operational autonomy pilot projects. It is contracting with increasing profits, profit reform and taxation, and contract management responsibility system, to adjust the responsibilities, rights and relations between the state and enterprises. This reform is carried out within the framework of not changing the original ownership, and it is only an adjustment of interests between the government and enterprises. Decentralization of power and transfer of interests have aroused the enthusiasm of managers and employees in production and operation. It enhances the vitality of firms and lays a preliminary foundation for enterprises to enter the market. However, serious negative problems have also emerged. For example, during implementing the contracting and leasing system, the situation of enterprise efficiency, economic growth, and decline in national fiscal revenue appeared, which aroused reflections from all walks of life.

In contracting and leasing, the state and enterprises have an unequal contractual relationship, and the government has insufficient information. In addition, the cost of one-to-one negotiation between the government and the enterprise is very high, and it is impossible to stipulate the details of the contract and lease contract one by one. Thus, business operators can pursue the maximization of their interests legally or illegally under contracting and leasing rights, disregarding the state's interests. These opportunistic behaviors are difficult for the government to restrain. From the perspective of business incentives, enterprises only bear profits, not losses, which reduce the national fiscal revenue and cause the short-term behavior of contractors and leasers. Even if a corresponding supervisory agency is established, the administrative cost is very high.

According to the theory of property rights, decentralization and profit distribution will adjust the residual control rights. It will also adjust the creditor's rights of the state and enterprises. In the residual control power aspect, although the state has increased the power of corporate leaders, it still maintains control over the major investment in companies and personnel matters through relevant departments. On the other hand, from the point of view of residual claim rights, since corporate leaders have not made equity investment, so as for capital investment, corporate leaders can only "gain profits" and not "take losses." Only the owners and banks of the company can "take a loss." And for the company leaders, only the level of their bonuses will be affected.

Furthermore, in terms of effect, the "delegating power and transferring profits" has re-adjusted property rights between the state and enterprises to a certain extent and improved the incentive effect under the planned economy system. And in terms of business decision-making, because enterprise leaders have a certain degree of autonomy, the efficiency of firms has improved in a certain period. However, the reform of delegating powers and transferring profits did not change the basic system of state-owned enterprises. It could not effectively solve many of the deep-seated problems related to the system of state-owned enterprises. In the end, it entered an unexpected dilemma: "decentralization" has led to the phenomenon of corporate leaders' departmentalism and "inside control," then to change these negative phenomena, the relevant government departments have to strengthen the control of enterprises, which is in contradiction with the policy orientation of "decentralization."

System Innovation Stage（1992—2002）

The dilemma of reforms is evident from the operating performance of state-owned enterprises, whose profits continued to decline in the 1990s, with one-third profits, one-third losses, and one-third false profits with actual losses (Chang et al., 2018). In the face of this situation, the reform of state-owned enterprises has reached a time of "no making without breaking." Further study on the causes of state-owned enterprises' losses has been carried out. It finds out that the losses between 1989 and 1994 were related to macroeconomic contraction at home and abroad, not just state-owned enterprises operations. However, after 1994, the economic situation improved, but they still suffered losses in general and even worsened year by year. The macroeconomy causes it, but the fundamental reason should be institutional arrangements.

A series of highly innovative achievements on state-owned enterprise reforms emerged in large numbers. Meanwhile, many theories were put forward during this period, such as the shareholding system, classification reform, property rights reform, human capital property rights, and market competition theory, etc. Specifically, the classification reform and property rights reform argue that state-owned enterprises withdraw from competitive fields, while competition theory emphasizes the importance of market competition. From the international background, the privatization trend of state-owned companies since the 1990s has significantly impacted the reform theory of Chinese state-owned enterprises (Lin 2021; Kwon and Kim, 2017; Chen et al. 2014; Hovey, Martin & Naughton, 2006). Therefore, the reform idea of advocating privatization prevailed before 2002.

In a market economy, a modern enterprise combines a set of contracts, stipulating a distribution of stakeholders' interests. Among them, ownership of equity is one of the key contracts. Although the concept of shareholder interest is challenged, equity is still the main basis for determining the residual claim and control of the enterprise in practice. In the last decade of the 20th century, property rights reforms were blustery. Starting from the "Zhucheng model," many state-owned small and middle-sized enterprises have carried out ownership reform, and "enterprise reform" has been put on the agenda. Ownership reform is an objective choice when state-owned enterprises face severe situations. "Decentralization of benefits" is no longer effective. Before 2000, the reformation was dominated by small and medium-sized enterprises (SMEs). And they gradually turned into large enterprises after 2000. As of the 16th National Congress of the Communist Party of China in 2002, more than 80% of China's state-owned SMEs had completed their restructuring and turned into private enterprises. After privatization, the government no longer had any property rights related to these enterprises, and the government gave the ownership and profit rights to the market.

Comprehensively Deepening Reform Stage（2003—2021）

In practice, this movement of state-owned property rights transactions and the entry of a private economy has aroused great debate. This completely privatized state-owned enterprise reformatting was suppressed after 2004. To solve the problem of the absence of owners, the Chinese government established the State-owned Assets Supervision and Administration Commission of the Stata Council (SASAC) in 2003. It can be seen as a special case starting from the reform of the enterprise management system to solve the problem of the reform of state-owned enterprises.

Under the leadership of the SASAC, although the reformatting of state-owned enterprises is still in progress, it is partly private with diversified property rights. Promoting the listing of large and medium-sized state-owned enterprises through the capital market has become the main form. In addition, the corporate governance structure of state-owned enterprises has been gradually improved. A mechanism has been established whereby shareholders' meetings, boards of directors, supervisors, and managers assume their respective responsibilities, coordinate their operations, and effectively check and balance the operations.

With the reform of state-owned enterprises, private enterprises have developed rapidly. It starts to occupy an important position in China's national economy. In 2018, President Xi Jinping stressed that the private economy has the characteristics of "5679", that is, the private economy contributes more than 50 percent of tax revenue, more than 60 percent of GDP, more than 70 percent of technological innovation, and more than 80 percent of urban labor employment. In other words, the private economy has become the main field of entrepreneurship and employment, an important source of technological innovation, and a crucial source of national taxation.

Both state-owned and private enterprises are important foundations for China's economic and social development and should be treated equally. In most sectors of the national economy, state-owned and private enterprises will face each other, compete, cooperate, and even merge. In this situation, the government proposed vigorously developing a mixed-ownership economy involving state-owned capital and non-public capital in 2013. The integration of state-owned and private enterprises is still in constant exploration at present. It is the same relationship between the State-owned Assets Supervision and Administration Commission and state-owned enterprises. It reflects that there is still uncertainty in the definition between government functions and the market mechanism.

Basic Experience of Chinese Enterprise Reform

This chapter focused on revealing historical and practical logic based on government function adjustment, summarized the historical experience and shortcomings in the development and transformation of enterprises in

China's modernization, and attached importance to the grasp and refinement of ownership reform government-enterprise relations. The results provide an empirical basis for the reformation of Chinese enterprise systems and the comprehensive construction of socialist modernization in the new era. Through summarizing and combing, it is found that: Firstly, government function adjustment has a fundamental role in promoting or inhibiting enterprise transformation. Whether it was the transition from an agricultural society to an industrial society or from a planned economic system to a market economic system, it is precise because of government function adjustment failure that modern Chinese enterprises have not developed. Secondly, to change the status quo of backwardness and achieve catch-up, the People's Republic of China adopted a planned economic system that sacrificed the independence of enterprises.

The system has a certain degree of rationality which realized the emergence of agriculture, industry, and transportation and thus laid a solid foundation for the advancement of modernization. However, the planned economy system regards the enterprise as an adjunct of the administrative department. It leads to the problems of insufficient power and vitality of the enterprise system. Therefore, after 1979, to improve the innovation enthusiasm of enterprises, the Chinese government carried out the social transformation toward the market economy. The state-owned enterprises' reform has shifted from decentralization to institutional innovation in this process. Since modern times, with the building of a well-off society in an all-around way, China has embarked on a new journey of building a modern socialist country in an all-around way. The enterprise also makes up the system defect in the management mechanism unceasingly. It truly becomes the modern enterprise in the market economy.

The world today is undergoing major changes in a century. It is necessary to have both a sense of risk and anxiety and historical opportunity. The novel Coronavirus disease, the global economic recession, the rise of unilateralism and protectionism not only mean that we must seize the opportunities of the new scientific and technological revolution and the rapid development of industrial reform. Thus, firstly, it is important to enhance Chinese society's transformation process further and build a high-level socialist market economy system. In particular, it is necessary to vigorously improve the level of the rule of law in the market economy and promote the transformation of the government's market role by further improving the rules and regulations and establishing a relevant legislative evaluation mechanism to create a legalized business environment.

Secondly, improve the socialist market economic system and strive to achieve the optimal allocation of resources. Make full use of the domestic and international markets and resources, and accelerate the construction of a new development pattern in which the big domestic cycle is the main body. The domestic and international double cycles promote each other. Give full play to integration and synergy, and actively promote the comprehensive docking of the consumer Internet and the industrial Internet.

Thirdly, actively develop the mixed-ownership economy. Explore a corporate governance mechanism in which capitals of different natures can be deeply integrated and realize fair competition and common development between the state-owned and private economies. Create more and more large Chinese enterprises with international competitiveness.

Finally, speed up the construction of science and technology power, realize high-level scientific and technological self-reliance, and enhance the overall effectiveness of the national innovation system. The forerunner of the fourth wave of the industrial revolution represented by intelligence and deep learning has arrived. Enterprises must accelerate their pace of adapting to the industrial revolution, enhance their competitiveness in artificial intelligence, green manufacturing, and big data security for modernization, and provide innovation momentum for modernization.

Afterword

After years of development, China has scored remarkable achievements in its modernization drive. On the world stage, China is playing a more important role. Therefore, periodical research and a summary of theories and practices in China's modernization process can be transformed into a powerful driving force for China's high-quality development. By introducing this book, which embodies China's recent development experience and lessons, to the world, other countries can gain useful reference and inspiration from it, thus contributing to the common development and progress of humankind.

This project was supported by the leaders of Huaihua College and Jishou University. Drs. Tian Guang, Lo Hong Long, and Chen Qian carefully edited the book with the efforts of all participants. Dr. Tian is a professor of business administration at Huaihua University, Hunan, China. He earned his Ph. D. in Economic Anthropology from York University, Ontario, Canada, in 1995 and used to work as a professor at colleges in Canada and the US. His major research interest is Economical Anthropology, Regional Development, and Cross-Cultural Administration. He has published over one hundred academic articles in peer-reviewed referral journals and authored and co-authored 25 books published in English and Chinese.

Dr. Luo works for Culture & History administration at Jishou University as a professor and the dean. He also is a visiting professor at Duke University, doctoral supervisor of Sun Yat-sen University and Jishou University. He has published over one hundred academic articles in more influential journals, authored and co-authored more than 20 books about Ecological Anthropology and Cultural Anthropology.

Dr. Chen, a lecturer of Culture & History administration at Jishou University, Hunan, China, earned her Ph. D. in Ecological Anthropology from Jishou University in 2018. Her major research interest is in Ecological Anthropology, Agricultural Cultural Heritage.

References

Abdi, Shadee. and Calafell, Bernadette Marie. (2017). Queer utopias and a (Feminist) Iranian vampire: a critical analysis of resistive monstrosity in A Girl Walks Home Alone at Night. Critical Studies in Media Communication. doi:10.1080/15295036.2017.1302092

Acemoglu, D. and Guerrieri, V. (2008). Capital Deepening and Nonbalanced Economic Growth. Journal of Political Economy, 116(3):467—498.

Acemoglue, D., and J. A. Robinson. 2013. *Why nations fail: The origins of power, prosperity and poverty*. London: Profile Books Ltd.

Alberti, F. G., and J. D. Giusti. 2012. Cultural heritage, tourism and regional competitiveness: The Motor Valley cluster. *City, Culture and Society*, 3(4): 261-273.

Alchian, A. A., & Demsetz, H. (1972). Production, information costs, and economic organization. *IEEE Engineering Management Review,* 62(2), 777-795. Available at: https://www.jstor.org/stable/1815199

Altonji, J. G., and Siow, A. (1987). Testing the Response of Consumption to Income Changes with (noisy) Panel Data. Quarterly Journal of Economics 102 (2): 293-328.

Yn, Y. and Fu, Y.Y. (2020). Regional Perspective and Emotional Framework: An Analysis of the Chinese Film and Television Culture Spreading Framework in South Korea. Modern Communication (Journal of Communication University of China), 42(06), 101-109.

Appadurai, A. (1986). Introduction: commodities and the politics of value. The Social Life of Things: Commodities in Cultural Perspective. New York: Cambridge University Press.

Baba, M. L. (1986). Business and industrial anthropology: an overview. Washington, DC: American Anthropological Association.

Babaii, E., and Asadnia, F. (2021). "If a black hole is an oyster, then. ": The discoursal trends of popularization in science fiction movies. Retrieved from https://orcid.org/0000-0001-9998-824710.1177/.

Baek, H., Oh, S., Yang, HD. And Ahn, J. (2017). Electronic word-of-mouth, box office revenue and social media. Electronic Commerce Research and Applications,22,13-23.

Bairoch P. (1988) *Cities and Economic Development: From Dawn of History to the Present.* Univ. of Chicago Press, Chicago, 1988 (English translation by Christopher Braider).

Baldwin, R.E. and Martin, P. (2004). *Agglomeration and regional growth.* In: Henderson, Vernon J., Thisse, Jacques-François (Eds.), Handbook of Regional and Urban Economics, vol. 4: Cities and Geography. Elsevier, North-Holland.

Bao, Hong, and Bi, Fangning. (2016). A strategic conception of "one belt and one road" under the perspective of Marx's doctrine. *Motherland*, 2016 (15): 116-117.

Bao, Jin (2012). Marx's Thought of "Consumption, Production and Production" and Its Enlightenment to Contemporary Times. Discussion on Modern Economy, 2012 (04): 50-53.

Bennett R. J. (1997) Administrative Systems and Economic Spaces, *Regional Studies*, Vol. 31.3, 323- 336.

BIELBY, D. D. and BIELBY, W. T. (1996). WOMEN AND MEN IN FILM: Gender Inequality Among Writers in a Culture Industry. Gender & Society, 10, 248-270.

Boivin， N. （2008）. Material Cultures, Material Minds: The Impact of Things Human Thought, Society, and Evolution. New York: Cambridge University Press.

Bourdieu, P. （1986）. The forms of capital. In Richardson, J (Ed), Handbook of Theory and Research for the sociology of education. Westport, CT: Greenwood Press.

Boyle, Ellexis., Millington, Brad, and Vertinsky, Patricia. (2006). Representing the Female Pugilist: Narratives of Race, Gender, and Disability in Million Dollar Baby. Sociology of Sport Journal, 23,99-116.

Bu, Xiting, and Qi, Ji（2013）. The Cultural Path of New Urbanization. Modern Communication, Vol. 2013 (07).

Buleca J. and Mura L. (2014) Quantification of the efficiency of public administration by data envelopment analysis. Procedia Economics and Finance 15, 162 – 168.

Cai, Fang (2019). Contributing Chinese wisdom to the relationship between government and market. *Theory Guide*,2019 (1): 16-18.

Carroll, C.D. (1994). How does future income affect current consumption? Quarterly Journal of Economics 109 (1): 111-147.

Chang, X. Z., Chang, X., Wen, Z.Y., Yu, J.G., Chen, Y.J., and Li, D. W. (2018). *Ownership reform and innovation-40 years of reform of China's ownership structure*, China: Guangdong Economic Publishing House.

Chen H.F and Zhang L.C. (2012) Shantou Daily 5 edition special reports on prospect of "agglomeration of Shantou, Chaozhou and Jieyang." Shantou Daily.

Chen J.B. and Zhao J.M. (2011) Thinking on the economic growth of Xiamen in the "12th Five-year Plan" – implications of the economic aggregate growth of other cities with independent planning, *Journal of the Party School of CPC Xiamen Municipal*, (06), 51-54.

Chen, C. W., and Zhao, X. Z. (2014). Social Governance: A Sociological Assessment of a Concept and Its Implications. Journal of Social Science of Hunan Normal University, Vol. 43(5):11-18.

Chen, Charles J. P., Du, Jun and Su, Xijia. (2014). A game of accounting numbers in asset pricing: Evidence from the privatization of state-owned enterprises. *Journal of Contemporary Accounting & Economics*, 10(2), doi: 10.1016/j.jcae.2014.05.001.

Chen, Feng (2005). Non-Mainstream Perspectives on China's Urbanization. City Planning Review, Vol. 2015 (12).

Chen, Gang (2012). The Influence of Tourism Development on Local Ethnic Relations in Multi-ethnic Regions--A Case Study of Lugu Lake in Sichuan, Yunnan, China. Journal of Tourism, 2012 (5): 94-102.

Chen, J., Chen, XT., Chao, XR.and Wang, HM. (2021). How electronic word of mouth dynamically influences product sales and supplies: an Evidence from China film industry, Economic Research-Ekonomska Istrazivanja. Retrieved from https://10.1080/1331677X.2021.1931910.

Chen, Q. (2018). Study on the value of Miao cultural resources in ecological poverty alleviation--Taking Zila village in Huawuan County as an example. Jishou University, 185.

Chen, Q., and Huang, X. F. (2020). Study on Innovative Inheritance Value of Agricultural Cultural Heritage from the Case of Zila Rice Tribute. Guizhou Ethnic Studies, Vol. 42(1):82-84.

Chen, Qingde (2012). Economic Anthropology. Beijing: People's Publishing House.

Chen, Yingfang (2004). Questions on Urbanization. Reading, Vol. 2004 (02).

Chen, Yingfang (2012). The Logic of Urban China. Beijing: SDX Joint Publishing Company. Chen, Yumei (1996). Cultural Contact and Material Culture Change: An Ethnoarchaeological Example from the Yami in Orchid Island, Taiwan. Bulletin of the Institute of History and Philology Academia Sinica, Vol. 2012 (06).

Cheng, Meibao (2014). How the Country "Escapes": The Paradox of Civil Society in China. Chinese Social Sciences Today, October 14, 2010, 11th Edition.

Cheung, S. (1983). The contractual nature of the firm. *Journal of Law and Economics,* 26(1). https://www.jstor.org/stable/725182?seq=1#metadata_info_tab_contents

China National Bureau of Statistics (2019). Significant Improvement of International Status and Continuous Enhancement of International Influence. http://www.stats.gov.cn/tjsj/zxfb/201908/t20190829_1694202.html, accessed in Dec. 2019.

China National Railway Corporation (2020). Railway statistical bulletin.

Chiu, YL., Chen, KH., Wang, JN. and Hsu, YT. (2019). The impact of online movie word-of-mouth on consumer choice A comparison of American and Chinese consumers. International Marketing Review,36, 996-1025.

Chung, J., and Eoh, J. (2019). Naming strategies as a tool for communication: application to movie titles. International Journal of Advertising,1139-1152.

Coase, R. H. (1937). The nature of the firm. *Economica, 4*(16), 386-405.

Cohen, D. and Soto, M. (2007). Growth and Human Capital: Good Data, Good Results. Journal of Economic Growth, 12(1):51—76.

Corresponding author: Wang Yazhou (1994 -), male, Han nationality, from Yulin, Shaanxi Province, Ph.D. candidate at Shinawatra University, Thailand, engaged in management research.

Dasgupta, S., and B. Gupta. 2019. Espoused organizational culture values as antecedents of internet technology. *Information and Management*, forthcoming.

Deiffield N. and Hughes D. (2003) Foreign and Domestic Investment: Regional Development or Crowding Out? *Regional Studies*, Vol. 37.3, 277–288. DOI: 10.1080/0034340032000065433.

del Barrio, M., M. Devesa., and L. C. Herrero. 2012. Evaluating intangible cultural heritage: The case of cultural festivals. *City, Culture and Society*, 3: 235-244.

Deng Zhiyang. (2004) Agglomeration of the regional public management and administrative resources of the great Pearl River Delta city agglomeration economic circle, *South China Journal of Economy*, (02), 55-58.

Department of Floating Population of National Health and Family Planning Commission of the People's Republic of China (2013). 2013 Report on China's Migrant Population Development. Beijing: China Population Publishing House.

Department of Housing and Urban-Rural Development of Chuxiong Yi Autonomous Prefecture (2014). Plan for New Urbanization in Chuxiong Yi Autonomous Prefecture (2014-2020). http://www.cxjs.net/file_read.aspx?id=2267.

Diamond, P. (1967). The Role of a Stock Market in a General Equilibrium Model with Technical Uncertainty. American Economic Review 57: 759-776.

Ding, H., C. Qin., and K. Shi., 2018. Development through electrification: Evidence from rural China. *China Economic Review*, 50: 313-328.

Ding, Yuanzhu (2014). Fei Xiaotong's Thoughts on Urbanizations: Characteristics and Enlightenment. Jianghai Academic Journal, Vol. 2014 (01).

DKJ, Donnelly. (2019). Film music: Critical approaches.

Dong, Defu and Su, Yu. (2018). "The Chinese Dream" and "the World Dream" are in common and win-win situations: An analysis based on the concept of "Community with a Shared Future for Mankind." *Journal of Jiangsu University (Social Science Edition)*, 2018, 20 (3): 6-11.

Dong, Yang, and Wang, Juan (2014). Seeing Like a State to Seeing of Social Constructionist: An Overview of New Urbanization. Urban Development Studies, Vol. 2014 (03).

Du, Shuhai (2014). Between the Hill People and the State: A Critical Review of James C.Scott's Study on Zomia. World Ethno-National Studies, Vol. 2014 (02).

Du, X.M., and Chen, Q. D. (2016). Gathering Economy from the Perspective of Economic Anthropology: A Case Study from Dulong River Gorge. Ethno-National Studies, Vol. 41(1):82-84.

Duan, Chengrong (1998). Theories and Methods of Research on Population Migration. Chongqing: Chongqing Publishing House.

Duong, L. (2015). Close up: The female gaze and ethnic difference in two Vietnamese women's films. Journal of Southeast Asian Studies, 46(3), 444-462.

Easton D.(1989) A System Analysis of Political Life. Beijing: Huaxia Publishing House, pp.492.

Erk, SM., Toet, A. and Van Erp, JBF. (2015). Effects of mediated social touch on affective experiences and trust. Retrieved from10.7717/peerj.1297.

Fairbank, John King, and Reischauer, Edwin Oldfather (1992). China Tradition and Transformation. Nanjing: Jiangsu People's Publishing House.

Fan, Jida (2019). China's Consumption Shows Four Significant Changes. Beijing Daily, April 08, 2019:14.

Fan, S., Zhang, X. 2004. Infrastructure and regional economic development in China. *China Economic Review*, 15(2): 203-214.

Fang, J. W. (2017). A review of social governance research in ethnic areas. Minzu Tribune, Vol. 35(4):100-106.

Fei, Xiaotong (1993). Reflections on the socio-economic development of ethnic groups in border areas. Journal of Peking University (Philosophy and Social Sciences Edition), 1993 (1): 12-20.

Fei, Xiaotong (1996). On the Development of Small Towns in China. Construction of Small Towns, 1996 (3): 40-43.

Fei, Xiaotong (1997). A Brief Introduction to My Experience and Reflection on Ethnic Studies. Journal of Peking University: Philosophy and Social Sciences, 1997 (2): 5-13.

Fei, Xiaotong (2001). Role and significance of human resources in the development of western China. Literature and Art Research, 2001 (2): 4-10.

Fei, Xiaotong (2002). Promoting balanced development between the east and the west and achieving common prosperity for all nationalities. Comments, 2000 (9): 6-9.

Fei, Xiaotong (2003). Some Confessions on "Cultural Consciousness." Academic Research, 2003 (7): 31-33.

Fei, Xiaotong (2004). Anthropology and Cultural Consciousness. Nanjing: Huaxia Publishing House, 2004.

Fei, Xiaotong, Dai, Kejing (2012). Peasant Life in China: The Life of Chinese Farmers. Beijing: Peking University Press, 2012.

Feng, W., Y. Liu., and L. Qu. (2019). Effect of land-centered urbanization on rural development: A regional analysis in China. *Land Use Policy*, forthcoming.

Flavin, M. (1981). The Adjustment of Consumption to Changing Expectations about Future Income. Journal of Political Economy, Vol. 89: 974-1009.

Fu, S.Y. (2013) Study on Evaluation and Selection of Our Country's Urban Advantageous Industries and Comparision of Their Competitiveness-- Based on analysis of Dalian, Qingdao, Ningbo, Xiamen Shenzhen 5 Separate Planning Cities' Panel Date. Qingdao University of Science and Technology (Master's degree).

Gao, P. (2020).Analysis of the modernization path for social governance. Public Relations Exploration, Vol. 21(24):171.

Gell A. (1998). Art and Agency: Towards a New Anthological Theory. Oxford: Clarendon Press.

Gopinath, Gayatri. (2000). Queering Bollywood. Journal of Homosexuality, 39(3-4), 283-297.

Grossman, S. J., & Hart, O. D. (1986). The costs and benefits of ownership: a theory of vertical and lateral integration. *Journal of Political Economy, 94*(4), 691-719.

Gu, A. H., and Wu, Z. J. (2017). Study on the Feature and Path Design of the Modern National Governance System with Chinese

Characteristics. The Journal of Shanghai Administration Institute, Vol. 18(02):78-80.

Guccio, C., D. Lisi, D., M. Martorana., and A. Mignosa. 2017. On the role of cultural participation in tourism destination performance: An assessment using robust conditional efficiency approach. *Journal of Cultural Economics*, 41(2): 129-154.

Gunn, W, Otto T, Smith R C. (2015). Design Anthropology: Theory and Practice. Journal of Design History, 2015(10):84-97.

Guo, Hongyu. (2014). The current situation of China's economic system reform and its implementation path. *Journal of Shanxi Agricultural University (Social Science Edition)*, 2014 (08): 766-769.

Guo, Xinying. (2014). Research on the Theory and Practice of the Chinese Dream. *Young Literator*, 2014 (6): 160-160.

Hahm, J. and Steigerwals, D. G. (1999). Consumption Adjustment under Time-Varying Income Uncertainty. Review of Economics and Statistics, Vol. 81:32-40.

Han, Xu. (2013). Moral lack and path choice of the socialist market economy. *Frontier*, 2013 (5): 98-100.

Hart, K. (1996). End of the World: Anthropologists Speechless. Anthropology Today, 1996(5):1-2.

Hart, O. (1989). An economist's perspective on the theory of the firm. Columbia Law Review, 89(7), 1757-1774.

Hausman, D. M. and Michael S. M. (1996) Economic Analysis and Moral Philosophy. Cambridge: Cambridge University Press.

Hawkins, J. N. 1988. The transformation of education for rural development in China. *Comparative Education Review*, 32(3): 266-281.

Henderson J.V. (2003) The urbanization process and economic growth: the so-what question. *Journal of Economic Growth*, 847–71.

Hennessy, Mary. (2016). Fassbinder's Female Complaint: Fassbinder's Female Complaint: Martha (1974) and the 1940s' Woman's Film.' The German Quarterly, 89,67-79.

Hennig-Thurau, T., Wiertz, C. and Feldhaus, F. (2015). Does Twitter matter? The impact of micro blogging word of mouth on consumers' adoption of new movies. Springer,43,375-394.

Herskovits, M. J. (1936). Applied Anthropology and the American Anthropologists. Science, 1936(83):215-222.

Hogan, S. J., and L. V. Coote. 2014. Organizational culture, innovation, and performance: A test of Schein's model. *Journal of Business Research*, 67(8): 1609-1621.

Hong, Yinxing (2013). Consumption Demand, Consumption Power, Consumption Economy, and Economic Growth. China's Economic Issues, 2013 (01): 3-8.

Hong, Yinxing (2013). Consumption Demand, Consumption Power, Consumption Economy, and Economic Growth. China's Economic Issues, 2013 (01): 3-8.

Hovey, Martin & Naughton, Tony (2006). A survey of enterprise reforms in China: The way forward. *Economic Systems,* 31(2), doi: 10.1016/j.ecosys.2006.09.001.

Hu, Z. F. and Yang, B. (2018). Communication Power: The Key Guarantee of Promoting the Cultural Soft Power of Chinese Film and TV. Journal of Tsinghua University (Philosophy and Social Sciences), 33(03), 140-147.

Hu, Ying. (2017). The new development of socialism with Chinese characteristics since the 18th National Congress - From "three self-confidence" to "four self-confidence." *Journal of Harbin University*, 2017, 38 (9): 19-22.

Huang, J., and S. Rozelle., 1996. Technological change: Rediscovering the engine of productivity in growth in China's rural economy. *Journal of Development Economics*, 49(2): 337-369.

Huang, Philip C. C. (2009). China's Neglected Informal Economy: Reality and Theory. Open Times, Vol. 2009 (02).

Huang, Qingying and Shen, Yaolin. (2012). Exploring the construction of four civilizations and optimizing the ideological and political education environment. Journal of *Huaihua University*, 2012, 31 (4): 36-38.

Huang, Renzong (2002). Urbanization or Freedom of Migration -- Reflections on the Value Orientation of China's Reform of Household Registration System. Truth Seeking, Vol. 2002 (05).

Huang, Renzong (2003). Reflections on the Value Orientation to China's Reform of Household Registration System. Chinese Public Administration, Vol. 2003 (01).

Huang, Shupin (2007). Fei Xiaotong's Theoretical Contribution to Chinese Anthropology. Journal of Central University for

Nationalities (Philosophy and Social Sciences Edition), 2007 (4): 22-31.

Huang, Y. (2015). Countermeasures for Improving the Communication Power of my country's Film and TV under the Background of New Media. Modern Literary Magazine, 2, 108-111.

Jia, L. J., Wang, J. M. and Xu, Y. (2021). The Unity of Nature and Man: A Methodological Leap from Quantitative Research to Qualitative Research. Enterprise Economy, 40(05),33-42. doi: 10.13529/j.cnki.enterprise.economy.2021.05.004.

Jiang, Xinjie (2008). Under the Eaves of the City. China Youth Daily, 9th Edition.

Jiggins, J. and Röling, N. (2000). Adaptive Management: Potential and Limitations for Ecological Governance. International Journal of Agricultural Resources Governance & Ecology. Vol. 1(1): 28-43.

Jin T. J. (2007) From Administering Administrative Districts to Regional Public Administration: A Game Theory Analysis of the Evolution of Governmental Forms of Governance. Social Sciences in China, (6): 53-65.

Jin，Bei (2019). The regional trend of China's economic development in the past 70 years. *Enterprise Vitality*, 2019 (4): 1-7.

John Tomlinson. (1999). Globalization and Culture. University of Chicago Press.

Johnson, J. P., and T. Lenartowicz. 1988. Culture, freedom and economic growth: Do cultural values explain economic growth? *Journal of World Business*, 33(4): 332-356.

Jonathan S. (1998). Consuming Representation: A Visual Approach to Consumer Research. London: Rout-ledge.

José L. and Deborah S. (2008) Metropolitan patenting, inventor agglomeration and social networks: A tale of two effects. *Journal of Urban Economics,* 63, 871–884. DOI: 10.1016/j.jue.2007.07.005.

Karl，Marx (1995). The german ideology.Beijing: People's Publishing House.1995.

Karl，Marx (2009). Manuscript of economics and philosophy in 1844. Beijing: People's Publishing House.2009.

Karl，Marx (2012). Socialism from empty to scientific development.Beijing: People's Publishing House.2012.

Keesing, R. M. (1981). Cultural Anthropology: A Contemporary Perspective. New York, NY, USA: Holt, Rinehart and Winston.

Kerlinová A. and Tomášková E. (2014) Approach to strategy at public administration organizations in the Czech Republic. Proceedings - Social and Behavioral Sciences 156, 88 – 92.

Keynes, John Maynard (2018). A General Theory of Employment, Interest and Money. New York, NY: Palgrave Macmillan

Kim, Yun K, Setterfield, Mark, and Yuan, Mei (2014). A theory of aggregate consumption. European Journal of Economics and Economic Policies: Intervention 11 (1): 31-49.

Kirby, DA. (2018). Harnessing the Persuasive Power of Narrative: Science, Storytelling, and Movie Censorship, 1930-1968. Science In Context,31,85-106.

Klein, B., Crawford, R. G., and Alchian, A. A. (1978). Vertical integration, appropriable rents, and the competitive contracting process. *Journal of Law & Economics, 21*(2), 297-326.

Koh, NS., Hu, N. and Clemons, EK. (2010). Do online reviews reflect a product's true perceived quality? An investigation of online movie reviews across cultures, Electronic Commerce Research and Applications,9,374-385.

Kong, Linggang, and Cheng, Biding (2013). Population Transfer Urbanization and Structural Transformation Urbanization--A Study on the Tendency of Urbanization Development in China. East China Economic Management, Vol. 2013 (07).

Kongsamut, P., Rebelo, S. and Xie, D. (2001). Beyond Balanced Growth. The Review of Economic Studies, 68 (4):869—882.

Kopytoff, Igor. (1986). The Cultural Biography of Things: Commoditization as Process," In Arjon Appadurai ed. the Social Life of Things: Commodities in Cultural Perspective. New York: Cambridge University Press.

Kroenig, Matthew, Melissa McAdam and Steven Weber (2010). Taking Soft Power Seriously. *Comparative Strategy*, Vol. 29 (5): 412-431.

Krugman, P. and Elizondo, R.L. (1996) Trade policy and the third world metropolis. *Journal of Development Economics,* 49 (1), 137–150.

Kwon, Seung-Ho & Kim, Joseph. (2017). Efficiency Versus Public Good: Electricity Privatization in South Korea. *Asian Perspective*, 41(2). https://muse.jhu.edu/article/713787

Lan, Xuehua, Tian, Guang (2011). The Application of Anthropology in Business Education and the Rise of Business Anthropology. China Management Informationization, 2011 (4): 70-75.

Lassiter, L. E. (2014). Invitation to Anthropology (4th Edition). Lanham, MD: Rowman & Littlefield Publishers:3.

Lee, S., C. Pantzalis., and J. C. Park. 2019. Does local culture trigger speculative investment behavior? *Journal of Business Research*, 103: 71-88.

Lei, Z.M. and Fu, S.Y. (2012) Empirical analysis on the evaluation of urban industrial competitiveness – taking Dalian, Qingdao, Ningbo, Xiamen and Shenzhen as samples, *Journal of the Party School of C.P.C. Qingdao Municipal Committee (Qingdao Administration College)*, (6), 12-18.

Lettau, M., and Ludvigson, S. (2001). Consumption, Aggregate Wealth and Expected Stock Returns. Journal of Finance 56 (3): 815-849.

Li, C. 2016. Research on the homogenization of contemporary Dong brocade. Chinese National Academy of Arts.

Li, Chunyan and Gao, Ruijing. (2013). Research on institutional mechanism design and supporting policies for promoting autonomous innovation in China. *Gansu Journal of Theory*, 2013 (04): 5-9.

Li, Congjun (2013). Migration Storm: Revelation from Urbanization. Beijing: Xinhua Publishing House.

Li, Dekuan, and Tian, Guang (2014). Dietary Anthropology. Yinchuan: Ningxia People's Publishing House.

Li, H. F., and Zhang, S. Z. (2021). The Development Path of Diversified Dispute Resolution Mechanism in Social Governance Modernization - An Examination of Sichuan Province as an Example. Social Science Trends, Vol. 5(07):48-55.

Li, Keqiang. (2010). Enhancing the endogenous power of economic growth to accelerate the transformation of development mode. *Theoretical reference*, 2010 (9): 5-5.

Li, Lan (2008). Generalized Ethnology--A New Peak of Ethnological Research--A Review of Shi Zhengyi's Introduction to Generalized Ethnology. Academic Forum, 2008 (12): 203-205.

Li, Qiang et al. (2013). Pluralistic Urbanization and China's Development. Beijing: Social Sciences Academic Press.

Li, S.L. (2011) Formation Mechanism of Regional Soft Power Based on Resource Endowment. *Chinese Journal of Systems Science,* Vol. 19 (1) 77-79.

Li, Wenrui, Chen Gang (2014). The Game of Pressure, Challenge, and Interest: A Case Study of Business Anthropology of Kunming Taxi Driver [J]. Ethnic Studies in Qinghai, 2014 (1): 12-21.

Li, Y. Z. and Zhao, F. (2015). Word-of-mouth and dissemination of Chinese films in the U.S. Based on the analysis of "New York Times" Chinese film reviews. Modern Communication, 37(12),74-78.

Li, Yajuan (2019). Market Equilibrium Dilemma between Consumption Upgrade and Development of Commercial Circulation Industry under Income Constraint. Commercial Economy Research, 2019 (19): 44-47.

Li, Yuehua. (2012). The Rise of Cultural China and the Chinese Dream. *Collection of Leaders*, 2012 (1): 24-26.

Liddy, Susan. (2016).' Open to all and everybody'? The Irish Film Board: accounting for the scarcity of women screenwriters. Feminist Media Studies,1-17.

Liinamaa, Sara. and Rogers, Malia. (2020). Women actors, insecure work, and everyday sexism in the Canadian screen industry. Feminist Media Studies,1-16.

Lin W.S. and Peng T. (2011) Extending Shantou SEZ to the whole city bringing about the large pattern, industry and business opportunity, Chaoshan Businessman, (02), 5-11.

Lin, Huocan (2019). Promoting Consumption Poverty Alleviation with Market Mechanism. Economic Daily, November 19, 2019 (009).

Liu R.C. (2010) Regional Governance: From Administrative-region Administration to Regional Public Administration: A Perspective of Regional Economic Cooperation. Journal of Guangxi Normal University(Philosophy and Social Sciences Edition), (4), 27-32.

Liu Zhijun and Meng Hua. (1999) On the functions of public management and administrative resources and the realization of sustainability, *Academic Forum*, (5), 64-67.

Liu, Feifei and Li, Haibo. (2018). On integrating the "Community with a Shared Future for Mankind" and the "Chinese Dream." *Frontier Economy and Culture*, 2018 (05): 50-52.

Liu, Guoguang. (2013). On the direction of China's economic system reform before the Third Plenary Session of the Eighteenth Central Committee -- guard against the privatization trend in the name of marketization. *Jianghuai Forum*, 2013 (5): 5-8.

Liu, Haiyang. (2012). The ethical perspective of fairness and efficiency under the socialist market economy. *Journal of Shangqiu Vocational and Technical College*, 2012 (1): 9-10.

Liu, J. T. (2019). The Audience Positioning and Cultural Function of Contemporary Film and Television Communication from The Perspective of Smart Media. View on Publishing, 2, 34-36.

Liu, Min, and Liu, Yuanxu (2014). Do not let the nostalgia become rural pain—Reflections on the phenomenon of urbanization becoming dismantling old buildings and building new ones in some regions. Country Agriculture Farmers, Vol. 2014 (01).

Liu, Qian, Zhang, Yinfeng (2016). Commodity Production and Consumption from the Perspective of Anthropology--From the Development of Western Business Anthropology. Journal of the Renmin University of China, 2016 (1): 138-146.

Liu, Yanchang. (2007). Focusing on China's vested interest groups. Beijing: Party School Press of the Central Committee of the Communist Party of China, 2007:60.

Liu, Yuan and Zhang Xinling. (2018). Research on financing strategy of privately-owned listed enterprises: Empirical analysis based on panel data from 2012 to 2015. *Rural Economy and Technology*, 2018 (09): 179-180.

Liu, Zhaohui. and Dahling, Robin. (2016). The quieter side of Chinese feminism: The feminist phenomenology of Li Yu's films. Asian Journal of Women's Studies, 22(1), 2-15.

Long, X. N. (2016). The Channel Construction and Its Effect Analysis of Chinese Film and TV's Communication to Africa. Contemporary Cinema, 3, 99-103.

Lu, C. T., and Zhu, Z. (2021). The modern connotation and system construction of environmental, social governance in China. Journal of Arid Land Resources and Environment, Vol. 35(09):4-6.

Lu, Yilong (2006). Embedded Political Influences on Economic Efficiency in a Village——A Case Study on Xiaogang Village. Journal of the Renmin University of China, Vol. 2006 (05).

Lu, Yilong (2007). Embedded Politics and Changes of Village Economy: A Survey of Xiaogang Village in Anhui. Shanghai: Shanghai People's Publishing House.

Lu， Fucai, Ma Shaoxiong, Xu Bin (2019). 70 years of industrialization in New China: From take-off to maturity. *Contemporary Finance and Economics*, 2019(10): 3-14.

Luisito B. and Duncan B. (2004) Urbanization and growth. *Journal of Urban Economics*, 56, 80–96. DOI: 10.1016/j.jue.2004.03.003.

Luo, K. L., and He, Z.M. (2019).On Ethnic Habitat and the Construction of Ethnic Culture. Journal of Ethnology, Vol. 12(05):19-20.

Luo, Yingguang (2014). The Road of Characteristic Urbanization in Yunnan. Kunming: Yunnan People's Publishing House.

Ma Q.Y. (2003) Vigorously develop tourism to promote the economy of Chaozhou and Shantou, Shantou Sci-Tech, (03), 34-35.

Ma, Aiping (2019). The Urbanization Rate Surged by Nearly 50%, and Big Data Reproduced the Process of Urban Expansion in New China. Science and Technology Daily, October 09, 2019:3.

Maddison, A. (2007). *Chinese Economic Performance in the Long Run, 960-2030 AD, Second Edition, Revised and Updated.* OECD.

Marius B. (2012) Economic growth, size of the agricultural sector, and urbanization in Africa. Journal of Urban Economics, 71: 26–36.

Marius B. and Federica S. (2009) Agglomeration and growth: Cross-country evidence. Journal of Urban Economics, 65, 48–63. DOI:10.1016/j.jue.2008.08.003.

Marquez, I. (2020). The Movie Poster in the Remix Culture. Historia Y Communication Social,25,161-169.

Martin, P. and Ottaviano, G. (1999) Growing locations: Industry location in a model of endogenous growth. European Economic Review 43 (2), 281–302.

Marx, Karl (2009). Introduction to Critique of Political Economy in Collected Works of Marx and Engels (Volume 8). Beijing: People's Publishing House, 2009: 5-36.

Marx. (1975). *Das Kapital*, Volume 1. Beijing: People's Publishing House, 1975:12.

Mcconnell C R. (2005). Microeconomics: Principles, Problems, and Policies. *Economics Principles Problems & Policies*, 2005.

Meng, Yue (2008). What Is Material and Its Culture – Thoughts on Studies of Material Culture. Meng, Yue, and Luo, Gang. The Material Culture Studies: A Reader. Beijing: Peking University Press, Preface.

Miller D. (2005). Materiality. Durham, NC: Duke University Press.

Ming, G. Y. and Bao, J. P. (2021). On The Paths and Strategies of The Spread of My Country's International Cultural Influence. Media Observer, 4, 14-18.

Ministry of Transport of the People's Republic of China (2020). Statistical bulletin on the development of the transportation industry.

Minoo Derayeh. (2010). Depiction of women in Iranian cinema, 1970s to present. Women's Studies International Forum, 33(3), 151-158.

Monaghan, J. and Just, P. (2000). Social and Cultural Anthropology: A Very Short Introduction. London, UK: University of Oxford Press,13.

Muellbauer, J., and Lattimore, R. (1995). The Consumption Function: A Theoretical and Empirical Overview." In Handbook of Applied Economics, edited by H. Pesaran and M. Wickens. Oxford: Blackwell: 187-267.

Mumford, Lewis. (2005). The City in History: A Powerfully Incisive and Influential Look at the Development of the Urban Form through the Ages. Beijing: China Architecture & Building Press.

Nakatsu, R., Tosa, N and Ochi, T. (2001). Concept and construction example of an interactive movie system, Journal of Vlsi Signal Processing Systems for Signal Image and Video Technology,27, 141-160.

Nie, X. R. (2019). Political Film as Genre Film. Hundred Schools in Arts, 2, 131-136.

Niu, Luqing. (2016). Agricultural UAV: Prospects and Constraints. *New Economic Guide*, 2016 (7): 42-48.

North, D. C. 1990. *Institutions, ideology, and economic performance.* Cambridge: Cambridge University Press.

O'Brien, A. and Liddy, S. (2021). The price of motherhood in the Irish film and television industries. Gender, Work & Organization. doi:10.1111/gwao.12612

Onaran, Ozlem, Engelbert Stockhammer, and Lukas Grafl (2011). Financialization, income distribution and aggregate demand in the USA. Cambridge Journal of Economics 35 (4): 637-661.

Park, Robert Ezra, et al. (2012). Urban Sociology: A Study of the Chicago School (Translated by Song Junling and Zheng Yefu). Beijing: The Commercial Press.

Peng, Lele, Shi, Qiuju (2014). Consumption Becomes a New Engine Driving Economic Development-Dynamic Analysis Based on Keynes's Effective Demand Theory. Journal of Taiyuan Municipal Party School of CPC, 2014 (04): 41-44.

Peng, Y., and S. Lin. 2009. National culture, economic development, population growth and environmental performance: The mediating role of education. *Journal of Business Ethics*, 90(2): 203-219.

Petronela, T. 2016. The importance of the intangible cultural heritage in the economy. *Procedia Economics and Finance*, 39: 731-736.

Plattner, S. M. (1974). Formal models and formalist economic anthropology: The problem of maximization. Reviews in Anthropology, 1974(4):572-582.

Power, D., R. Klassen., T. J. Kull., and D. Simpson. 2015. Competitive goals and plant investment in environment and safety practices: Moderating effect of national culture. *Decision Science*, 46(1): 63-100.

Putterman, L. (1993). Ownership and the nature of the firm. *Journal of Comparative Economics, 17*(2), 243-263.

Qi, Y.Z. (2019). Changes of Social Governance Model and Effective Governance in Ethnic Areas —From "Rule By Rite" To "Good Governance." Guangxi Ethnic Studies, Vol. 35(2):47-56.

Qian, Q., J. H. Holland., and D. D. Brown. 2016. Social and economic impacts of subsidy policies on rural development in the Poyang

Lake region, China: Insights from an agent-based model. *Agricultural Institutions*, 148: 12-27.

Qian， Jin (2019). On the industrialization construction of new China. *Economic Aspect*, 2019 (3): 1-7.

Quan, Jingxiu, Cui, Haiyang (2013). A Probe into Fei Xiaotong's Anthropological Research Methods--An Intensive Reading of Peasant Life in China. Journal of Guangxi University for Nationalities (Philosophy and Social Sciences Edition), 2013 (4): 58-64.

Ren， Jianlan, Wang， Yaping, Cheng， Yu (2018). From ecological environment protection to ecological civilization construction: A review and prospect of 40 years. *Journal of Shandong University (PHILOSOPHY AND SOCIAL SCIENCES EDITION)*,2018 (6): 27-39.

Ren, Jie. (2018). Community with a Shared Future for Mankind: China's program for global governance. *Southeast Academy*, 2018 (1).

Rodriguez-Pose A. (2013) Do Institutions Matter for Regional Development? *Regional Studies*, Vol. 47, No. 7, 1034–1047. DOI: 10.1080/00343404.2012.748978.

Rodzi, N. I. M., S. A. Zaki., and S. M. H. S. Subli. 2013. Between tourism and intangible cultural heritage. *Procedia-Social and Behavioral Science*, 85: 411-420.

Rowe, M. (2012). Anthropological Practice: Fieldwork and the Ethnographic Method. Journal of Organizational Ethnography. Vol. 19(2): 90-91.

Schumpeter, J. A. 1911, (2008). The theory of economic development: An inquiry into profits, capital, credit, interest and the business cycle, translated from the German by Redvers Opie, New Brunswick (U.S.A) and London (U.K.): Transaction publishers.

Scott, James C. (2009). The Art of Not Being Governed: An Anarchist History of Upland Southeast Asia, New Haven: Yale University Press.

Scott, James C. (2012). Seeing Like State: How Certain Schemes to Improve the Human Condition Have Failed (Translated by Wang Xiaoyi). Beijing: Social Sciences Academic Press.

Shao, L., C. Y, Kwok., and R. Zhang. 2013. National culture and corporate investment. *Journal of International Business Studies*, 44(7): 745-763.

Sharma, R. and Wherry, B. (2009). Software Development for Disney Animated Feature Film Production. Agile 2009 Conference. doi:10.1109/AGILE.2009.60

Shen, Lisheng (2009). Evaluating the Contribution of Three Components of GDP ("Troika"). Quantitative Economics, Technology, and Economics, 26 (04): 139-151.

Shi Y.P. and Zhou L.A. (2007) Regional decentralization and economic efficiency – demonstrated by independent planning, *Economic Research*, (1), 17-28.

Shi, Lin (2002). Economic Anthropology. Beijing: Central University for Nationalities Press.

Shi, Lin (2011). Ethnography of the Frontier: Perspective and Methodology of Economic anthropology. Journal of Guangxi University for Nationalities (Philosophy and Social Sciences Edition), 2011 (3): 35-38.

Shi, Lin (2016). An African Approach to Ethnic Diversity: Ethnic Governance in Ethiopia from a Multidimensional Perspective. Heilongjiang Ethnic Series, 2016 (3): 59-67.

Shi, Y. (2019). On the particularity and remarkable characteristics of social governance in ethnic areas in China. Journal of Shaanxi Institute of Socialism, Vol. 26(4):40-43.

Shi, Zhengyi (1985). On Socialist Nationality--On Stalin's Theory of Socialist Nationality. Ethnic Studies in Guizhou, 1985 (3): 1-9.

Shi, Zhengyi (1986). "Accelerating Strategy" of Economic Development in Western Minority Regions. Chinese Nationalities, 1986 (11): 8-10.Shi, Zhengyi (1983). From concrete to abstract and then from abstract to concrete is the scientific method of theoretical thinking--Reading Marx's Introduction to Critique of Political Economy, Section III, Methods of Political Economy. Journal of Central University of Finance and Economics, 1983 (3): 52-55.

Shi, Zhengyi (1986). Some issues of economic system reform in minority areas. Exploration of Economic Problems, 1986 (1): 18-20.

Shi, Zhengyi (1987). Ethnic Economics and the Four Modernizations in Ethnic Regions. Beijing: Ethnic Publishing House.

Shi, Zhengyi (1988). A Study on the Economic Development of Ethnic Regions in Western China. Beijing: Nationalities Press.

Shi, Zhengyi (1989). Acceleration and Equilibrium of Disparity-Exploration of Economic Development Strategy in Ethnic Minority Regions. Heilongjiang Ethnic Series, 1989 (3): 29-45.

Shi, Zhengyi (1990). On the Research Object of Generalized Ethnology. Heilongjiang Ethnic Series, 1990 (4): 66-70.

Shi, Zhengyi (1991). Economic Dictionary of China's Ethnic Minorities. Shanghai: Shanghai Lexicographic Publishing House.

Shi, Zhengyi (1992 a). Generalized Ethnology. Beijing: Guangming Daily Press.

Shi, Zhengyi (1992 b). Research methods of generalized ethnology. Heilongjiang Ethnic Series, 1992 (4): 91-97.

Shi, Zhengyi (1992 c). Strategic policy on accelerating development. Journal of Central South University for Nationalities (Humanities and Social Sciences Edition), 1992 (4): 18-20.

Shi, Zhengyi (1993 a). Introduction to Ethnic Economics. Beijing: Ethnic Publishing House, 1993.

Shi, Zhengyi (1993 b). On the Strategic Policy of Accelerating Development in Ethnic Minority Regions--Learning from Comrade Deng Xiaoping's Strategic Guiding Thought on Accelerating Development. Inner Mongolia Social Sciences (Chinese Version), 1993 (2): 35-41.

Shi, Zhengyi (1996). A Brief Discussion on the Religious and Cultural Morphology of Ethnic Minorities in China. Journal of Guangxi University for Nationalities, (Philosophy and Social Sciences), 1996 (2): 51-55.

Shi, Zhengyi (2000). Several relations should be dealt with correctly in implementing the strategy of developing the western region--Re-discussion on the "New Ideas of Developing the Western Region." Journal of Central University for Nationalities, 2000 (5): 58-61.

Shi, Zhengyi (2001). A Course in Ethnic Economics [M]. Beijing: Central University for Nationalities Press, 2001.

Shi, Zhengyi (2002). A new approach to the study of Ethnic minority economies. Chinese Nationalities, 2002 (4): 56-57.

Shi, Zhengyi (2002). Forum on Ethnic Economics and Western Development [M]. Beijing: Ethnic Publishing House.

Skinner, G. William. (2000). The City in Late Imperial China, Ye Guangting et al. (Trans). Beijing: Zhong Hua Book Company.

Smith, A. 1776. *The inquiry into the nature and causes of the wealth of nations*. London: for W. Strahan and T. Cadell.

Song, Junling (2001).15 Lectures on Urbanization in China. Beijing: China City Press.

Song, K., Kim, H., Lee, J.and Kim, YG. (2017). Dissecting movie performance across multiple distribution channels: An elastic justification theory perspective. Telematics And Informatics,159-167.

Stott, Alan. (1993). Significance and Social Origin of Expositions on the Spatial Foundation of Society. Readings in Social Theories and the Cultural Form of Space (Translated by Xia Zhujiu et al.). Taipei: Mingwen Book Company.

Strange W., Hejazi W. and Tang J.M. (2006) The uncertain city: Competitive instability, skills, innovation and the strategy of agglomeration. *Journal of Urban Economics,* 59, 331–351. DOI: 10.1016/j.jue.2005.10.006.

Strasburger, VC., Donnerstein, E. and Bushman, BJ. (2014). Why Is It So Hard to Believe That Media Influence Children and Adolescents? Pediatrics,133,571-573.

Strengers, Y., 2004. Environmental culture change in local government: a practiced perspective from the international council for local environmental initiatives Australia/New Zealand. Local Environ. 9 (6), 621-628.

Sun Y.H. (2001) Comprehensive evaluation on the economic benefits of China's 35 provincial capital and cities with independent planning, *Statistics & Information Forum,* (9), 14-18.

Sun, Feiyu (2017). From Social Change to Social Balance: Fei Xiaotong's Thoughts before Jiang Cun Investigation. Sociological Review, 2017 (1): 76-84.

Sun, Hangsheng. (2011). Research on the transformation and upgrading of China as the "world factory." *Industry Development*, 2011, (03): 76-78.

Sun, Jian. (2010). The economic system, resource allocation, and the model of economic development. *Economic System Reform*, 2010 (5): 5-11.

Sun, S. S. (2010). Comparative Analysis of the Application of Qualitative and Quantitative Methods in Brand Image Research. Commercial Times,18,29-30.

Sun, Wensheng. (2004). Note on the Amendment (Draft) to the Land Management Law of the People's Republic of China - Eleventh Meeting of the Standing Committee of the Tenth National People's Congress, 2004.

Swank, D. 1996. Culture, institutions, and economic growth: Theory, recent evidence, and the role of communitarian politics. *American Journal of Political Science*, 40(3): 660-679.

Talor D. (2014) In vogue and at odds: systemic change and new public management in development.Enterprise Development and Microfinance Vol. 25 No. 4, pp.271-287.

Tang, H. 2014. The research of Dong brocade art in Hunan province. *Hunan Normal University.*

Tang, Xi and Ren, Zhijiang (2018). Research on "Shortage of Migrant Workers" and "Lewis Turning Point" in China. Journal of Northwest A&F University (Social Science Edition), Vol. 18(2):101-107.

Tavassoli, Nader T. and Lee, Yih Hwai. (2003). The Differential Interaction of Auditory and Visual Advertising Elements with Chinese and English. Journal of Marketing Research, 40(4), 468-480.

Teece, D. J. (1982). Towards an economic theory of the multiproduct firm. *Journal of Economic Behavior & Organization, 3*(1), 39-63.

The Bureau of Statistics of the People's Republic of China (2021). Bulletin of the seventh national census.

The Ministry of Health of the PRC (1985). China Health Yearbook. People's Health Publishing House.

The State Council (2014). Opinions of the State Council on Further Promotion of Reform of the Household Registration System. Beijing: People's Publishing House.

The state council document (2011). The Reply of the State Council on Expanding Shantou Special Economic Zone. http://zwgk.gd.gov.cn/006939748/201104/t20110428_49455.html.

Theodore W. Schultz. (1990) Human Capital Investment and Urban Competitiveness.Beijing; Beijing: Beijing Economic College Press.

Thompson, L. (1944). "Some Perspectives in Applied Anthropology. Applied Anthropology. Vol. 3 (3):12–16.

Throsby, D. 1999. Cultural capital. *Journal of Cultural Economics*, 23: 3-12.

Tia Julien. (2015). A Review of Kevin J. Donnelly's Occult Aesthetics: Synchronization in Sound Film. Retrieved from https://journal.lib.uoguelph.ca/index.php/sofammj/article/view/3428

Tian G. and Dai Q.Q. (2012) Criticism on market orientation: theoretical thinking on the economic system reform of contemporary China. Beijing: China Financial & Economic Publishing House.

Tian G. and Dai Q.Q. (2013) Administrative resources and independent planning – strategic new thought on the agglomeration of Shantou, Chaozhou and Jieyang, *Journal of Southern Vocational Education*, (03), 53-61.

Tian G., Dai Q.Q. and Qi X.G. (2012) Strategic thinking on national operation; criticism on market orientation thinking, *Journal of Shijiazhuang University of Economics*, (2), 92-95.

Tian Guang, Dai Qinqin (2013). Thinking on the Path of Indigenization of Anthropology and Business Administration in China. Journal of Management, 10 (6): 78-89.

Tian, G. (2011) Soft Power and Construction of Shantou Economic Special Zone: A New Breakthrough Point.Journal of Applied Business and Economics, (6), 121-131.

Tian, G. Wang, Y., and Wang, H. (2017). From Ethnography to Business Ethnography. Qinghai Journal of Ethnology, Vol. 29(3):89.

Tian, G., and Yu, H. (2017). Leading Officials Should Know Anthropology—Academic Preparations for Improving Leadership Abilities and Skills, Renming Luntan·Xueshu Qianya. Vol. 6(23):74-83.

Tian, G., Tian, K. , and Wang, H. et al. (2017). Independent Planning System and Public Administration in Metropolitan Development: Agglomeration Strategies of Greater Chaoshan in Southern China.

Contemporary Chinese Political Economy and Strategic Relations: An International Journal, Vol. 3(1):395-432.
Tian, Guang (2012). The rise and application of business anthropology. Managers: Practical Edition, 2012 (12): 39-48.
Tian, Guang (2013). Consumption-driven and Market-driven: New Thoughts on China's Macroeconomic Strategy. Entrepreneur Daily, January 12, 2013: W03.
Tian, Guang (2014). On Some Economic anthropology Issues. Guangxi Ethnic Studies, 2014 (5): 41-48.
Tian, Guang (2015). Anthropological interpretation of economic evolution. Qinghai Ethnic Studies, 2015, 26 (4): 24-29.
Tian, Guang, and Dai, Qinqin. (2012). Criticism of Pan-marketization. Beijing: China Financial and Economic Publishing House, 2012.
Tian, Guang, Feng, Jiao, and Wang, Ying (2017). Marketing Anthropology. Yinchuan: Ningxia People's Publishing House.
Tian, Guang, Liu, Yu, and Wang, Yifan (2015). Qualitative Research and Management Discipline Construction: Reflections Based on Business Anthropology. Journal of Management, 2015 (1): 1-12.
Tian, Guang, Liu, Yu, Wang, Shuting (2014). On the Role of Market and Consumption in Promoting China's Macroeconomic Development. China Market, (45):46-52.
Tian, Guang, Luo, Kanglong (2013). Economic Anthropology. Yinchuan: Ningxia People's Publishing House.
Tian, Guang, Shao, Huan (2014). Anthropological thinking on cross-cultural and cross-ethnic marketing. Journal of Hebei University of Economics and Business (Comprehensive Edition), 2014 (2): 5-10.
Tian, Guang, Tao Ketao, and Lv, Li (2019). Management Anthropology. Yinchuan: Ningxia People's Publishing House.
Tian, Guang, Wang, Ying (2016). Supply-side reform from the perspective of critique of pan-marketization. Friends of the Leader, 2016 (15): 17-25.
Tian, Guang, Zhou, Daming (2013). A General Theory of Business Anthropology. Beijing: China Financial and Economic Publishing House.
Tian, Guang, Zhou, Tao, and Ma, Jianfu (2018). Management and Business Anthropology. Yinchuan: Ningxia People's Publishing House.

Triandis, H. C., Mccusker, C. Betancourt, H. et al. (1993). An Etic-Emic Analysis of Individualism and Collectivism. Journal of Cross-Cultural Psychology. Vol. 24(3): 366-383.

Uzkurt, C., R. Kumar., H. S. Kimzan., and G. Eminoğlu. 2013. Role of innovation in the relationship between organizational culture and firms performance. European Journal of Innovation Management, 16(1): 92-117.

V. L. Eaklor. (2012). The Kids Are All Right but the Lesbians Aren't: The Illusion of Progress in Popular Film. Berghahn Journals,38,153-170.

Wan, F. K. (2018).The current situation, obstacles, and modernization reform measures of social governance in ethnic minority areas: the case of Enshi Tujia and Miao Autonomous Prefecture in Hubei. Theoretic Observation, Vol. 34(05):69-73.

Wang X.L. and Yang P.Q. (2012) A research on the symbiosis theory of tourism cooperation model in Chaoshan regional. Journal of Chongqing University of Science and Technology (Social Sciences Edition), (23), 69-71.

Wang, Bin, Hu Yucui (2020). The process and experience of cultural construction in New China in the past 70 years. *Contemporary World Socialist Issues*, 2020 (1): 57-67.

Wang, Dongjing. (2019). Establishing a socialist market economic system is a great creation. *Wisdom China*, 2019 (01): 55-57.

Wang, Ning (2015). The Advent of the Era of Mobility, Sun Yat-Sen University.

Wang, Q.C. (2009) Overall Evaluation and Research on Urban Competitiveness of Provincial Area. *Journal of Anhui Agricultural Sciences*, (8) 25-28.

Wang, Renyuan (1995). The City History of Zigong. Beijing: Social Sciences Academic Press, Preface.

Wang, Wenjun (2013). Population, Resources and Environmental Economics. Beijing: Tsinghua University Press.

Wang, Xiaolu (2016). A New Understanding of the Demand Theory of the "Three Drivers." In Li, Zuojun, Wei, Yun, Tian, Huimin, and Zhao, Xijun (Eds.) Report on China's Development Driving Factors. Beijing, PRC: Social Sciences Academic Press:110-120.

Wang, Y. W. (2001). Western Development and Social Development in Ethnic Areas. Social Science Research, Vol. 23(02):22-24.

Wang, Y. W., and Wang, J. (2015). Social governance in ethnic autonomous areas in the context of national governance modernization. Journal of Ethnology, Vol. 6(1):63.

Wang, Z. Q. (2020). On Legal Protection of Promoting Modernization of Social Governance in Ethnic Areas of China. Journal of Tibet University (Social Sciences), Vol. 35(1):158-165.

Wang， Shaojie (2007). Resource system and the growth and distribution of national wealth. *Inner Mongolia Social Sciences,2007* (2): 75-79.

Ward N. and Brown D. L.(2009) Placing the Rural in Regional Development, *Regional Studies*, Vol. 43.10, 1237–1244. DOI: 10.1080/00343400903234696.

Waynes, Menena. (2008). Fascinating Things. Meng Yue, Luo Gang: The Material Culture Studies: A Reader. Beijing: Peking University Press.

Wen L. (2011) Comprehensive evaluation on the economic benefits of China's provincial capital and cities with independent planning, *CO-Operative Economy & Science*, (4), 18-19.

Wen, Guanzhong (2014). There is No Land for Our People: the Internal Logic of Urbanization, Land System and Household Registration System. Beijing: Oriental Press.

Wen, J., and Hu, A. G. (2003). Nationalities and Development in the New Modernization. Journal of Southwest University for Nationalities (Philosophy and Social Science). Vol. 24 (02):9-11.

Wilk, R., Liggett, L. (2007). Economies and Cultures: Foundations of Economic anthropology. New York, NY: Westview Press.

Williams, B., Wilmshurst, T., Clift, R., 2011. Sustainability reporting by local government in Australia: current and prospects. Acc. Forum 35, 176-186.

Williams, Paul. (2003).' What A Bummer for the Gooks': representations of white American masculinity and the Vietnamese in the Vietnam War film genre 1977-1987. European Journal of American Culture, 22, 215–234.

Williamson, O., Wachter, M., and Harris, J. (2009). *The economic nature of the firm: Understanding the employment relation: the analysis of idiosyncratic exchange*. Cambridge: Cambridge University Press.

World Bank, World Development Report, Oxford Univ. Press, Oxford, 2000.

Wright, Andrea. (2012). A sheep in wolf's clothing? The problematic representation of women and the female body in 1980s sword and sorcery cinema. Journal of Gender Studies, 21(4), 401-411.

Wu, Jiang et al. (2009). The behavior of Local Governments in the Process of New Urbanization in China. Chinese Public Administration, Vol. 2009 (03).

Wu, Liangyong (2002). Be sober-minded with the third planning boom. City Planning Review, Vol. 2002 (02).

Xiang, D. B., and Wang, J. J. (2020). International Media Effects of and Strategies for The Wandering Earth from Intercultural Communication Perspective. Global Journal of Media Studies, 7(04),59-71.

Xie, Di, and Xie, Siru. (2014). An Economic Analysis of the Chinese Dream. *Economist*. 2014 (01): 14-21.

Xie, Z. and Sun, Q. (2013). Cultural Differences, Audience Acceptance and Communication Effects in Cross-Cultural Communication——Take the Sino-British Documentary BBC Wild China and CCTV"Beautiful China" As Examples. Modern Communication (Journal of Communication University of China), 35(10),91-94.

Xin, Xiangyang (2018). Historical Philosophy of Xi Jinping's Socialism with Chinese Characteristics in the New Era. Learning Forum, 2018 (09): 5-9.

Yang , Weizhong (2019). 70 years' achievements in public health in China. *Modern Preventive Medicine*, 2019 (6): 7-10.

Yang X.T. and Pu Y.J. (1998) Resource economics – economic analysis of the optimal allocation of resources. Chongqing: Chongqing University Press, 10.

Yang, Chengbiao (2005). Volume 1 "Residence" of "Chronicles of Baiyanjing during the Qianlong period" of "The old local chronicles of Chuxiong Yi Autonomous Prefecture (Dayao Volume)." Kunming: Yunnan People's Publishing House.

Yang, Dongchang, Tian, Guang (2018). On the Development of Marxist Economic anthropology in the New Era. Academic Frontiers, 2018 (8): 88-103.

Yang, Qiyu. (2016). Pan-marketization and moral dilemma. *Mao Zedong and Deng Xiaoping Theory Research*, 2016 (4): 44-47.

Yang, Yunli (2006). A Breakthrough Study on Marx's Thinking Method of Scientific Theory by Representation-Abstract-Concrete--Reading Professor Shi Zhengyi's On the Thinking Method of Scientific Theory. Journal of Jining Normal University, 2006 (2): 47-52.

Yang, Z. Y. (2016). Path Analysis of Modernization Process in Less Developed Ethnic Regions in the West. Journal of Southwest Minzu University (Humanities and Social Science), Vol. 38(6): 130-134.

Yang, Zhiming (2015). There are a total of 274 million migrant workers in China, and 168 million go out for work with an average monthly income of 2,864 Yuan, the China News Service: http://news.china.com.cn/2015-02/28/content_34912197.htm (visit the page on January 5, 2016).

Yeh, R., and J. J. Lawrence.1995. Individualism and Confucian dynamism: A note on Hofstede's cultural root to economic growth. *Journal of International Business Studies*, 26(3): 655-669.

Yin, Xingshan (2008). Research on the Development of Financial Services. Nanjing Agricultural University, 2008.

Yn, Y. and Fu, Y.Y. (2020). Regional Perspective and Emotional Framework: An Analysis of the Chinese Film

Yoon, Y., Polpanumas, C. and Park, YJ. (2017). The Impact of Word of Mouth via Twitter on Moviegoers' Decisions and Film Revenues Revisiting Prospect Theory: How about Movies Drives Loss-Aversion and Reference-Dependence Behaviors, Journal of Advertising Research,57,144-158.

Yu X.Q. (2005) Selection of the optimal allocation of administrative resource, *Theory and Reform*, (2), 83-85.

Yu, Lin. (2010). The impact of technological innovation on the trade competitiveness of high-tech products. *Forum on Statistics and Information*, 2010, 25 (5): 76-80.

Yuan L. (2003) Regional economy agglomeration and the meso-control of the government, *Gansu Social Sciences*, (3), 86-87.

Yuan, Y. (2021). Several Countermeasures on Strengthening Geographical Indication Protection and Brand Building--Analysis on the Current Situation of Geographical Indication Protection in the Northern Guangdong Ecological Development Zone. New Agriculture, Vol. 50(14):62-65.

Yun, Z. (2017). Dilemmas and initiatives to promote social governance modernization in minority regions. Modern Economic Information, Vol. 14(12): 463-464.

Zang, Xuheng and He, Yang (2016). Insisting on Guiding the Theoretical Research of Consumer Economy with Marxist Political Economics. Marxism and Reality, 2016 (05): 15-20.

Zha, Zhengquan (2019). The Promotion of Consumer Culture to Economic Development-Comments on Principles of Marxist Political Economy. Journal of Guangdong University of Finance and Economics, 34 (05): 113.

Zhan, Z. R. (2001). Reflections on Western Development and Economic and Social Development in Ethnic Areas. Studies on the Socialism with Chinese Characteristics, Vol. 7(01):52-55.

Zhang L. (2014) A Comparative Study of the coordinated development of economic growth and environmental construction planning cities. Liaoning Normal University (Master's degree).

Zhang Z.S and Bai B. (2015) Public Management under the New Normal: the Dilemma and Way Out. Chinese Public Administration, (3): 38-42.

Zhang, Deyong (2019). New Consumption Trend Reflects New Economic Kinetic Energy. People's Liberation Army Newspaper, 2019-11-21 (010).

Zhang, Hongyan (2011). Reflection of Western Urbanization Theory and Theoretical Model Constructionism of Chinese Local Urbanization. Social Sciences in Nanjing, Vol. 2011 (09).

Zhang, Jihai (2012). Shiyang Town actively carried out the transfer of agricultural to non-agricultural status. The old Shiyang Town Newspapers.

Zhang, Jijiao (2014). Corporate Anthropology as a World Frontier Discipline. Journal of Hangzhou Normal University (social science edition), 2014 (4): 71-82.

Zhang, Jijiao (2016). Urban Revival and Cultural Value of Old Brands: A Comparative Analysis of Seoul and Beijing. Ethnic Forum, 2016 (5): 55-58.

Zhang, Xinguang (2009). The Change of and Reflection on Life Style of New China's Farmers. Modern Economic Research, Vol. 2009 (09).

Zhang, Yonghong. (2017). Generation, value, and realization of the concept of "Community with a Shared Future for Mankind." *Ideological and Theoretical Education*, 2017 (08): 33-39.

Zhang, Yulei (2014). Adjustment of the Relationship between Market and Government in the Process of New Urbanization: A New Analytical Framework. Journal of Socialist Theory Guide, Vol. 2014 (09).

Zhang, Zhongtao. (2005). Corruption and Anti-corruption in the Perspective of the Institution. *Hubei Social Science*, 2005 (11): 44-46.

Zhao, Shukai (2013). Reforms of Farmers. Beijing: The Commercial Press.

Zheng H.J. (2007) The Greater Pearl River Delta economic development and Regional Public management Innovation. Journal of Sun Yatsen University(Social Science Edition), (2), 82-85.

Zheng L.Z. (2011) Reflections on the development of extended Shantou SEZ, *China Urban Economy*, (26), 40-41.

Zheng, Z. H. (2019). The Path of Modernization of China's National Governance Capacity. Gansu Social Sciences, Vol. 40(03):36-40.

Zhou L.A. (2004) Incentives and cooperation of government officials in promotion gaming – on the reasons for the long-standing issues of China's regional protectionism and repeated construction, *Economic Research*, (6), 33-40.

Zhou S.P. (2004) Theoretical location and practice thinking on political resources. *Journal of Social Sciences*, Hunan Normal University, (1), 42-45.

Zhou, Daming, Yang, Xiaoliu (2014). From Migrant Workers to New Urban Migrants: A Concept and a Way of Thinking. Journal of Sun Yat-sen University, Social Sciences Edition, 2014 (5): 144-154.

Zhou, Ronghui (2011). Research on the Core Values of Socialism with Chinese Characteristics. Central School of the Communist Party of China.

Zhu L. (2007) Strengthen Soft Power Construction and Societal Innovation. *Shantou Daily*, December 31, 2007, theory and practice page.

Index

A

B

C

D

E

F

G

H

I

O

P

Q

R

S

T

U

Made in United States
Orlando, FL
23 June 2026

83290744R00177